A special boxed edition of two thousand copies of this work include an original drawing by Nicolas de Crécy printed on handmade paper: 10 copies numbered I to X and signed by the artist, 190 copies numbered HC11 to HC200, and 1,800 copies numbered 1 to 1800.

Notice to the reader

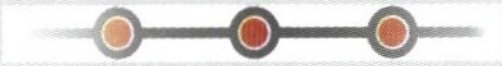

The designation of stops shows the order in which the drawings were done.

SKETCHTRAVEL

CHRONICLE BOOKS
San Francisco

A B C D E F G

1 2 3 4 5 6 7

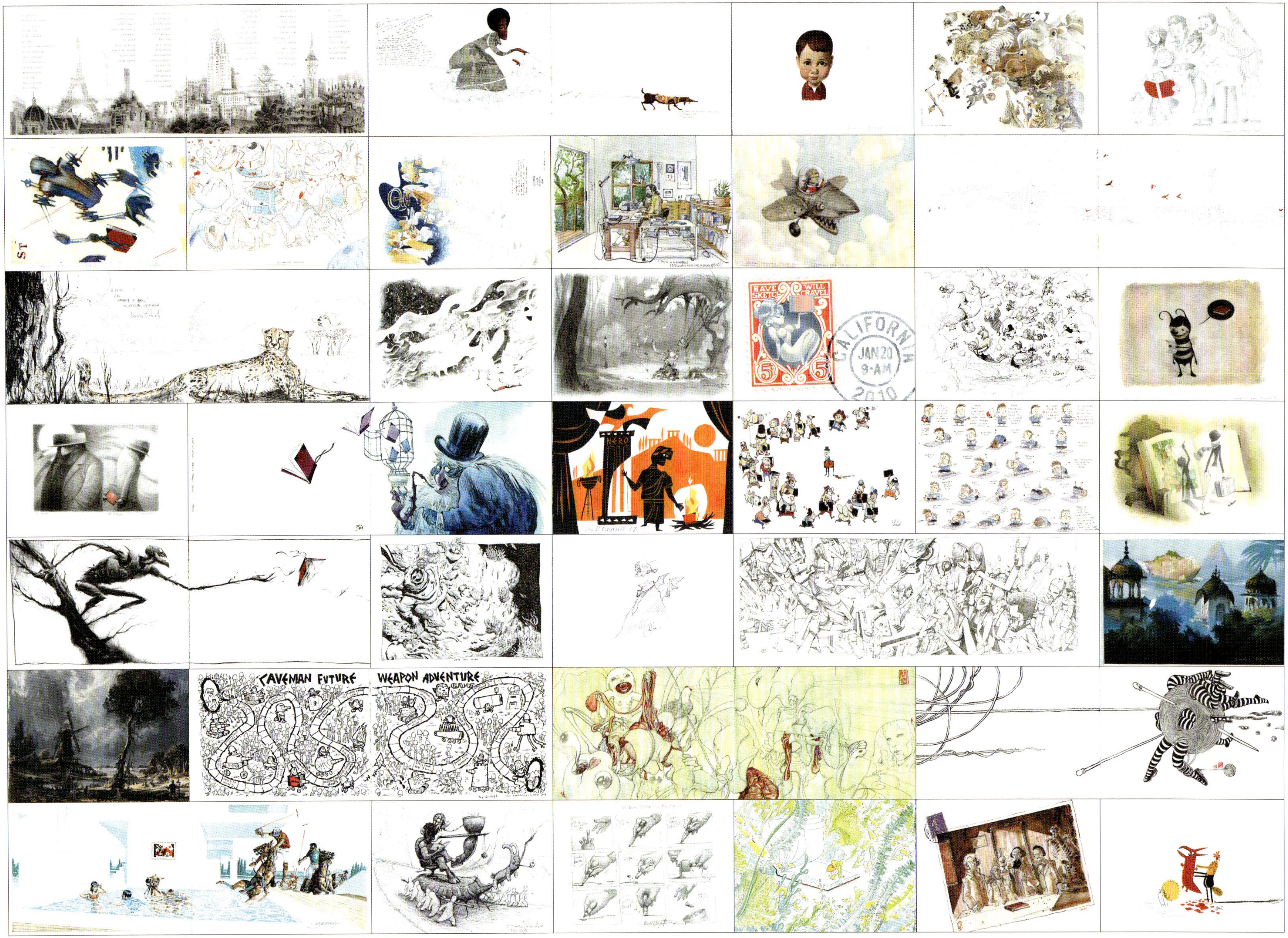

H I J K L M N

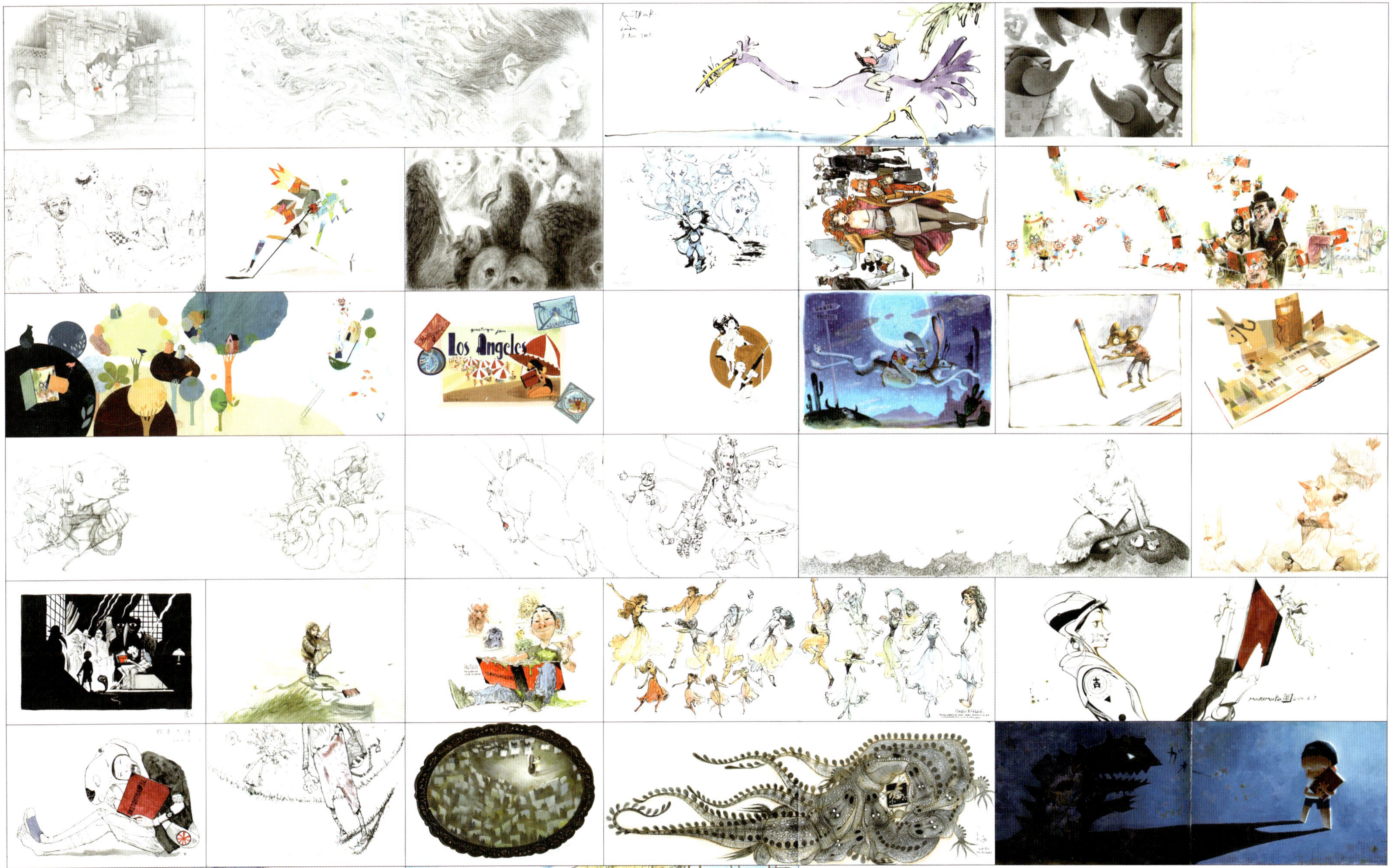

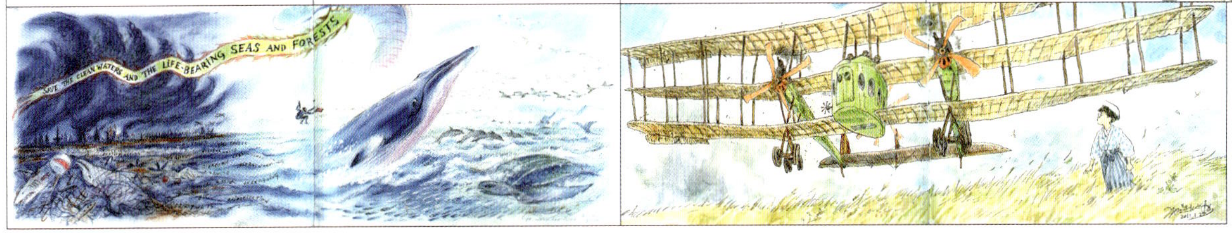

Foreword by

Gérald Guerlais

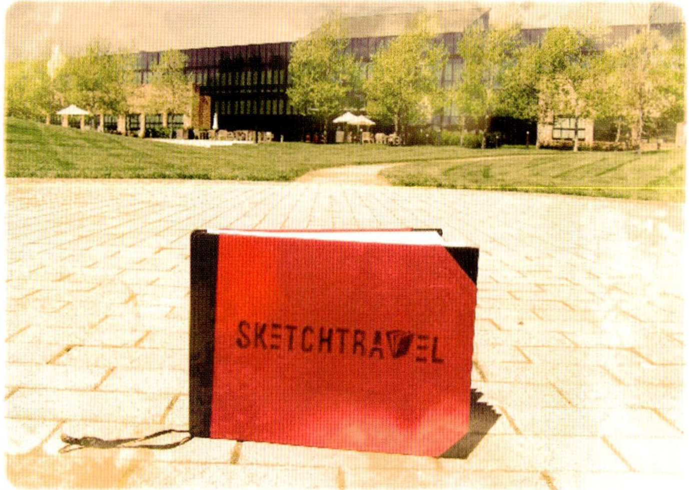

Sketchtravel at Pixar Studios

In September 2006, my friend Daisuke Tsutsumi was visiting Paris, and the creative energy that he put into his sketchbook inspired me to suggest that we share one. My idea was that we could also share this sketchbook with our friends and colleagues and the artists who made us dream—a sketchbook that would take a trip around the world.

We drew up a list of the artists we wanted to see in the book, artists of all ages and all graphic styles. And then, we started dreaming aloud. It took hundreds of e-mails, telephone calls, meetings, and miles.

Daisuke put a crazy, unbelievable energy, a contagious passion, and a lot of time into the project. As the aliens in *Toy Story 3*, a film on which Daisuke worked as artistic director, say, "I owe him eternal gratitude." Without his unflagging support, I would never have been able to convince so many artists to participate.

Five years have gone by. In your hands, you hold a work of pure persistence, a struggle, a bet on each page, a promise kept, a wanderer, a talent sponge, a test of friendship, a benign virus, a connecting thread, a witness, a storyteller, and the answer to the question, "What will happen when two strangers invite seventy international artists, coming from the fields of animation, comics, and illustration, to express themselves in the same notebook?"

Understand: This is more than a compilation of individual images. There are already many of those. No. Here is a real traveling sketchbook, carried around the planet like the Olympic flame, from hand to hand, in a rhythm created through inspiration and availability. A tower of Babel in pictures in which no one speaks the same language but in which everyone surely possesses the same language. A fruit of complicated passion inscribed on a walking tree.

We often wrongly imagine artists holed up in their studios working ceaselessly to polish their work, sometimes in a group, sometimes alone in the face of their doubts. But here, in conversation with one another, these illustrators banded together to create a work of enormous visual appeal for a good cause. In this case: rarely in competition, yet often striving with a spirit of generosity and curiosity to produce an image equal to those already in place. Here you will find previously unknown talents who deserve a spotlight and legends who were thought to be unreachable.

Globalization is not always a bad word. Sometimes people around the world can join their talents and their efforts, use their resources, and, without considering the personal cost, contribute to a collective work that surpasses what each one could achieve alone without losing the individuality of any. The artists donated their work, and the income from the book benefits the nonprofit literacy organization Room to Read. Thanks to them, thousands of children in disadvantaged countries will be able to read, discover, and, in their turn, share.

In these pages you will find gouache, oil, acrylic, ink, charcoal, pastel, and even collage; the desire to surpass oneself, the poetry of childhood, fantasy, humor, tears, first steps and maturity; ghosts, sweat, fears, dreams and nightmares, tears of joy and pain, demons and angels, inspiration, mistakes, slip-ups, passions, provocations, tributes, winks, smiles, and fingerprints. Proof of love itself. Great friendships. The sum of everything human.

Welcome. We thank you for choosing *Sketchtravel* and wish you a pleasant voyage on our lines, curves, and flourishes.

—G. G.

Foreword by

Daisuke "Dice" Tsutsumi

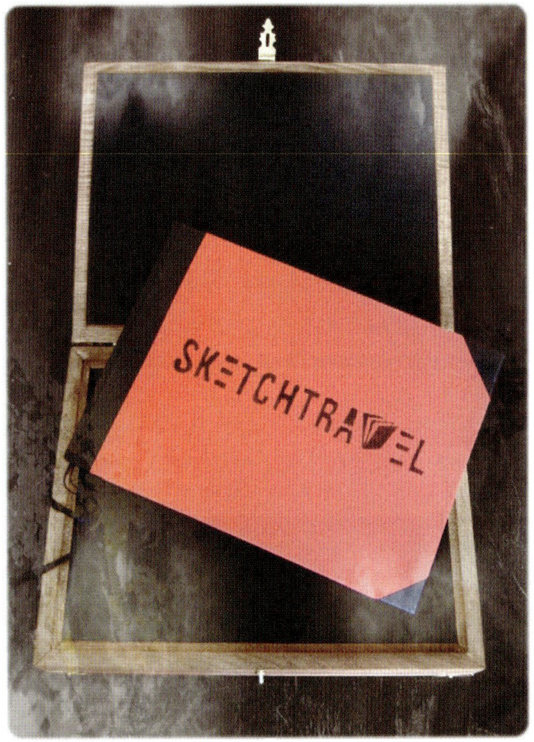

The notebook in its carrying case.

Staring at the gray, November Montreal sky through the airplane window on my flight back to San Francisco, I held the red sketchbook tight in my arms, deep in recollection of the forty-eight hours I had just spent in the French Canadian city.

I had never dreamed I would have the opportunity to meet the animation legend Frédéric Back. But just a few weeks after our mutual friend Charles Solomon connected us, I set foot in Montreal to visit the atelier of one of the masters who had made me want to start my career in animation.

The selection of the seventy-one artists participating in *Sketchtravel* was all based on the connections between us. Everyone in this book is someone linked to us by the delicate thread of personal connection, the lines along which invitations traveled and were accepted. Many were our friends already, and many more became friends of ours through this project.

Frédéric Back, the man whom I had admired ever since I first saw his Oscar-winning short, "The Man Who Planted Trees," was full of spirit despite his eighty-six years. I was much younger, but his everlasting passion and dedication and charming sense of humor made me feel old by comparison. He has dedicated his life to animation and to communicating his sociopolitical views in the form of animated films. His technical achievements have been respected by animation communities around the world, but it is the content of his films that has struck the hearts of audiences from generation to generation. His films have always had a purpose.

"If your art doesn't have a purpose for the world, what is the point?" he said, his one eye flashing with determination. The sparkling eye of this legendary figure made me realize I had not taken my own art as seriously. All artists start studying art with the desire to be able to express something, not just to make a living and comfortably sit on the nest of "a successful career." I had worked hard to achieve certain things in my career to be viewed as somewhat "successful." But had I been really following my heart with such dedication, as Frédéric had? Overwhelmed by the weight of his words, I suddenly found tears running down my cheeks.

There are seventy-one unique stories in this book, and seventy-one face-to-face encounters between artists went into its four-and-a-half year journey. The extraordinary experiences I have had through Sketchtravel—spending all afternoon with Carlos Nine in Buenos Aires, his atelier full of his family's good humor; figuring out the eccentricity of the mysterious Nicolas Marlet at his beautiful home garden in Los Angeles; being scolded with words full of wisdom and life by Hayao Miyazaki—these are memories I will treasure for the rest of my life.

The mind-boggling images inscribed in these pages are well deserving of praise. But for me, and I know for many of the other artists who participated, this project cannot be described without the personal encounters between artists on its journey. We established the rule that the book must be handed off in person because we knew this rare international collaboration was not just about the artwork, but about the connection between artists.

As I was on my way out of Frédéric Back's atelier, he stopped me and told me I had forgotten something.

"This will be better off in your hands," he said, handing me an original animation cel from "The Man Who Planted Trees."

It was an image of the young man following old Elzéard Bouffier.

—D.T.

Making Use of a Notebook, from Dürer to *Sketchtravel*

by Fabien Simode

In 1521, at the end of a year's travel that took him from Cologne to Anvers, from Aix-la-Chapelle to Bruges, passing through Tiel on the Rhine, Albrecht Dürer came back to Nuremberg with a little cabinet of curiosities in his trunk: a baboon, coral, fish fins, parrots (alive), mussel shells, elk hooves . . . In a corner, a logbook and two sketchbooks of different sizes and uses. The smaller one contained pen portraits, the second, a number of ordinary objects, landscapes and architecture, people and animals, in silverpoint. Records of fleeting memories as much as study notebooks, they were the extension of the master's eye, noble recipients of the hand of genius, as were the notebooks of da Vinci at about the same time.

More than four centuries went by before Vincent van Gogh covered several thousand stunning pages in his turn. In the meantime, in 1832, Eugène Delacroix came back from his travels in North Africa and Spain with several albums completely filled with drawings and notes. Later, Pablo Picasso never ceased scribbling everything that went through his head—what a head—in his notebooks! These notebooks led to the birth of *Demoiselles d'Avignon* and with it, modernity in painting.

The Invention of the Artist's Notebook

The sketchbook has seen the birth of each moment in the history of art. It has been the first step in developing a work of art since the Italian Renaissance: noble Moleskine or simple collection of lined or blank sheets, graph paper prized by Bouguereau or white or pink paper such as we find in Dürer's notebooks, spiral bound or with glued binding, with stiff covers with marbled paper like some of Delaunay's, or simply soft covered. Sketchbooks—works in themselves, no less! In the nineteenth century, the sketchbook acquired its own respectability when new kinds of high-quality paper appeared. Artists crossed the English Channel to obtain English-made paper, the highest quality; for example, the Whatman paper that Manet made into a notebook when he stayed in Boulogne in 1868. Of course, the artist didn't forget to bring back from his travels a box or two of pocket watercolors from Rowney, there again much better than the French watercolors. The quality of a notebook, its paper, and the way it feels in the hand all invite the artist to choose one technique over another, sometimes even a style. This thin sheet won't support the weight of a brush swollen with gouache, while that lightweight paper won't survive the scars inflicted by the aggressive weight of graphite. Thus, thanks to the perfecting of the sketchbook and of its traveling companion watercolor, Turner, Jongkind, and Boudin could finally leave the studio to paint directly from nature. Impressionism had just been born. Having become an identifiable genre, the notebook was filled up with its lively graphite sketches, sometimes highlighted with colors, a few notes jotted in the margin. We see in these pages a genuine witness to creation, perhaps the only witness, with its hesitations, its regrets, its dazzling speed. Then, the book was taken apart for collectors. From the intimacy of the artist's desk drawer to the library of a collector, the painter's notebook gained the nobility of art and its picture rails. Edward Steichen showed the erotic nudes torn from Rodin's notebooks at Gallery 291 in New York in 1908, and in 1929, Paul Signac continued the tradition with his sketches of famous French ports.

The Discovery of the World:
The Travel Notebook

Dürer, Delacroix, Manet, Signac . . . The sketchbook is indisputably linked to travel. Maurice Denis, great master of the sketch because he was a great traveler, or great traveler because he was a master of the sketch, moved from Pont-Aven to Moscow with a notebook in his pocket. Under its green morocco leather cover, the journal of Duplessis, an engineer onboard the ship *Comte-de-Maurepas*, brought back images from faraway worlds, among which were extraordinarily colored fish and, more than two centuries before Signac, views of ports. In the eighteenth century, navigators and naturalists came back from their expeditions with, as witness to their journey, drawings of previously unknown exotic animals or flowers, sketched on large, annotated pages. Can you imagine the fascination of looking for the first time at a tamarind? At that moment in history, the notebook did the work that photographs would later do. One discovered the world at the same time as one committed it to paper. The pages of notebooks became as precious as those of the Bible, the only irrefutable proof of the existence of another world. Samuel Fallours would amuse himself, populating his world with a carnival of animals as fanciful as fantastic.

And then in the nineteenth century exploration was slowly replaced by the contours of the voyage. Writers, painters, and dreamers left to discover Europe, their destination Italy and the Grand Tour. All through his life, Girodet filled hundreds of pages with poems and sketches. We have very few of his notebooks, but those we do possess document his thinking as much as his move to Naples between 1793 and 1794. After Girodet, the list of great French sketchers might begin under the pencil of Prosper Mérimée. Victor Hugo, too, seized upon the notebook to use it for his art. In the hands of the poet, it took a definite romantic turn. But in the twentieth and twenty-first centuries, what has happened to the artist's notebook? We might think it dead, killed on the altar of abstraction . . . This would be to forget Mondrian working out his grids on the pages of a notebook, indicating in the margin what is blue, yellow, or red. It would also be to forget Zao Wou-Ki, another great sketcher in notebooks, bringing back from his maiden voyage in a Volkswagen, in 1948, six notebooks of ink and watercolor full of Cézanne's Saint-Victoire, the French countryside, Italy, and Spain, as well as his own abstraction. Was the sketchbook weakened by photography? Consider the prints glued into the logbook of Laurent Tixador and Abraham Poincheval, who set out from Nantes by foot to go over to Caen and Metz (*L'Inconnu des grands horizons,* 2002). Supplanted by the digital? To animate her sketches, Blanca Casas Brullet today tests the plasticity of the sketchbook in video format. Has it fallen into disuse? One single notebook of the student Thibaut Waré is enough to stand witness to the interest of young artists today.

Sketchtravel, an Artistic and Human Adventure

Then, what happened? Drunk on the freedom obtained through pencil marks, the artist's notebook has slid toward the artist's book. The formats and techniques have adapted. The artists' intentions are not the same as they were in the eighteenth and nineteenth centuries: to make a work, to live an artistic and sometimes human adventure, to explore the infinite possibilities of the sketchbook.

This is the way to understand *Sketchtravel*, this incredible artistic experience carried out by two illustrators, French and Japanese, Gérald Guerlais and Daisuke Tsutsumi, who, between 2006 and 2011, carried this sketchbook around the world. A traveling notebook more than a traveler's notebook, this blank book was passed from hand to hand to make, in the end, an artistic chain of more than seventy artist-illustrators of whom the last contributor is no doubt not the least—Hayao Miyazaki. It isn't just the audacity of the artists that overwhelms the story, but also sometimes their union, their brotherhood. A sign of the times and the abolition of borders, *Sketchtravel* reminds us of the book that the French writer Alain Robbe-Grillet and the American visual artist Robert Rauschenberg created across a great distance with their two pairs of hands between 1972 and 1978—*Traces suspectes en surface*. *Sketchtravel* required more than seventy pairs of hands, and with them almost as many practices, styles, approaches, and commitments. All collaborated in an aesthetic event that resulted in a single, unique notebook, indivisible in its diversity. A global positive, then, the book expresses itself as one of the last avatars of postmodernism that brought down the walls between genres. In spite of the little consideration that they enjoy in the art world, in spite of Daumier, Steinberg, and even Dalí and his unrealized *Destino*, illustration, animation, and comics are writing a new and beautiful page in the history of the sketchbook that has been held hostage by art for a long time. Friends of *Sketchtravel*, welcome to your new family.

Sketchbook artists, do not be ashamed.

Notebook for drawing, notebook of drawings. Notebook of notes. Notebook for models or logbook.

The labels don't define genres even though we can sometimes define their fields. And after all, what artist hasn't taken pleasure in filling them up, from Michelangelo to François Morellet, from the poet Apollinaire to, from now on, master Miyazaki? What artist doesn't owe much, if not everything, to his notebooks? In the end, it is the only thing that matters . . . "In the street, I have almost always my sketchbook in my hand, to be able to little by little master the movements of people and animals," August Macke says in a letter to his parents. A sentiment understood by the sculptor Alexander Calder, author of a notebook of animal caricatures in 1926, *Animal Sketching*, that urged young artists to "Have a pencil and paper with you all the time. And use them, do not be embarrassed." To sketch from their imaginations and participate in a collective adventure, the artists of *Sketchtravel* are not embarrassed.

Introduction by Charles Solomon

The original *Sketchtravel* book was passed from hand to hand like an Olympic torch in an artistic relay of more than 120,044 kilometers (almost 75 thousand miles). The results represent the personal visions of seventy exceptional illustrators, animators, and comic book artists from North and South America, Europe, and Asia.

Like many artistic endeavors, from Walt Disney's *Fantasia* to a Christo installation, the Sketchtravel project began modestly. While working at Blue Sky Studios on the *Ice Age* films, Japanese artist Daisuke "Dice" Tsutsumi compiled *Out of Picture: Art from the Outside Looking In*. The book presented personal work of some of the artists he'd met at Blue Sky, including Mike Knapp, Vincent Nguyen, Nash Dunnigan, Robert MacKenzie, Daniel López Muñoz, and Peter de Sève.

When Tsutsumi went to Paris to promote *Out of Picture*, he met illustrator Gérald Guerlais, who recalls, "I was inspired by the paintings Dice did for *Ice Age* that I saw on the DVD. I discovered his website and wrote to him how impressed I was with his work. When he told me he was coming to Paris in January 2005, I offered to serve as his guide: I hope he doesn't regret accepting."

During that visit, Guerlais got the idea that would grow into the Sketchtravel project: "We were coming back from a bookstore on the bus, and Dice was drawing in his sketchbook, which he did constantly. I said to him, 'Imagine how cool sharing the same sketchbook among all of us would be!' It's pretty hard to break Dice's concentration when he's drawing, but he looked up at me and we started talking about artists we'd like to get."

"Gérald and I are just big fan boys ourselves: Interacting with other artists inspires us to push our own work," Tsutsumi says. "Passing sketchbooks has been done many times—that's not new. But as we developed the idea, we realized it's not the drawings that would make this book special, it's the connections between the artists. That's why we decided on the hand-delivery rule between participating artists."

"When I had a gallery exhibit in Paris, I asked Gérald if he knew Rébecca Dautremer, who's one of my favorite children's book artists in France," Tsutsumi adds. "Gérald said he'd arrange a meeting, and introduced me to my idol artist in Paris! I found out later Gérald hadn't known Rebecca: He looked her up in the phone book and called her. That convinced me he would be the right partner for this project."

Tsutsumi and Guerlais began by talking about artists they knew as friends, then expanded their list to include artists whose work they respected. But they agreed the list should balance illustrators, animation artists, and comic book artists, as well as animation studios and artistic styles.

Guerlais explains, "By the end of that day we had a list—and one that wasn't very different from the final list. The process was very subjective: We invited artists we admire. Some of the artists suggested others they knew. Pierre Alary introduced us to Juanjo Guarnido; Peter de Sève arranged for us to meet Mike Mignola and Carter Goodrich. We drew from a global network of people who love sharing in the name of Art. At the time, including Hayao Miyazaki and Glen Keane was a dream: I didn't believe it would be possible."

Not every artist they invited agreed to participate. Some couldn't fit the additional work into already overcrowded schedules; others were too difficult to reach—or too modest to accept.

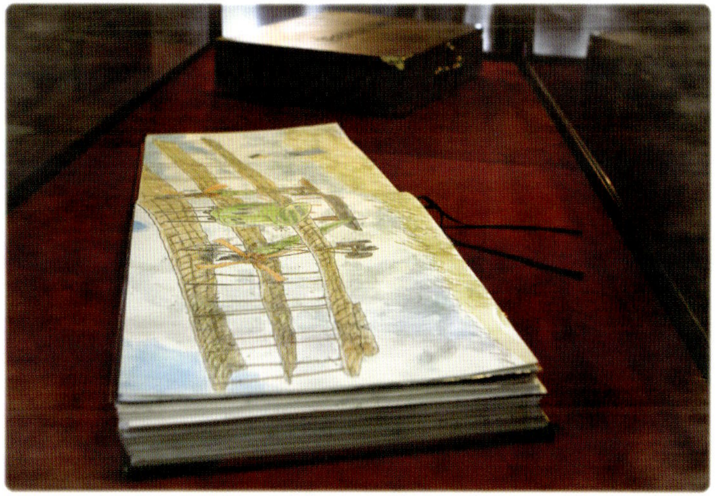

"Nicolas Marlet said no the first time I asked him: He's so humble he didn't feel he deserved to join the other artists!" Guerlais says. "Three years later, I insisted and he finally said OK. I was surprised that famous artists were afraid of not being good enough."

"The book was in and out of my hands at least three times before I could commit to putting anything in it," Peter de Sève confesses. "The final hand-off was probably one of the most unusual: Greg

Couch secreted the sacred tome in a locked file cabinet at Blue Sky and hid the key in the shavings compartment of his pencil sharpener. When I saw his masterpiece, I put my head in my hands. There was no good way to follow that act. I think the final image captures my ambivalence and, let's be honest, terror about committing an image to paper."

De Sève shows a mouse who bears more than a passing resemblance to the artist nervously preparing to pick up a pencil. But he wasn't the only participant to poke fun at his own talent. Guerlais drew himself attempting to sketch while a crowd of onlookers stares over his shoulder. Paul Felix caricatured himself blithely slopping paint over the sketchbook, like one of the Queen of Hearts' attendants painting a rosebush red.

The *Sketchtravel* book reflects the diversity of contemporary graphic art. Erik Tiemens evokes the look of seventeenth-century Dutch landscape in his brooding landscape, while Dominique Bertail gives new meaning to the term *water polo* in a sunlit scene that recalls David Hockney's Southern California landscapes. M. C. Escher might envy the interlocking patterns of the crocodiles in Nicolas Marlet's sketch, while Juanjo Guarnido pays homage to some of his favorite cartoon characters. Husband-and-wife team Sylvain Marc and Véronique Joffre share their visions through a small window cut into the page they share.

Not surprisingly, many of the illustrations echo the artists' other works. Taiyo Matsumoto drew White from his celebrated manga *Tekkon Kinkreet* clutching the book. Frédéric Back's delicate colored pencil drawing of a whale fleeing a sea humankind has fouled recalls his ecologically themed films. Glen Keane's vivid studies of dancers were drawn at a reference performance during the making of Disney's *Tangled*. Hayao Miyazaki's striking watercolor of a boy staring at a fantastic flying machine echoes the soaring imagery of his animated features.

Yet each drawing reflects the reactions of a talented artist to the threats and promises of the world around him, rendered in a style that is as personal as a signature. These drawings were done not to impress viewers, but to reveal a little of each artist's heart and mind.

"To me, the most appealing thing about the project is that we each have given a moment of our lives to create a time capsule," comments Mike Lee. "Each image reflects who we were as artists and how much of ourselves we chose or were able to give."

As the *Sketchbook* passed from hand to hand and country to country, its edges began to fray and its red cover to show signs of wear. When he saw the damage the book had suffered, Daniel López Muñoz suggested buying some sort of bag or case to protect it. "A few days later Dice and I received an e-mail from Dan with a blueprint of the wooden case, which he built," Guerlais recalls. "We were flabbergasted. But Dan is an incredible artist, and his wooden case quickly became the signature of the project. The publisher is even having copies of it built for the deluxe edition of the book."

Is the *Sketchtravel* book a completed work, or is it the first installment in an ongoing series? Guerlais answers cautiously, "Dice and I need to end this first chapter before we begin writing another. But if we launch a second book, we will do it very differently: We learned a lot in 4½ years."

But Tsutsumi counters with characteristic enthusiasm, "Our goal is to have one sketchbook on an interesting journey somewhere in the world perpetually! Wouldn't it be wonderful if we had sketchbook #10 connecting 700 artists around the world in 2050?"

Although the artists who participated in the Sketchtravel project represent the pinnacle of their professions, no one took any money for their work. The book was conceived as a benefit, and the recipient the artists chose is Room to Read.

In 1998, Microsoft executive John Wood was trekking through Nepal and visited a school where more than 200 children shared a library of thirty books—which were locked away, too precious to be handled. A year later, Wood returned with 3,000 books, and Room to Read began to take shape. It became an official 501(c)(3) charity in 2000, and now operates in Bangladesh, Cambodia, India, Laos, Nepal, South Africa, Sri Lanka, Vietnam, and Zambia.

According to UNESCO, more than three-quarters of a billion people cannot read or write. In addition to acquiring the basic skills, children need access to engaging books to become lifelong readers. Many of the books available in the developing world are old, in foreign languages, of low quality, and/or written for older audiences. In addition to establishing more than 10,000 libraries, Room to Read hires indigenous writers and illustrators to create new, culturally relevant children's books. By February 2010, Room to Read had published more than 4.1 million copies of over 430 original titles.

A disproportionate number of illiterate children are girls, due to economics, cultural bias, and gender discrimination. In 2000, Room to Read established the Girls' Education program, which identifies girls at risk of dropping out of school and provides the support needed to motivate, educate, and empower them to continue their education through secondary school. The program currently supports more than 6,800 girls through long-term scholarships.

Literacy skills and the habit of reading are mutually reinforcing: The goal of Room to Read is to create literacy interventions that can be replicated, enabling millions of children to acquire the skills and resources needed to become lifelong learners. Further information about these programs can be found at Roomtoread.org. The extent to which *Sketchtravel* would benefit Room to Read would not be known until more than six years after it was initially conceived, when the French edition was published and the original sketchbook was put up for auction.

On the evening of October 17, 2011, artists, collectors, and fans from the around the world converged on the Pierre Bergé & Associés auction house in Brussels, Belgium. Some came in person; others were present electronically on the Web.

"Having the completed book in my hands, in January 2011, was the first climax of this adventure; the auction in Brussels was the second," says Guerlais. "The auction was both stressful and a real joy. Having the event in Brussels, the home of many international organizations and the capital of European comics, seemed highly appropriate. But those six days were like a marathon: We had a signing in a bookstore, plus radio interviews and a TV show on the same day."

"The events surrounding the auction were incredible, emotional, and REALLY difficult to plan," agrees Tsutsumi. "Some of us went without any sleep at all leading up to the event. We had some bumpy roads behind the scenes, but in the end, it went beyond our expectations."

"Some of the contributors met each other for the first time in Brussels," Guerlais continues. "It felt like a family get-together, but it looked like an international convention of artists and collectors. Although not all of the seventy-one artists were able to be present, the dozen who were made the week memorable. I felt like an organizer, a spy on a mission, a producer, a circus manager, a diplomat, a rep, a poker player, and a construction worker on the Tower of Babel."

"Artists from Japan, England, France, and the United States came to the event; ultimately, I consider that more important than the auction itself," Tsutsumi adds thoughtfully. "The camaraderie and mutual respect the artists shared over Belgian beer and mussels really confirmed that we had done a good thing."

The climax of the evening came when the original *Sketchbook* was sold to an anonymous buyer for €70,000 (US$97,160 / ¥7,499,800); nine signed *Sketchbooks* brought in an additional €6,000 (US$8,328 / ¥642,840), bringing the auction's total to €76,000 Euros (US$105,488 / ¥8,142,640). "I consider the buyer the seventy-second contributor," says Guerlais. "This great person spent so much money to get the original book, proving our efforts weren't in vain."

"When we started the project, money wasn't a consideration," Tsutsumi says. "Once we got serious about the potential results of an auction, we set a goal of around US$30,000, to build a library and sponsor one children's book. Obviously, it earned substantially more."

Room to Read founder and board chair John Wood says his reaction to the book was "total and complete awe. First, for the creativity that went into each sketch, but also for the passion that so many of the contributors have for learning, creativity, and exploration."

Wood calls the results of the auction, "Incredibly important for Room to Read . . . . We will open five libraries—one each in Cambodia, Laos, Nepal, Sri Lanka, and Vietnam," he explains. "We will also publish one new local language children's book in each of those countries. More than 2,000 children in five countries will benefit from this project. Each of those children will now have access to a brightly colored children's book in their mother tongue, as well as in English, in a well-stocked and well-run library."

"Many of us in the developed world take libraries for granted, as we grew up with them," he continues. "Try to imagine what life would be like if we'd had to grow up without Dr. Seuss and Harry Potter. Yet there are hundreds of millions of kids across the developing world who don't have access to books. Their parents can't afford them, so for-profit publishers have no incentive to publish them. This contribution helps us reverse that inequality for a large number of students."

The libraries will be open and the books printed by the middle of 2012. "A group of Sketchtravel artists is planning to visit the libraries when they're completed," Tsutsumi concludes. "I feel we'll get a sense of closure on this project once we see the effect of our adventure in person."

"I thought the auction would feel like the final chapter," Guerlais concludes. "But if something ended there, something else began."

That something else might be the gratitude of thousands of children who will be able to read through the efforts of Tsutsumi, Guerlais, and the other *Sketchtravel* artists.

—Charles Solomon
Los Angeles, 2012

ROBERT KONDO
RÉBECCA DAUTREMER
FRANÇOIS ROCA
LEUYEN PHAM
GÉRALD GUERLAIS
ELI HARRIS
CLAUDE-WILLIAM TRÉBUTIEN
ALEXANDRA BOIGER
BENOÎT LE PENNEC
ROBERT MACKENZIE
TADAHIRO UESUGI
ANDREA BLASICH
YOKO TANJI
NASH DUNNIGAN
BILL PRESING

SANG JUN LEE
VINCENT DI NGUYEN
MICHAEL KNAPP
DANIEL LÓPEZ MUÑOZ
LOU ROMANO
LUIS GRANÉ
ENRICO CASAROSA
RONNIE DEL CARMEN
JEROME OPEÑA
PETER NGUYEN

MIKE MIGNOLA
ROBERT VALLEY
DOMINIQUE LOUIS
ERIK TIEMENS
SCOTT CAMPBELL
JAMES JEAN
YUKO SHIMIZU
DOMINIQUE BERTAIL
DAVID GORDON
BILL PLYMPTON
THE KERASCOËT
PIERRE ALARY
ÉRIC GOSSELET
GRÉGOIRE VILLERMAUX
JOHN HOWE

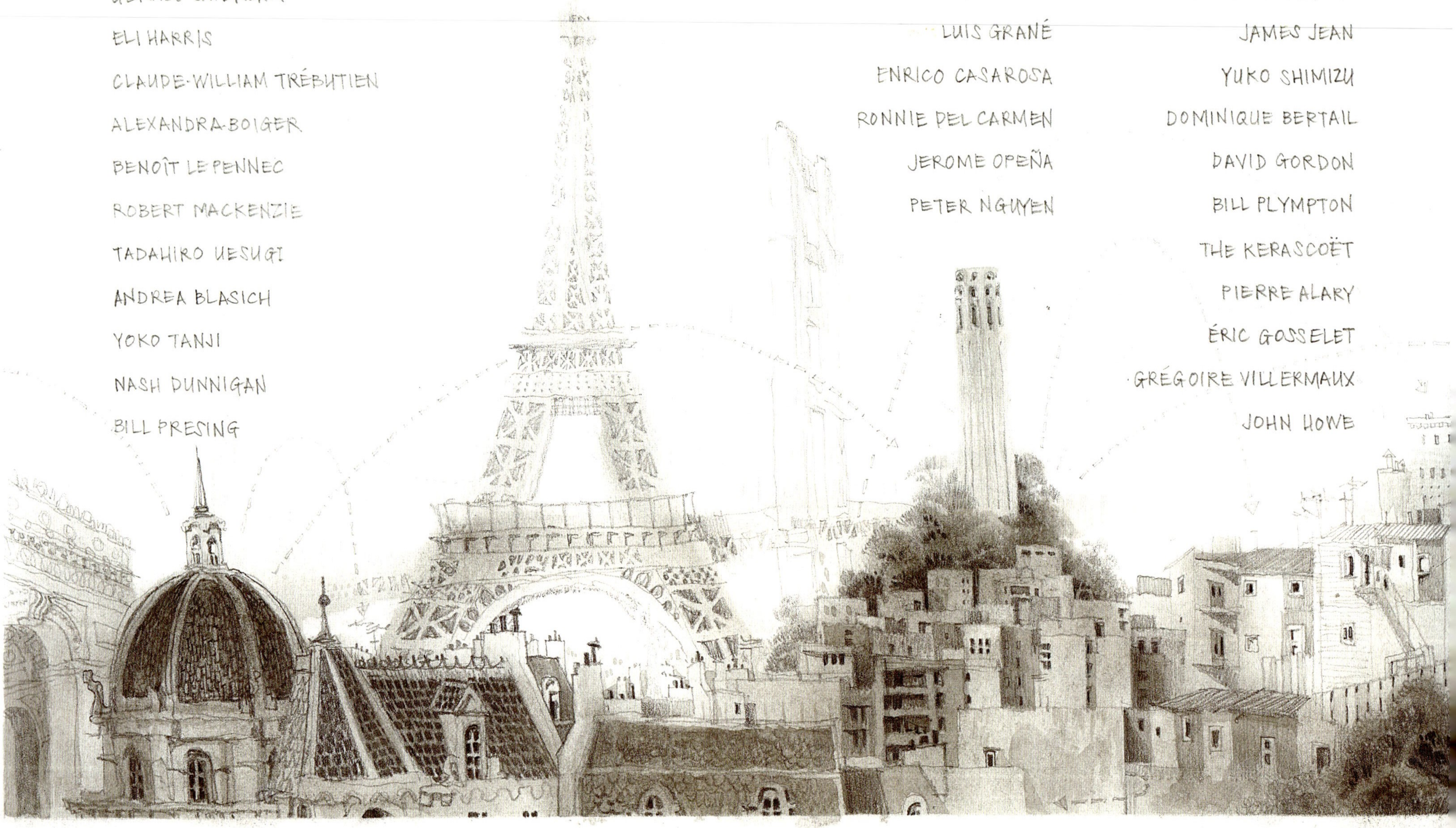

QUENTIN BLAKE
MIKE LEE
DANIEL ADEL
NICOLAS DE CRÉCY
AURÉLIEN PREDAL
MAÏLYS VALLADE
ENRIQUE FERNANDEZ
JUANJO GUARNIDO
SYLVAIN MARC
VÉRONIQUE JOFFRE

LORELAY BOVE
TOMER HANUKA
GREG COUCH
PETER DE SÈVE
BEN BUTCHER
NATALIE ASCENCIOS
KATSUYA TERADA
CARTER GOODRICH
CARLOS NINE
ALEX PUVILLAND
CHRIS APPELHANS

PAUL FELIX
GLEN KEANE
KOJI MORIMOTO
ATSUKO FUKUSHIMA
TAIYO MATSUMOTO
CATIA CHIEN
NICOLAS MARLET
DAISUKE TSUTSUMI
FRÉDÉRIC BACK
HAYAO MIYAZAKI

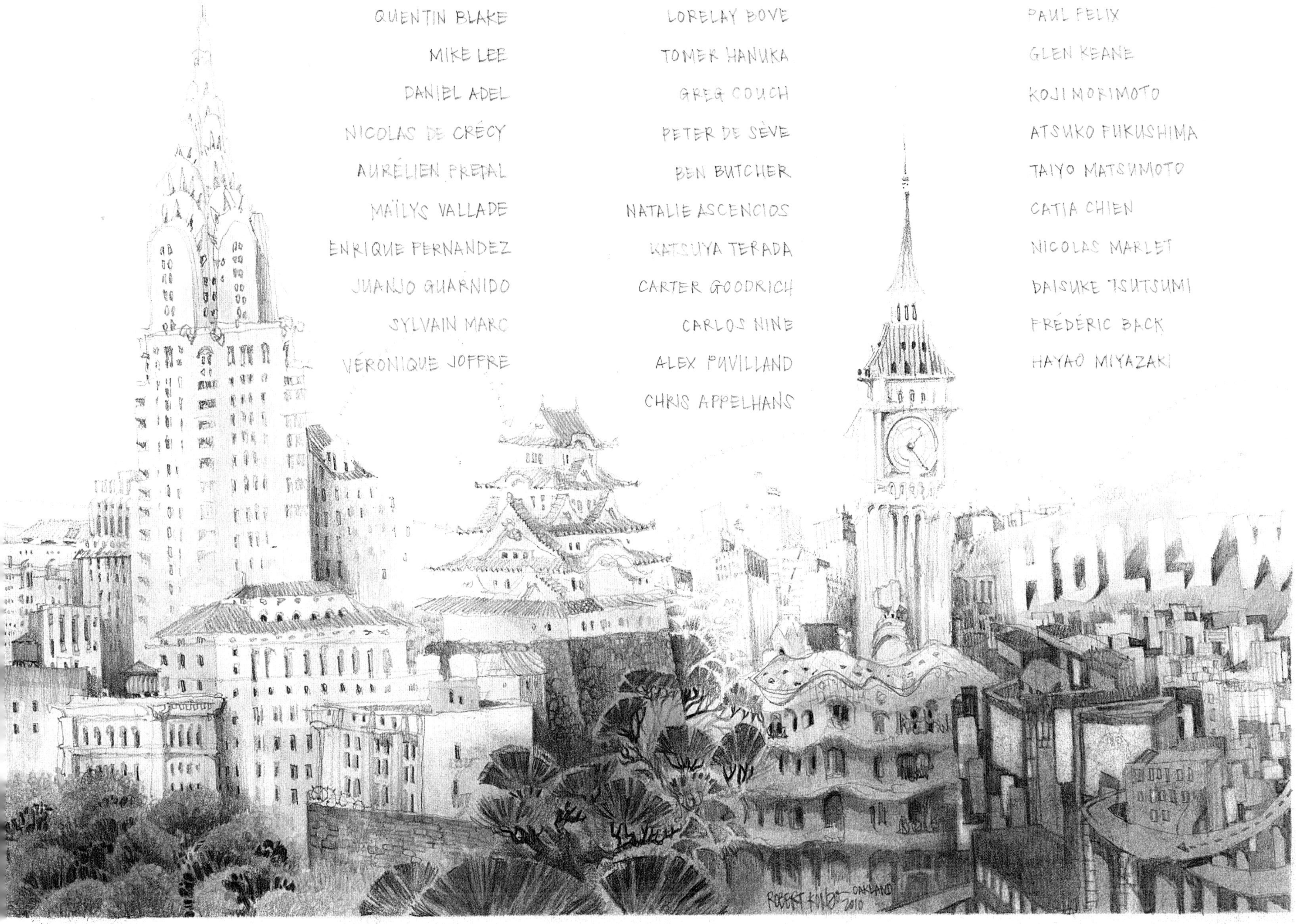

Robert Kondo

ROBERT KONDO

"This project is unbelievable. Thank you for including me."

OAKLAND
2010

Robert Kondo received *Sketchtravel* from the hands of **Nicolas Marlet** on March 10, 2010, in Burbank and gave the book to **Daisuke Tsutsumi** a few days later in San Francisco.

Stop 58 — Stop 59 — Stop 60

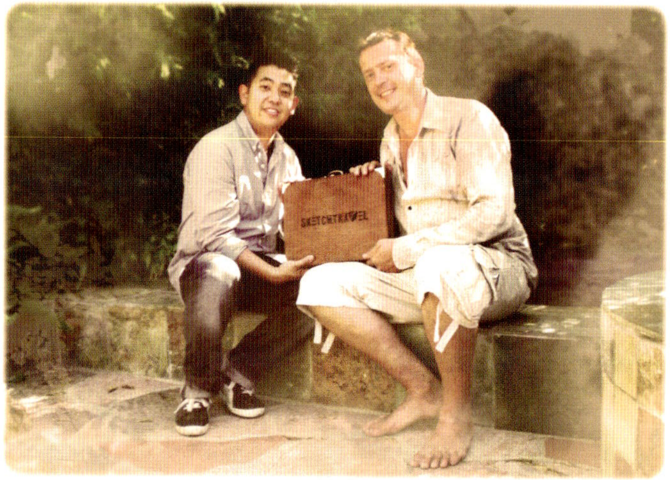

Robert Kondo and Nicolas Marlet

Rébecca Dautremer

Rébecca Dautremer

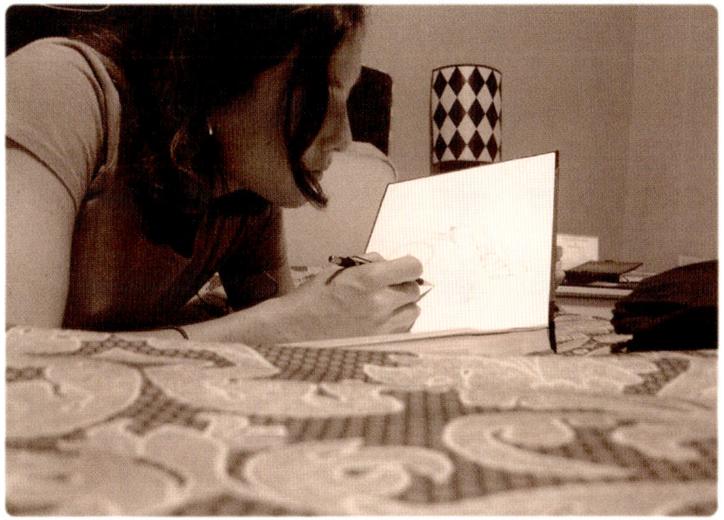

Rébecca Dautremer

"I took the notebook with me to San Francisco before I made my contribution. Because I was doing the first page, I didn't have the pressure that the other contributors did to compare, so I chose very calmly to play the game of sketchbook. I mean that I painted on a red Formica table in a donut shop on Mason Street. The waitress wanted to bring me a glass of water rather than have me dip my brush in my too-sweet chocolate. She was studying at the California College of Art, by coincidence.

Then, I made an appointment with Alexandra Boiger in a noisy café. She spoke good English with a German accent, and I spoke badly with my French one. Who knows what the real topic of conversation was?

If I had had the last page, I would have done something different. But that's another story."

le 10 novembre 2006.

Rébecca Dautremer received *Sketchtravel* from the hands of **Gérald Guerlais** on November 6, 2006, in Paris and gave the book to **Alexandra Boiger** November 14, 2006, in San Francisco.

Stop 3 — Stop 4 — Stop 5

Alors.... je.... bon....
Alors... Sketch Travel.... Sketch Twavelle ... yer
je vais..... je vais faire... je vais faire pour ce carnet....
je... .... Bon,, je vais faire... donc, je vais faire ce carnet... je vais.... je vais dessiner..... mmm....
... ...Ben.... qu'est ce que.... je..... je pourrais... peut.être...
Il faut... Il faudrait... donc... que.... Bem.... une.. idée?
je.... alors .....il faudrait que je trouve... il faudrait....
une idée .... UNE I-DÉE... oui ... une... je ne sais....
mais ...je ... je suis pas sûre ... que ... je sais... où.... un homme
une femme ...oui une femme.... mais... où....
oui... alors je vais dessiner... un homme... ou... à moins que...
ou une femme...non.... quand même ... donc c'est un homme ... mais ... aussi
un ... un chien...je dessine un chien... oui mais...un homme aussi... alors
Un homme et un... un chien... oui un homme ET... un chien. oui ... Bon
alors un chien ... un chien vert ... et l'homme ... une .. tiens ...
le chien enlaisse oui... non un chien bleu qui tient un homme ... qui attrape ...
non... un chien noir qui mort un homme vert... un chien vert ...oui
qui tire le... le pantalon... oui un homme vert non... non ...non
un chien ... un chien ... qui tire... l'homme... il ... est ...vert non!
non... noir ...un noir... un chien qui tire... le noir.. le but...

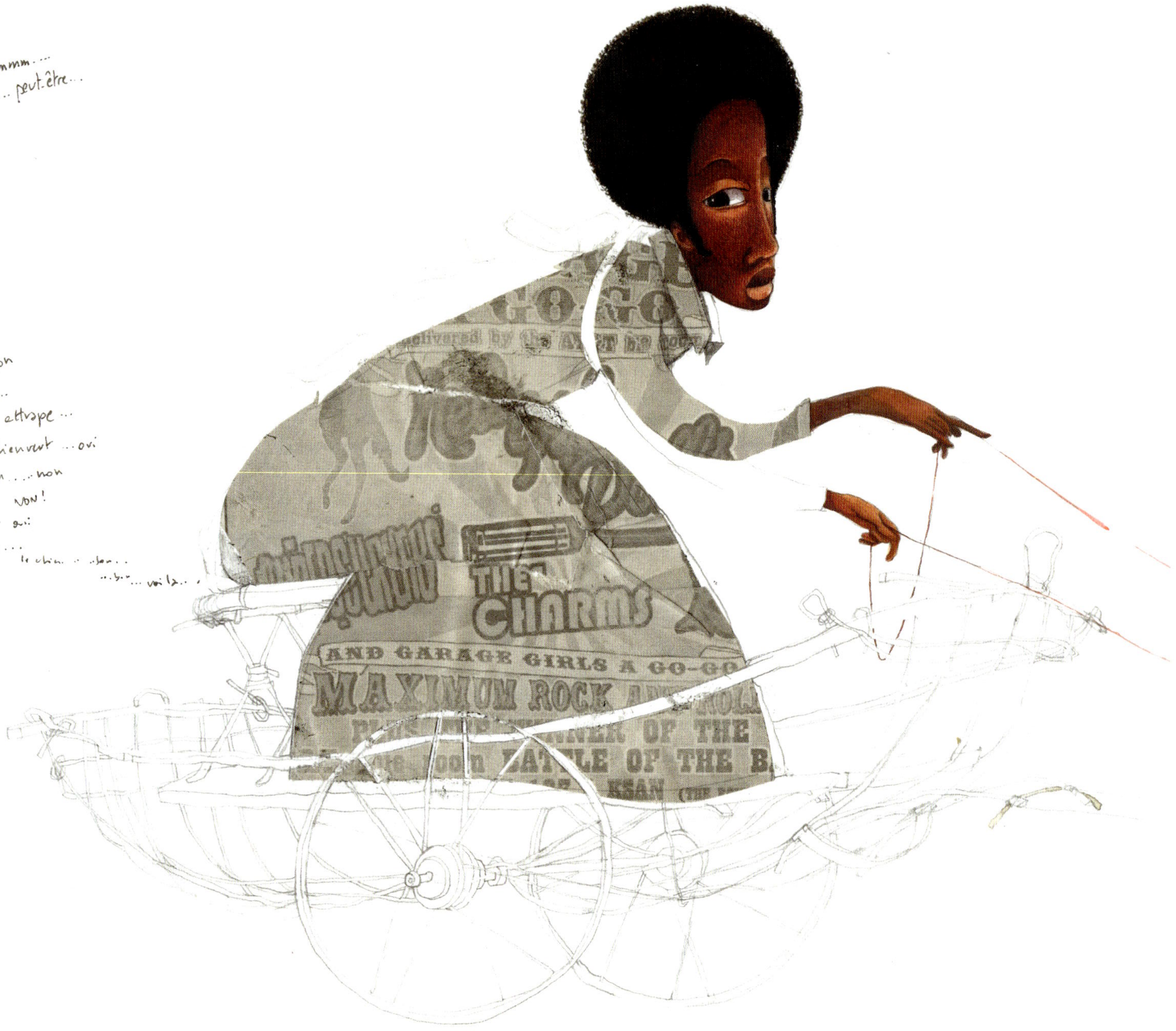

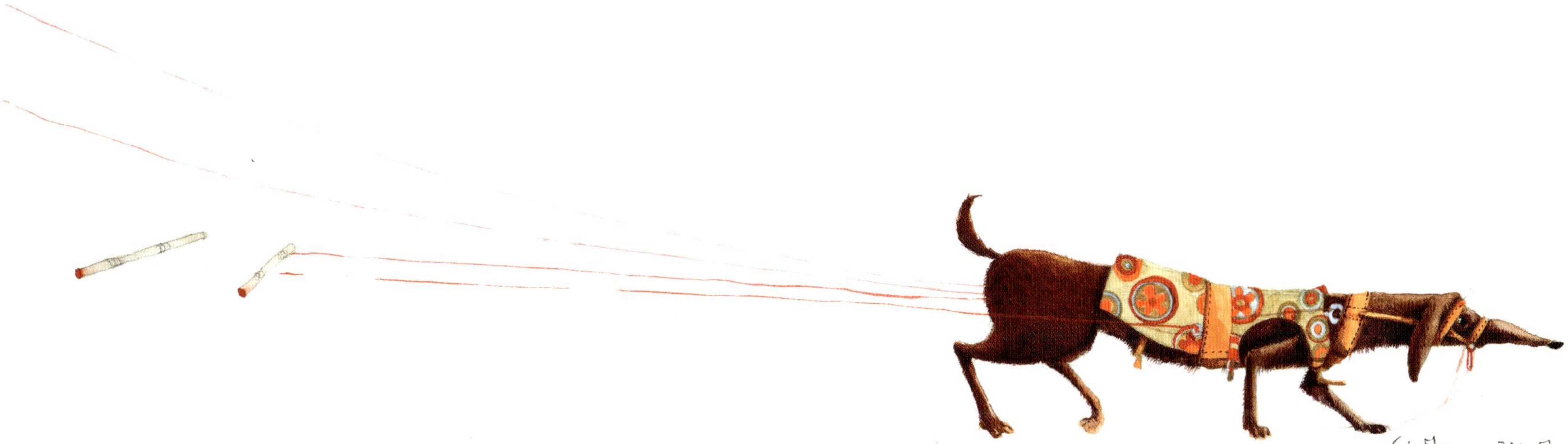

café Mason – 336 Mason street . San Francisco / CA.
le 10 novembre 2006.
Rébecca Dautremer

François Roca

François Roca

"It was after I met Gérald and Dice in Paris that they asked me to contribute to *Sketchtravel*. I was the first contributor to the project, but I didn't dare take the first page. Ladies first, in this case, Rébecca Dautremer.

I was far from suspecting the importance and the duration of the voyage of this notebook, enriched by each of the many contributions by so many talented artists.

I have only one regret, that the adventure is over, for now? . . ."

19 octobre 2006

? **François Roca** received *Sketchtravel* from the hands of **Gérald Guerlais** on October 10, 2006, in Paris and gave it back to **Gérald Guerlais** on October 20, 2006, in Paris.

Stop 0 · Stop 1 · Stop 2

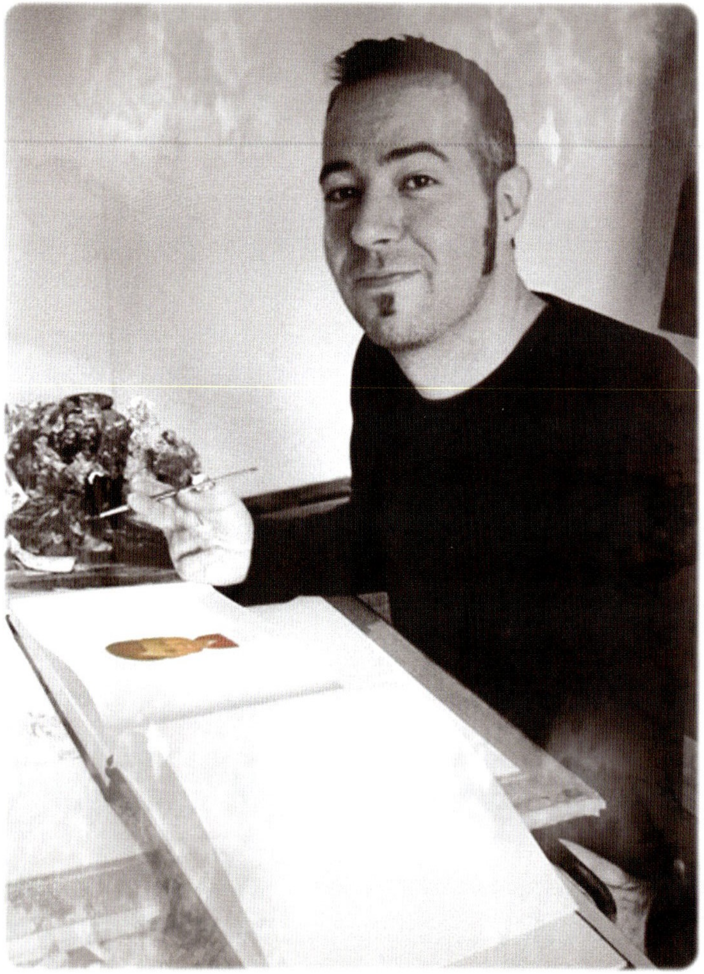

François Roca

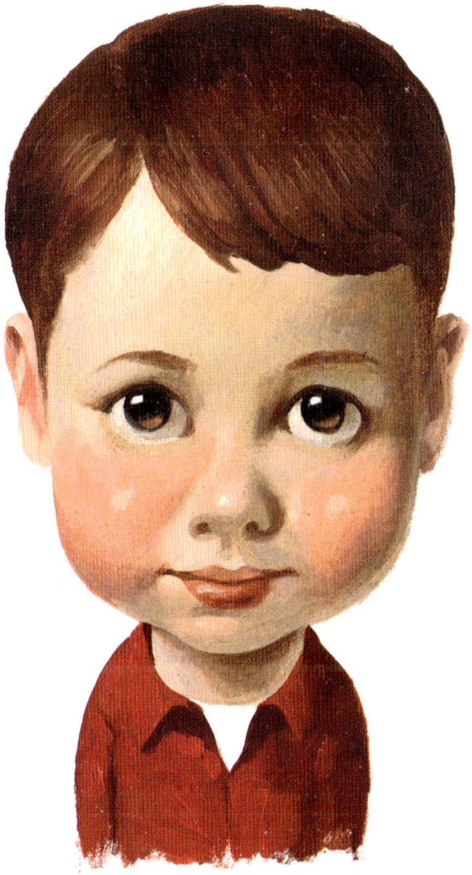

François Roca 19 octobre 2006

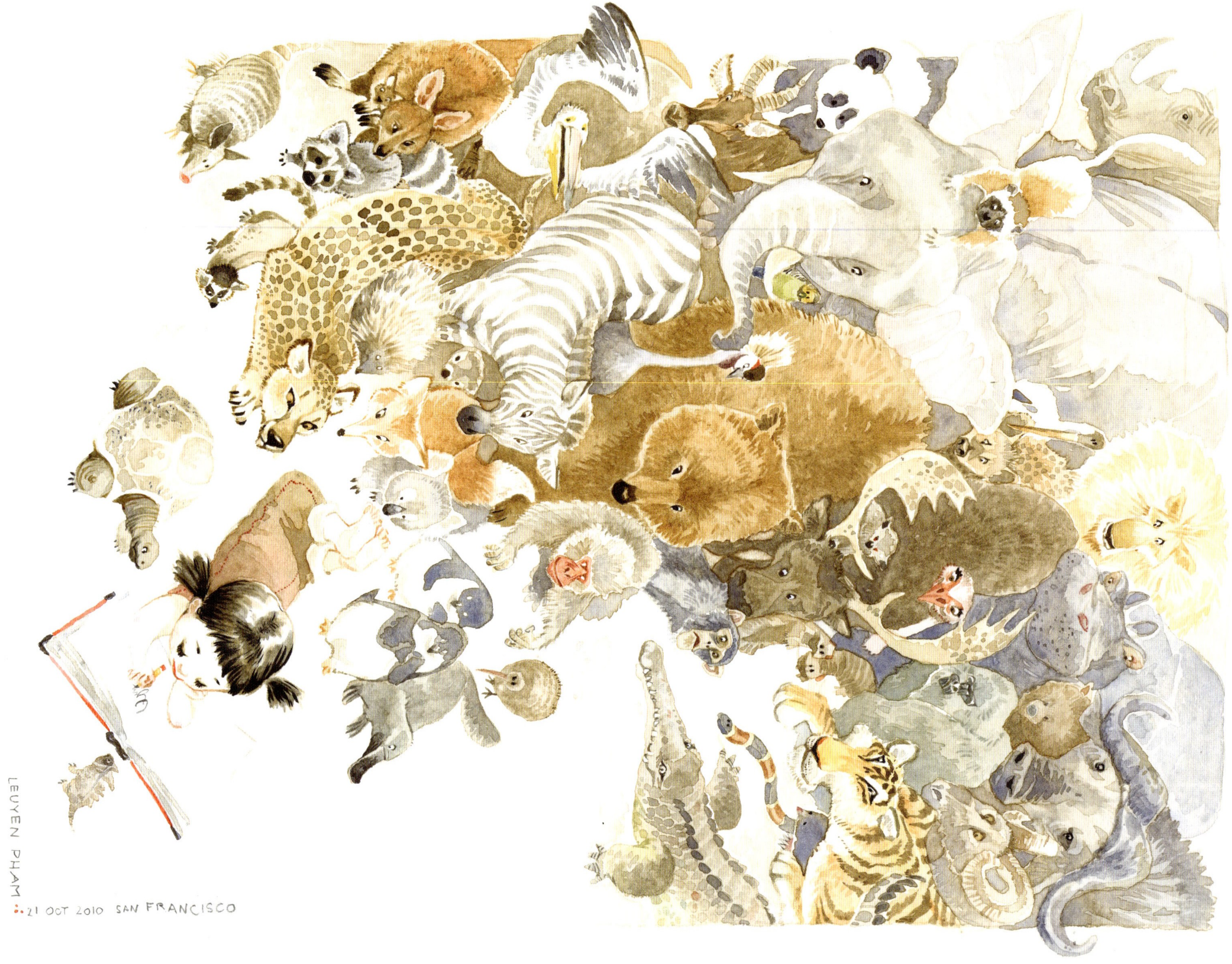
LEUYEN PHAM
21 OCT 2010 SAN FRANCISCO

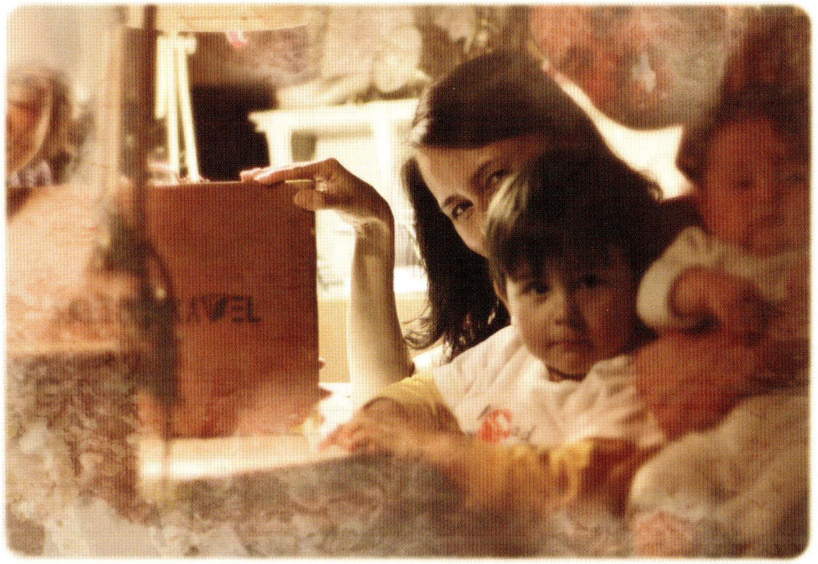
Daisuke Tsutsumi, Leuyen Pham, and Alex Puvilland with their children

LEUYEN PHAM

Leuyen Pham

"I was very happy to be one of the last to receive the book, because it gave me the opportunity to see it when it was almost done. I needed an extraordinary effort not to steal anything, there were so many beautiful things . . ."

21 OCT 2010 SAN FRANCISCO

Leuyen Pham received *Sketchtravel* from the hands of **Daisuke Tsutsumi** on October 20, 2010, in San Francisco and gave it to **Alex Puvilland** on October 21, 2010, in San Francisco.

Stop 65 Stop 66 Stop 67

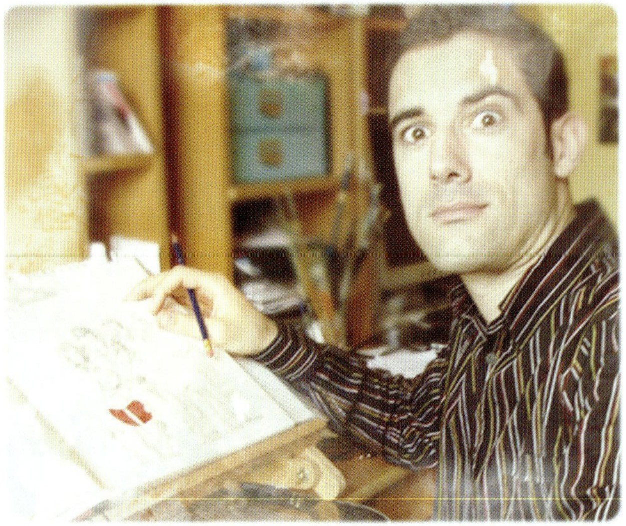

Gérald Guerlais

Gérald Guerlais

Gérald Guerlais

"Having started the project, I couldn't keep myself from worrying that I was not of the stature of the artists that inspired me so much. In this picture, I only succeeded in drawing a bit like Mike Knapp.

If I could do it over, I would change the composition and add color. We were supposed to sketch, but then in the following pages, the idea evolved . . ."

24 octobre 2006

?

Gérald Guerlais received *Sketchtravel* from the hands of **François Roca** on October 20, 2006, in Paris and gave it to **Claude-William Trébutien** on October 28, 2006, in Paris.

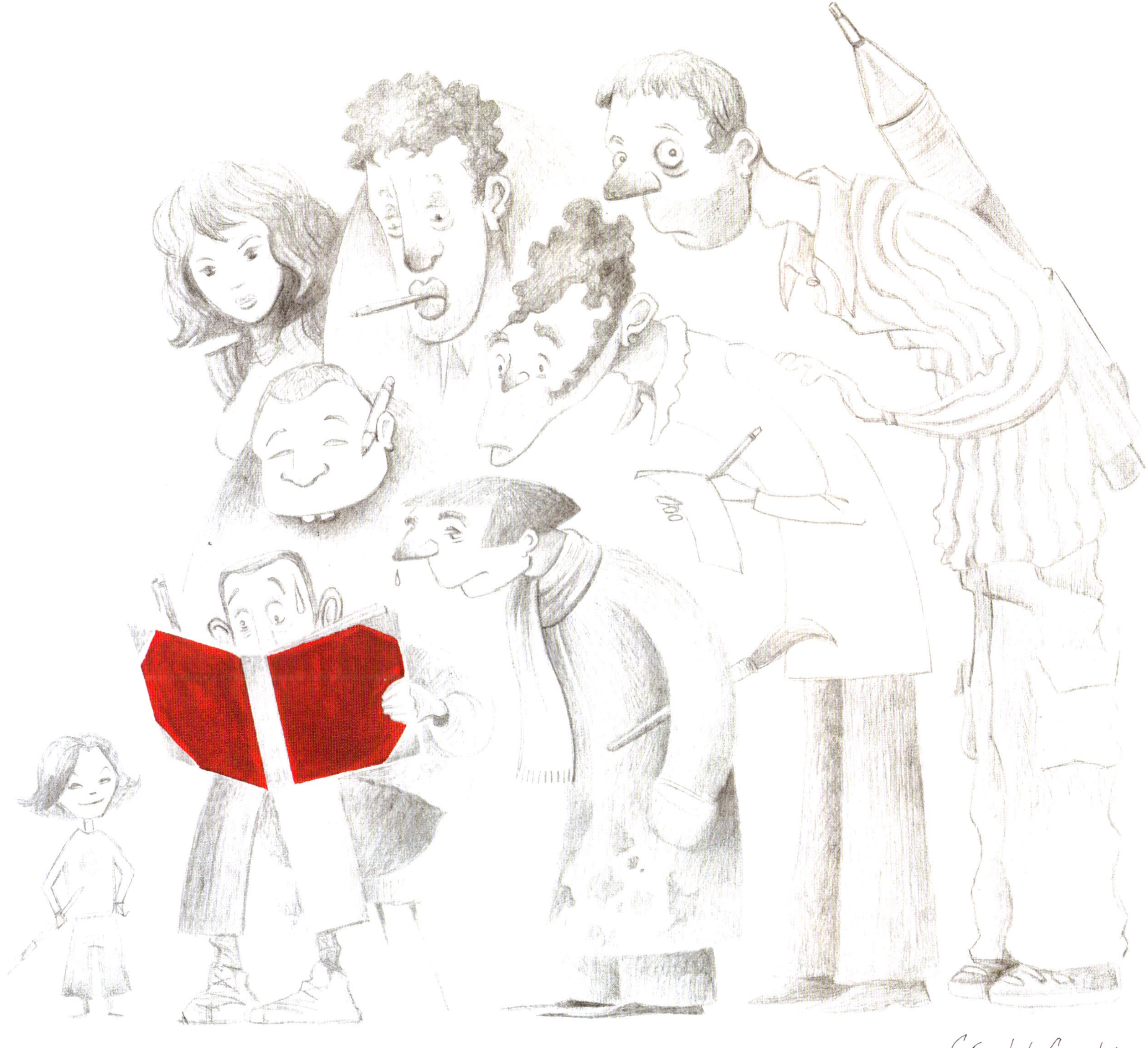

24 octobre 2006 - GÉRALD GUERLAIS -

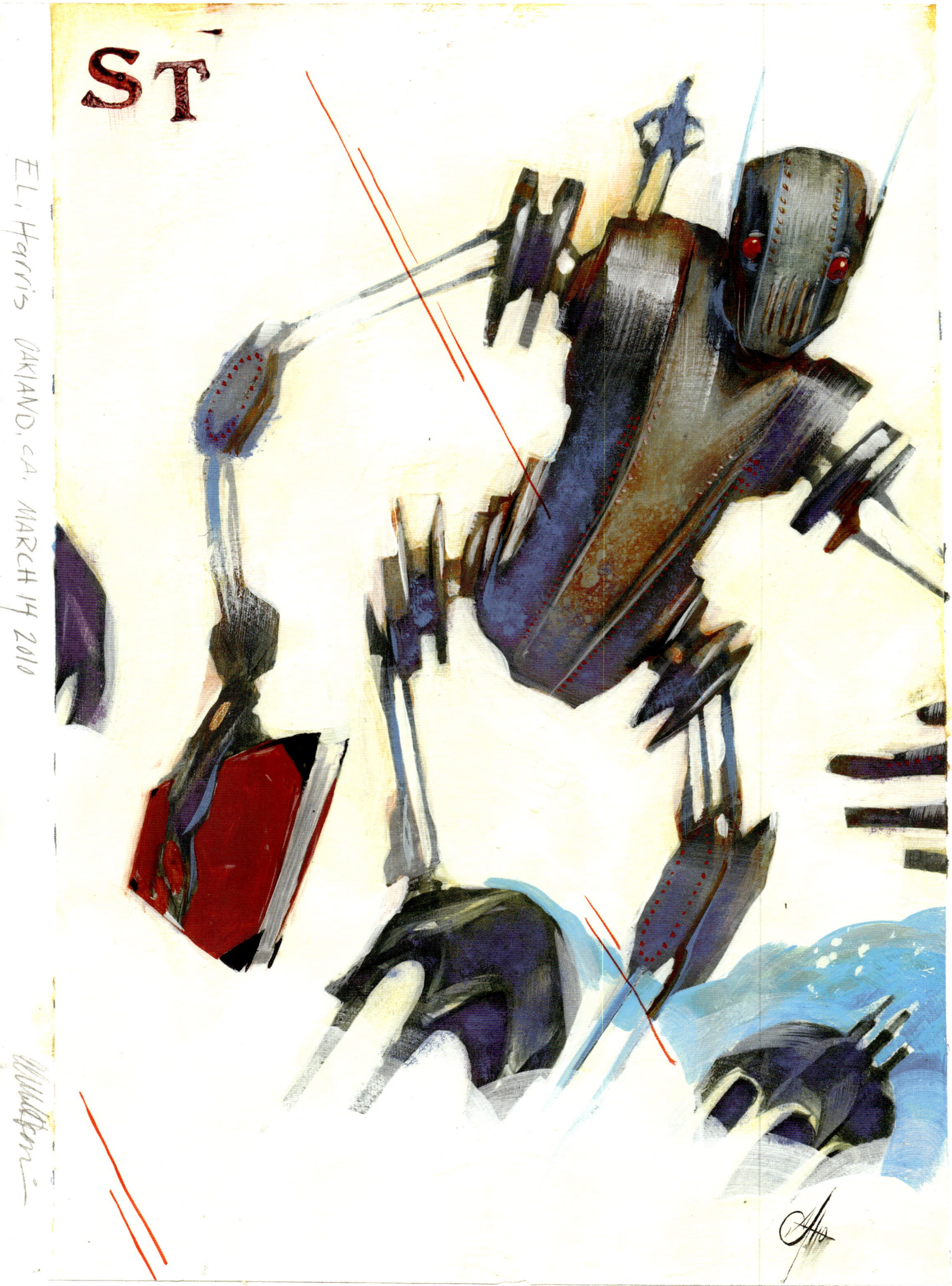
ST
E.L. Harris OAKLAND, CA. MARCH 14 2010

Eli Harris

Eli Harris

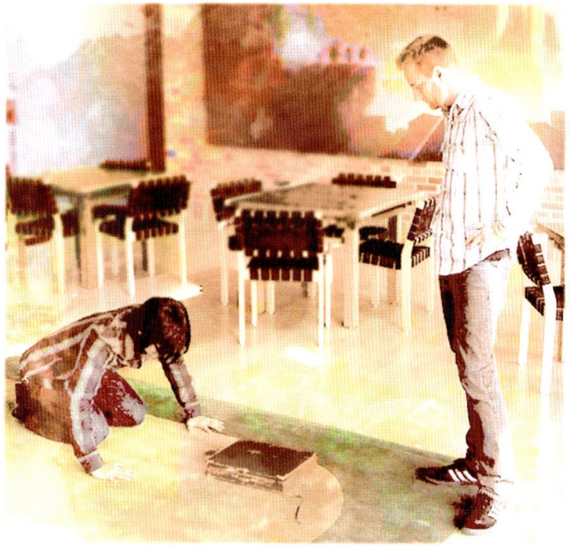

Daisuke Tsutsumi and Eli Harris

"I had the great honor to be invited by Dice Tsutsumi to contribute to *Sketchtravel*. This project brought together a large number of artists, and it was a real lesson in humility for me. The list of participants can be found on the *Sketchtravel* Web site, along with the story of its birth."

OAKLAND, CA.
MARCH 14 2010

? **Eli Harris** received *Sketchtravel* from the hands of **Daisuke Tsutsumi** on March 12, 2010, in San Francisco and gave it to **Robert Kondo** on March 19, 2010, in San Francisco.

CLAUDEWILLIAM

Claude-William Trébutien

"*Sketchtravel* is a formidable project that lets today's great illustrators and all the talents working a bit in the shadow to come together, at least from the point of view of the public.

Animation and the world of illustration are small communities, but one doesn't meet or exchange ideas with all these artists: often, one knows the work of each without knowing anything about him or her.

I myself discovered new artists and met people through *Sketchtravel.*"

30 OCTOBRE 2006

? **Claude-William Trébutien** received *Sketchtravel* from the hands of **Gérald Guerlais** on October 28, 2006, in Issy-les-Moulineaux and gave it back to **Gérald Guerlais** on October 31, 2006, in Paris.

Stop 2 Stop 3 Stop 4

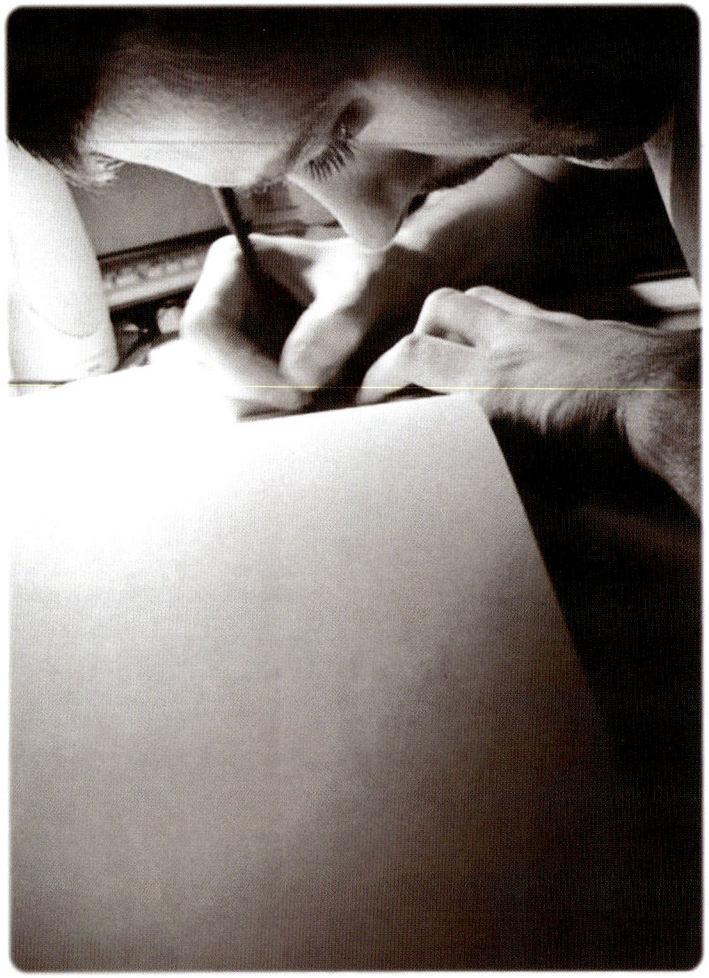

Claude-William Trébutien

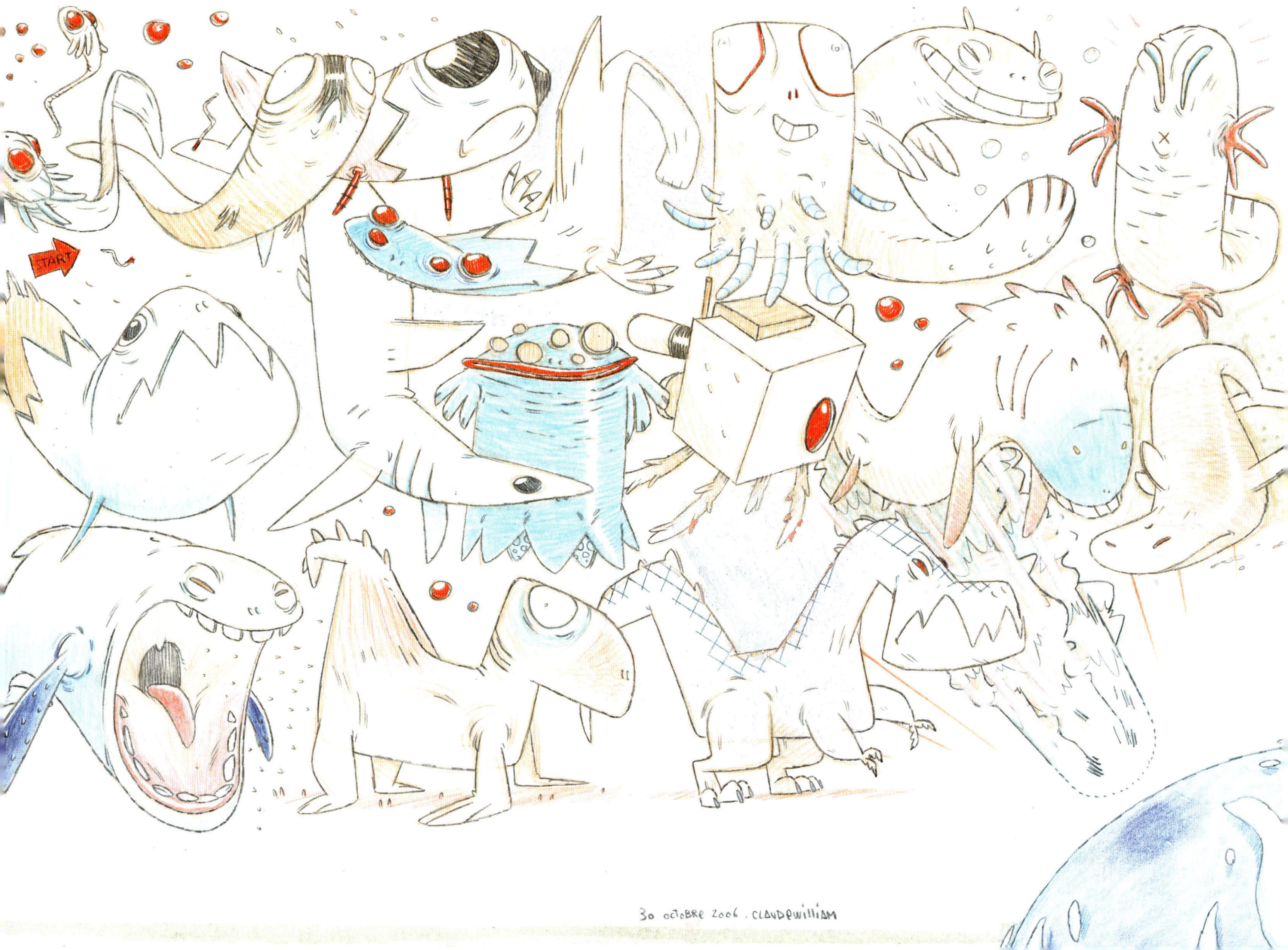
START
30 octobre 2006 . CLAUDEWILLIAM

ALEXANDRA BOIGER

Alexandra Boiger

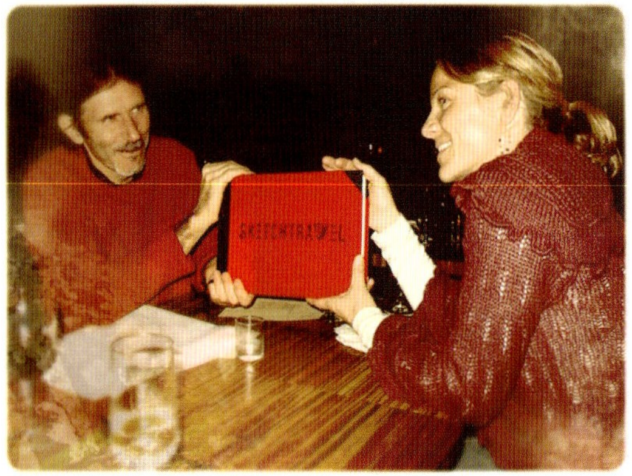

Benoît Le Pennec and Alexandra Boiger

"For me, the important thing is that the project brought together a large number of artists from different countries around an exchange of ideas and inspiration.

It also let me meet people I admire, and it finances a worthwhile cause . . . I can't find adequate words.

Sketchtravel is a book with its own history, that of a journey from artist to artist, from studio to studio. When you have the habit of working closed up in your own small studio, it is unbelievably stimulating to be part of this kind of project."

16. november 2006

? **Alexandra Boiger** received *Sketchtravel* from the hands of **Rébecca Dautremer** on November 14, 2006, in San Francisco and gave it to Benoît Le Pennec on November 24, 2006, in San Anselmo.

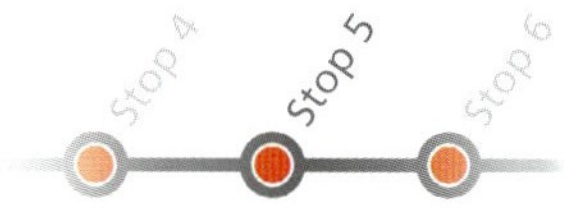

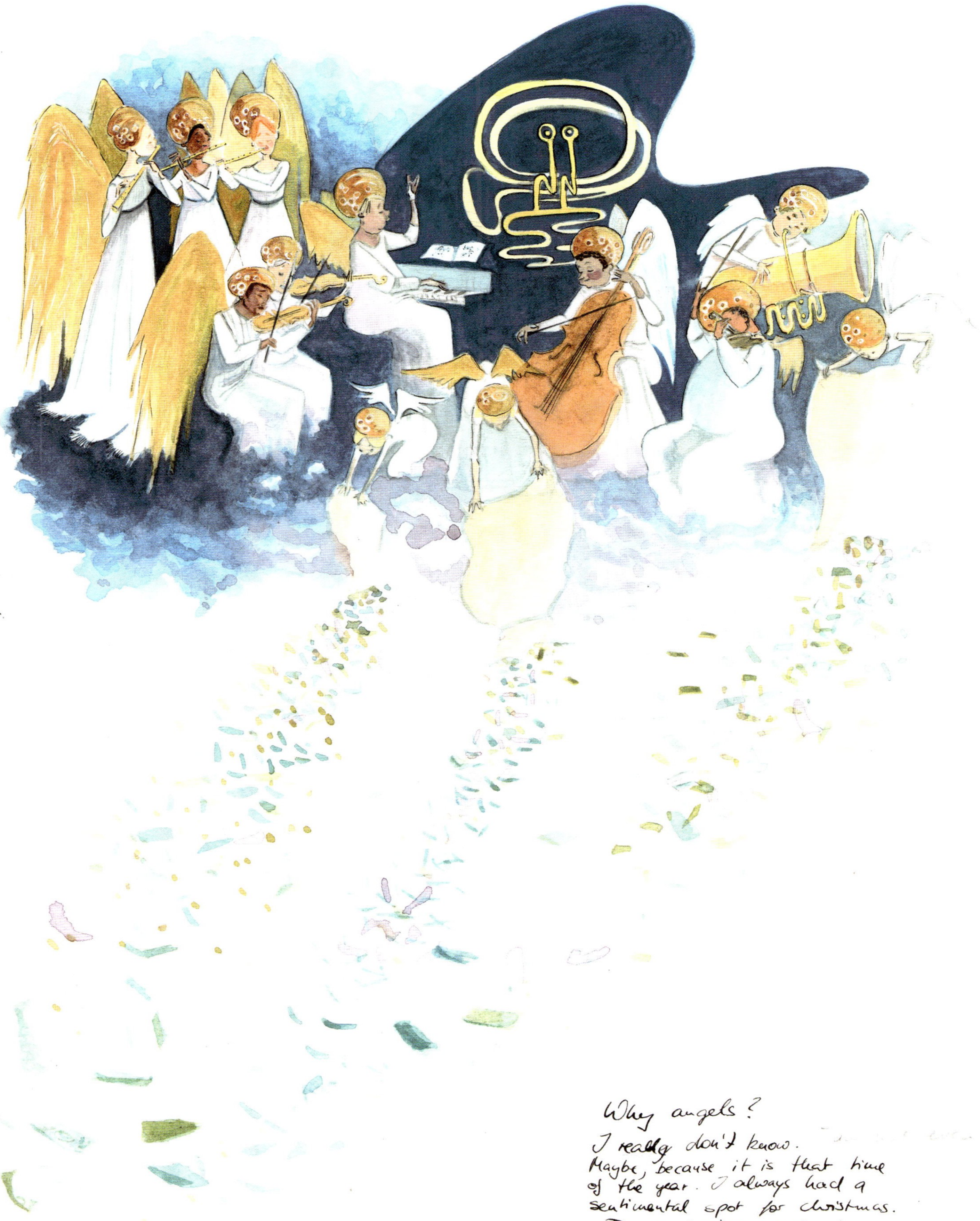

Why angels?
I really don't know.
Maybe, because it is that time
of the year. I always had a
sentimental spot for christmas.
FROHE WEIHNACHTEN!

Oh yes, and there is a
friend I have. She plays the
violin. And unfortunately I
couldn't go to her latest
recital with her chamber quartett

ALEXANDRA
BOIGER
16. november
2006

San Anselmo, USA

BENOÎT

Benoît Le Pennec

"The motivation is obvious, something fun to do and share with brilliant colleagues. You couldn't ask for more!"

11/24/06 IN ALEXANDRA'S STUDIO, SAN ANSELMO, CALIFORNIA

Benoît Le Pennec received *Sketchtravel* from the hands of **Alexandra Boiger** on November 24, 2006, in San Anselmo and gave it to **Andrea Blasich** on December 5, 2006, in San Francisco.

Stop 5
Stop 6
Stop 7

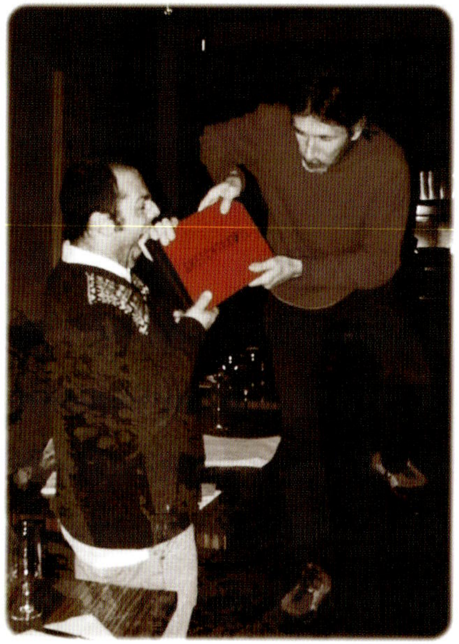

Andrea Blasich and Benoît Le Pennec

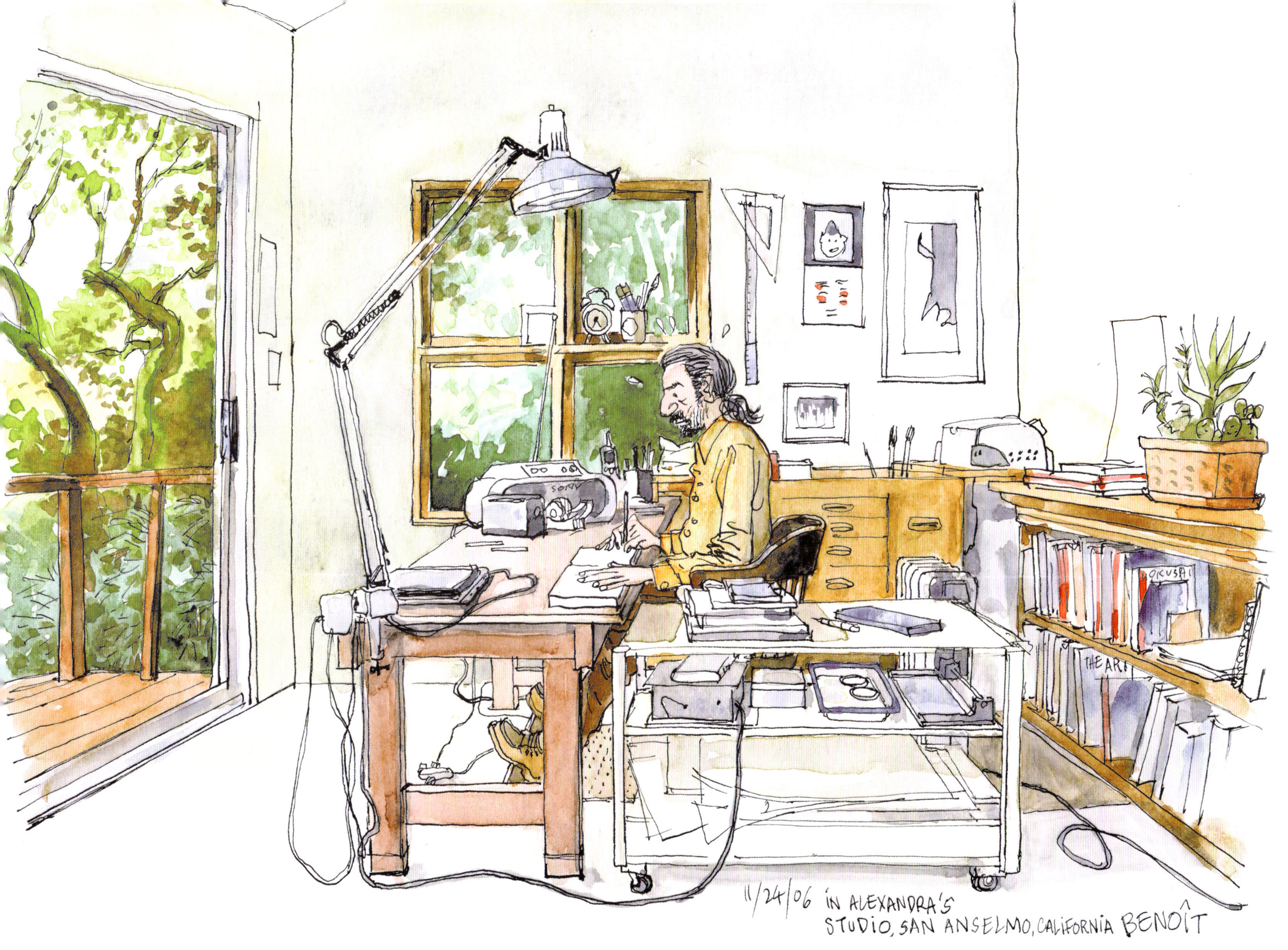
SONY
OKUSAI
THE ART
11/24/06 IN ALEXANDRA'S
STUDIO, SAN ANSELMO, CALIFORNIA BENOÎT

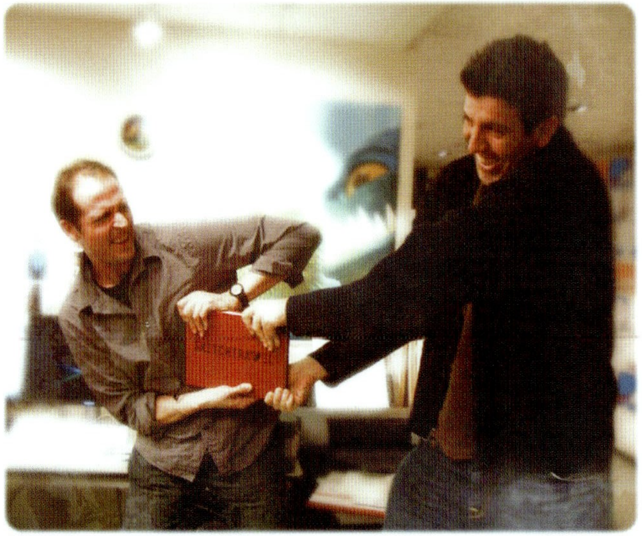

Nash Dunnigan and Robert MacKenzie

ROBERT MACKENZIE.

Robert MacKenzie

"It is good fortune and an immense honor to appear on the pages with all these talented artists, even more that it is for a charitable cause. Together, we created this book for a better world, and in the end, that is what is important about the project.

I was among the first to receive the book, and I didn't feel the same stress as those who got the book later when it had already been worked on.

That said, I was still inspired by several drawings that preceded mine; that each image had an influence on the one that followed is part of the magic of *Sketchtravel.*"

7, December 2006, New York City

Robert MacKenzie received *Sketchtravel* from the hands of **Daisuke Tsutsumi** on December 8, 2006, in New York and gave it back to **Daisuke Tsutsumi** on December 9, 2006, in New York.

Stop 7 Stop 8 Stop 9

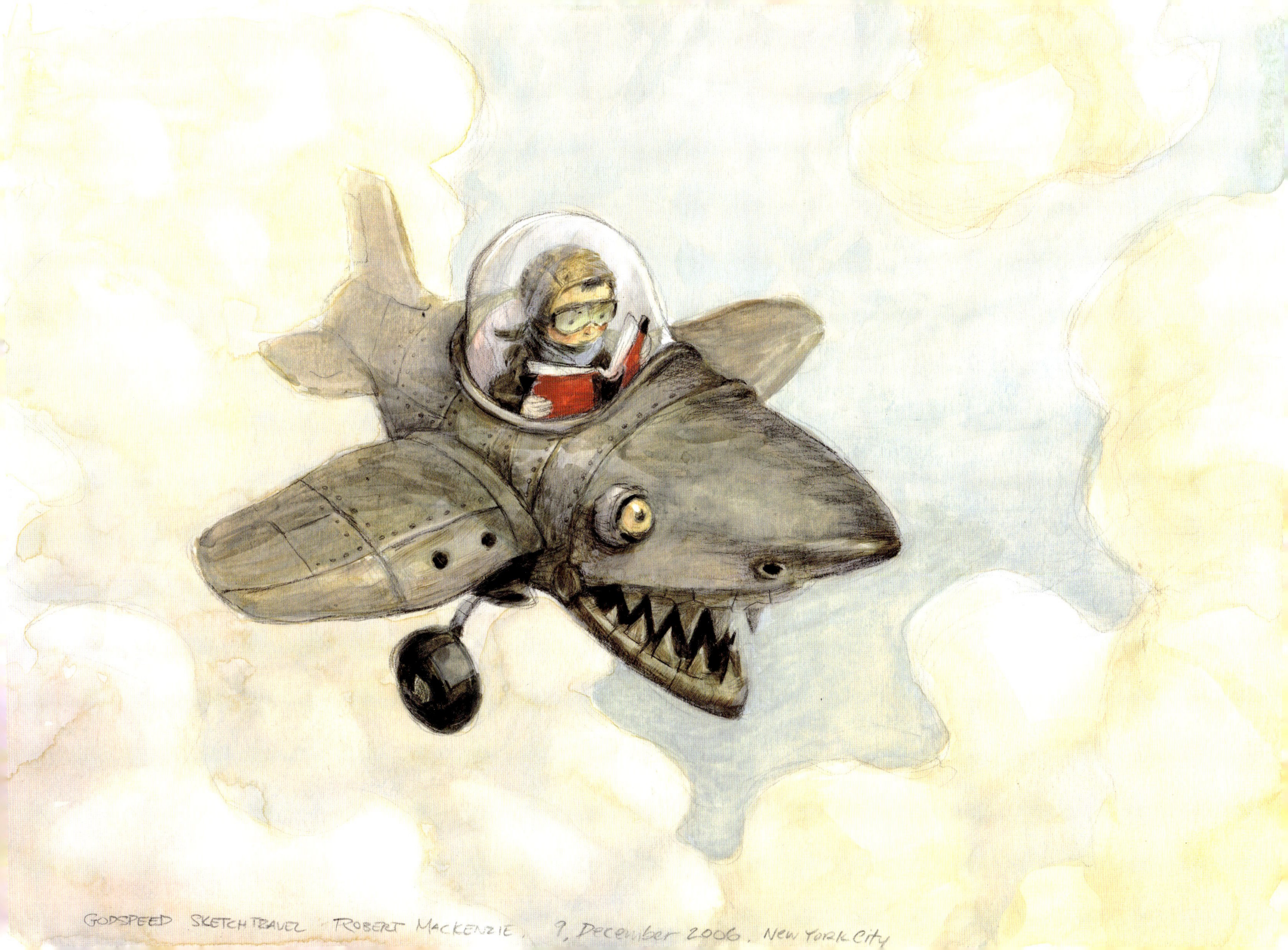
GODSPEED SKETCHTRAVEL ROBERT MACKENZIE, 9, December 2006, New York City

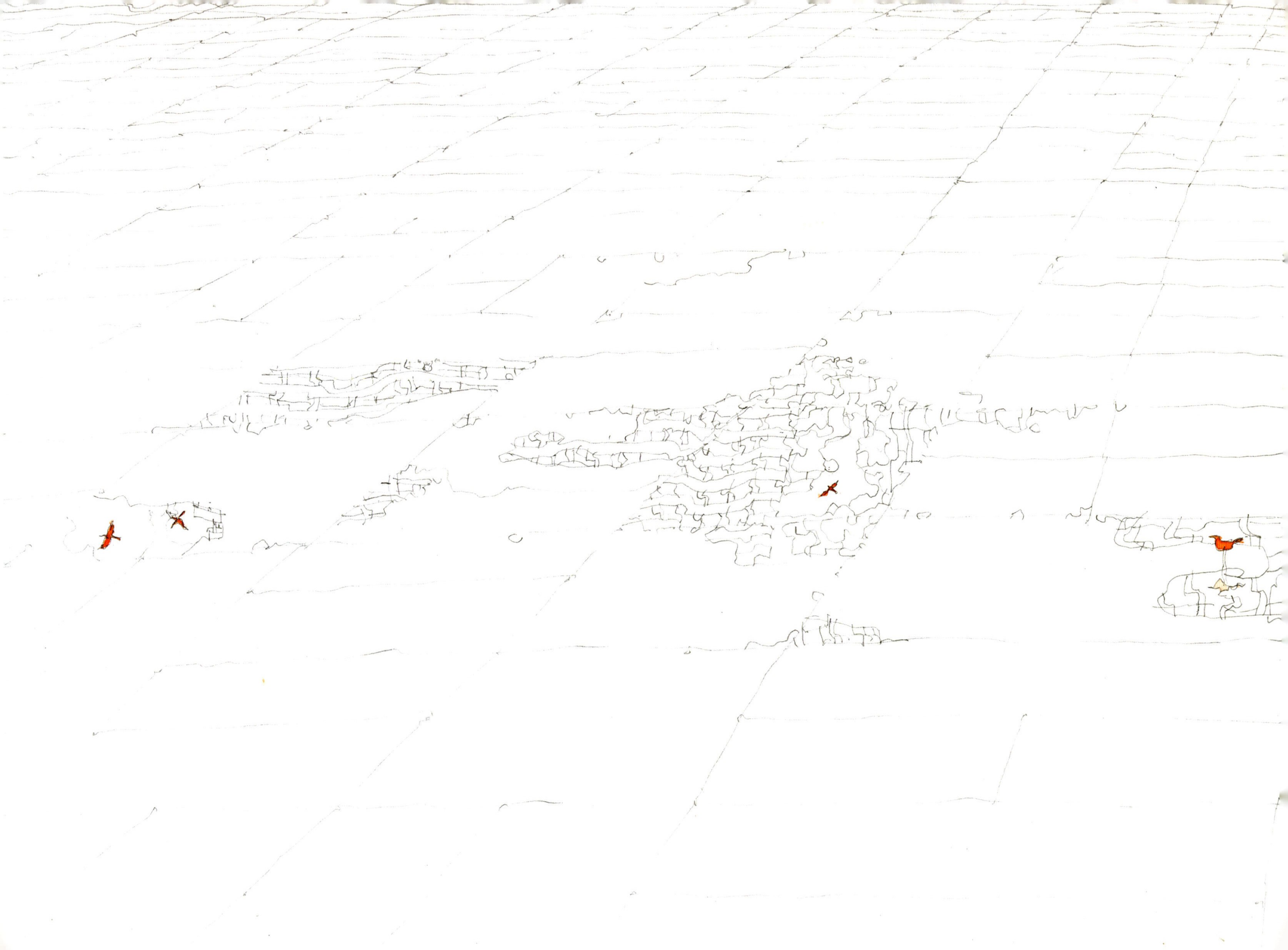

"The initial instruction I received when I was handed the sketchbook was 'do a sketch in an hour, please.' It is interesting how that escalated into *this*! I mean, can I redo my sketch?"

Tadahiro Uesugi

Tadahiro Uesugi

2006.

Tadahiro Uesugi received *Sketchtravel* from the hands of **Daisuke Tsutsumi** on December 11, 2006, and gave it to **Yoko Tanji** on December 28, 2006, in Tokyo.

Stop 8 Stop 9 Stop 10

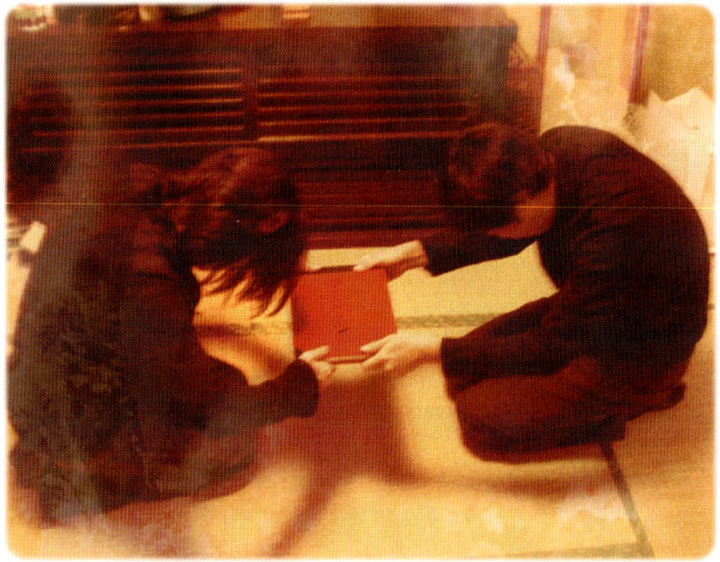

Daisuke Tsutsumi and Tadahiro Uesugi

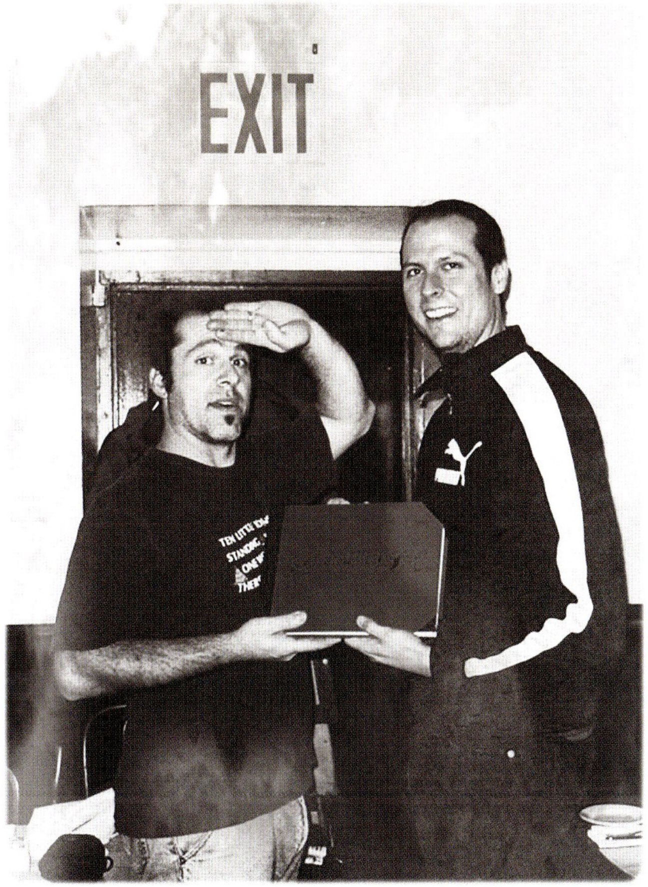

Andrea Blasich and Nash Dunnigan

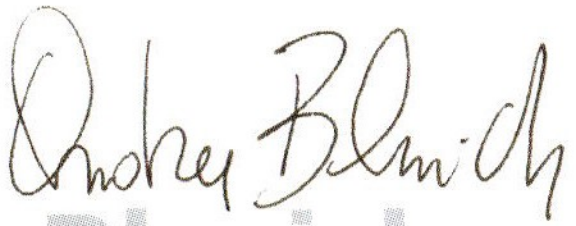

Andrea Blasich

"It is a magnificent book, and I can't believe that I am part of it."

Andrea Blasich received *Sketchtravel* from the hands of **Benoît Le Pennec** on December 5, 2006, in San Anselmo and gave it to **Nash Dunnigan** on January 15, 2007, in New York.

Stop 6 Stop 7 Stop 8

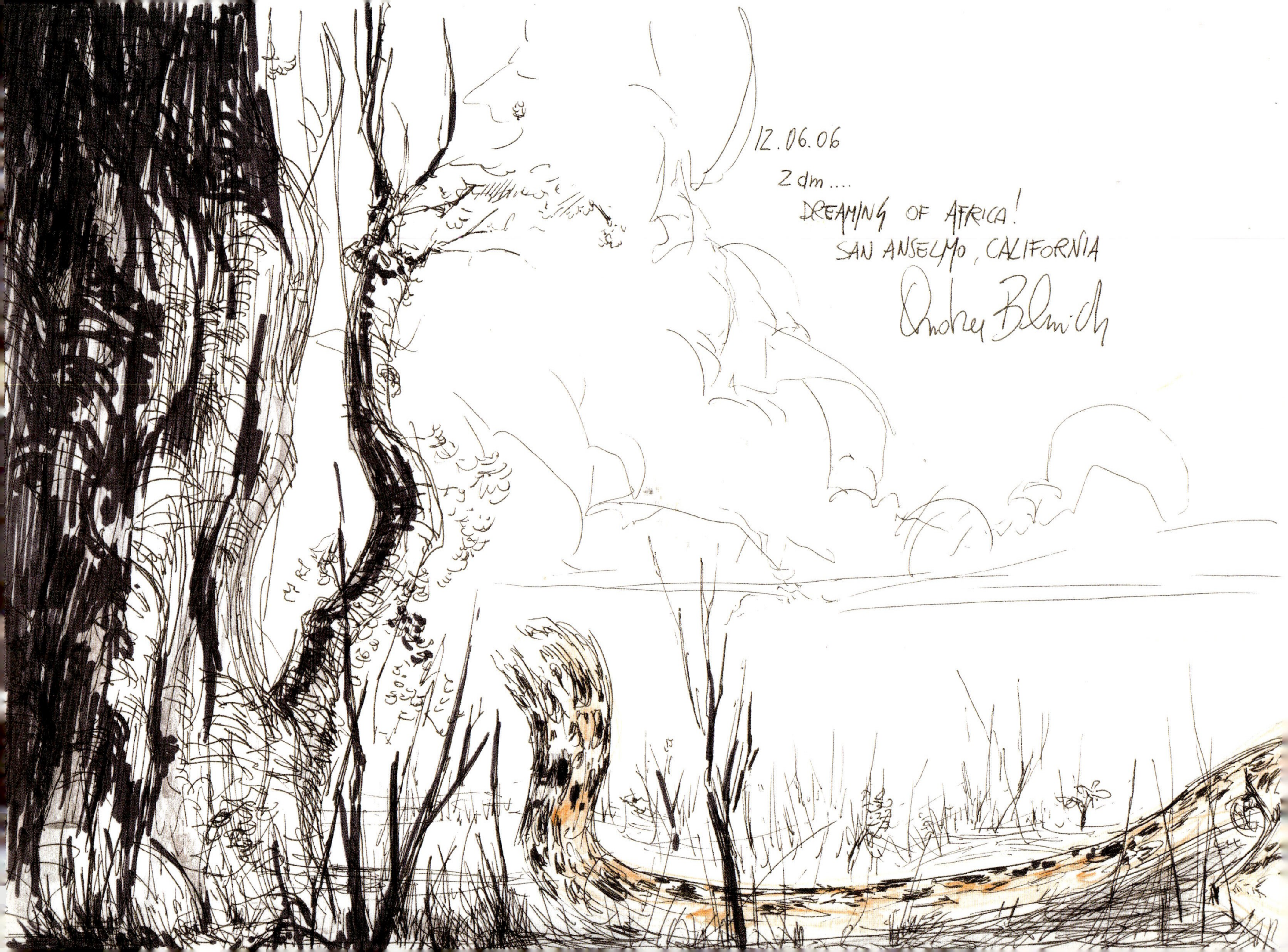
12.06.06
2 dm....
DREAMING OF AFRICA!
SAN ANSELMO, CALIFORNIA

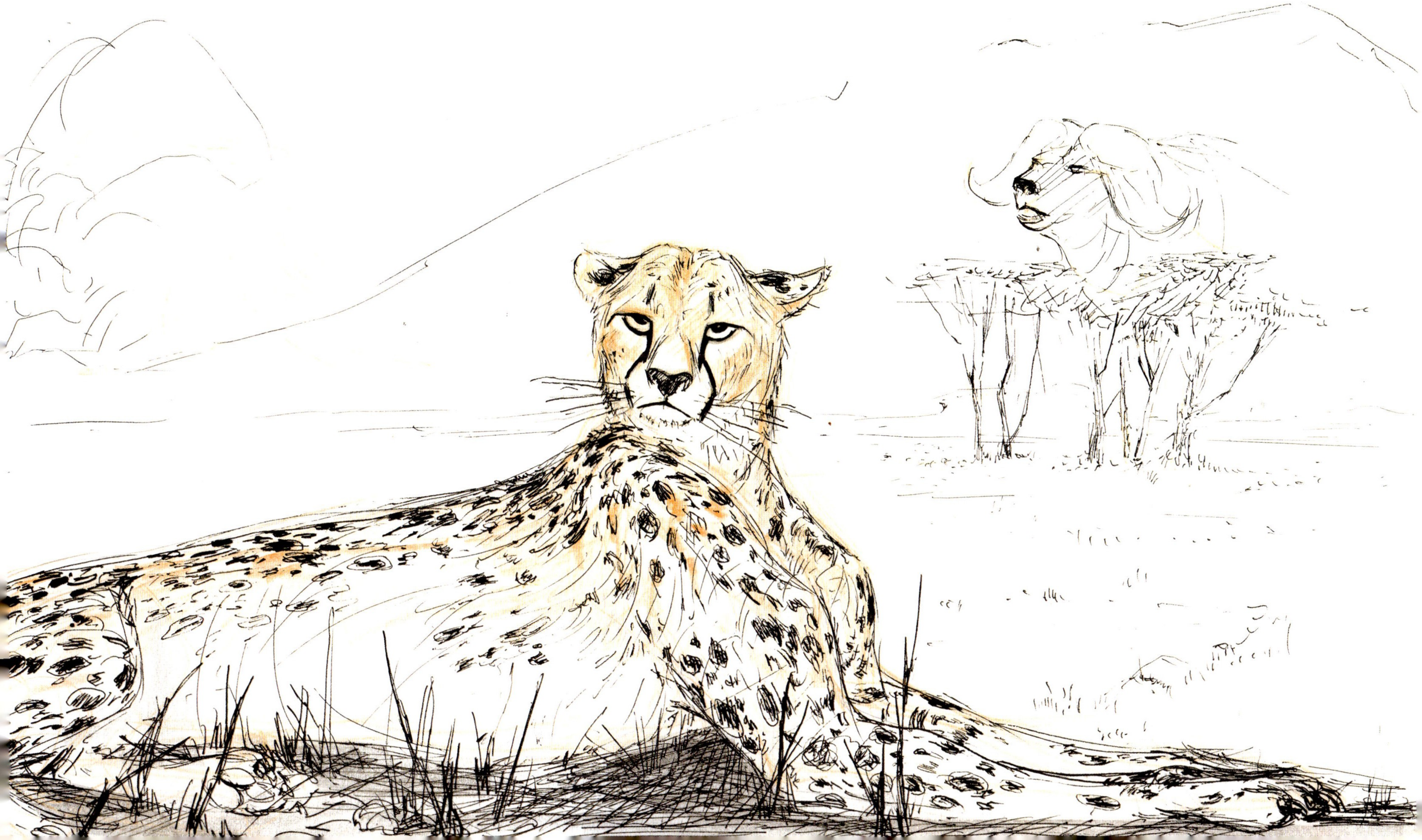

"It was at the end of 2006 that I accepted the invitation to be a part of this fun-sounding project. I returned the book after completing my sketch over the New Year without imagining it would end up being part of such a prolonged epic adventure. It was wonderful to follow the way a simple idea turned into such a terrific project. I feel fortunate to be a part of it."

Yoko Tanji

Yoko Tanji

20070104. TOKYO. JPN

?

Yoko Tanji received *Sketchtravel* from the hands of **Tadahiro Uesugi** on December 11, 2006, in Tokyo and gave it to **Daisuke Tsutsumi** on January 4, 2007, in Tokyo.

Stop 9 — Stop 10 — Stop 11

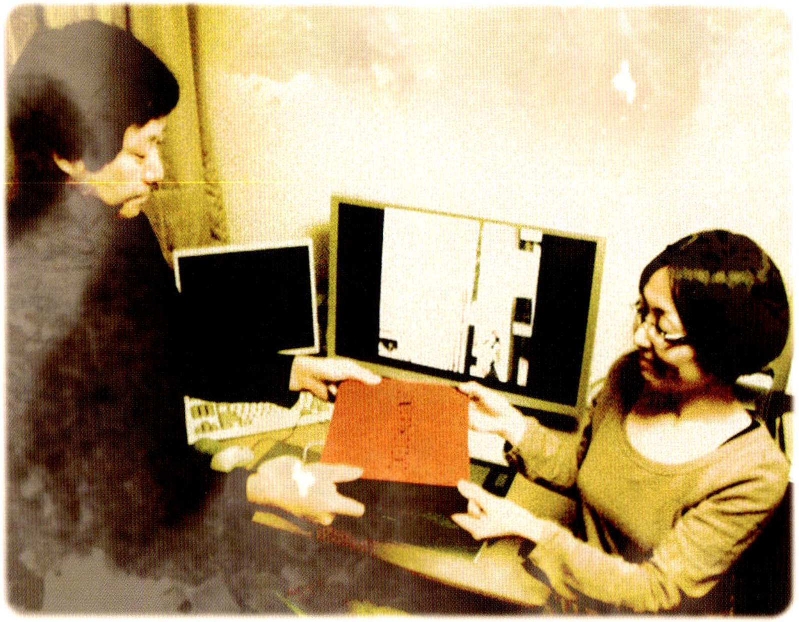
Tadahiro Uesugi and Yoko Tanji

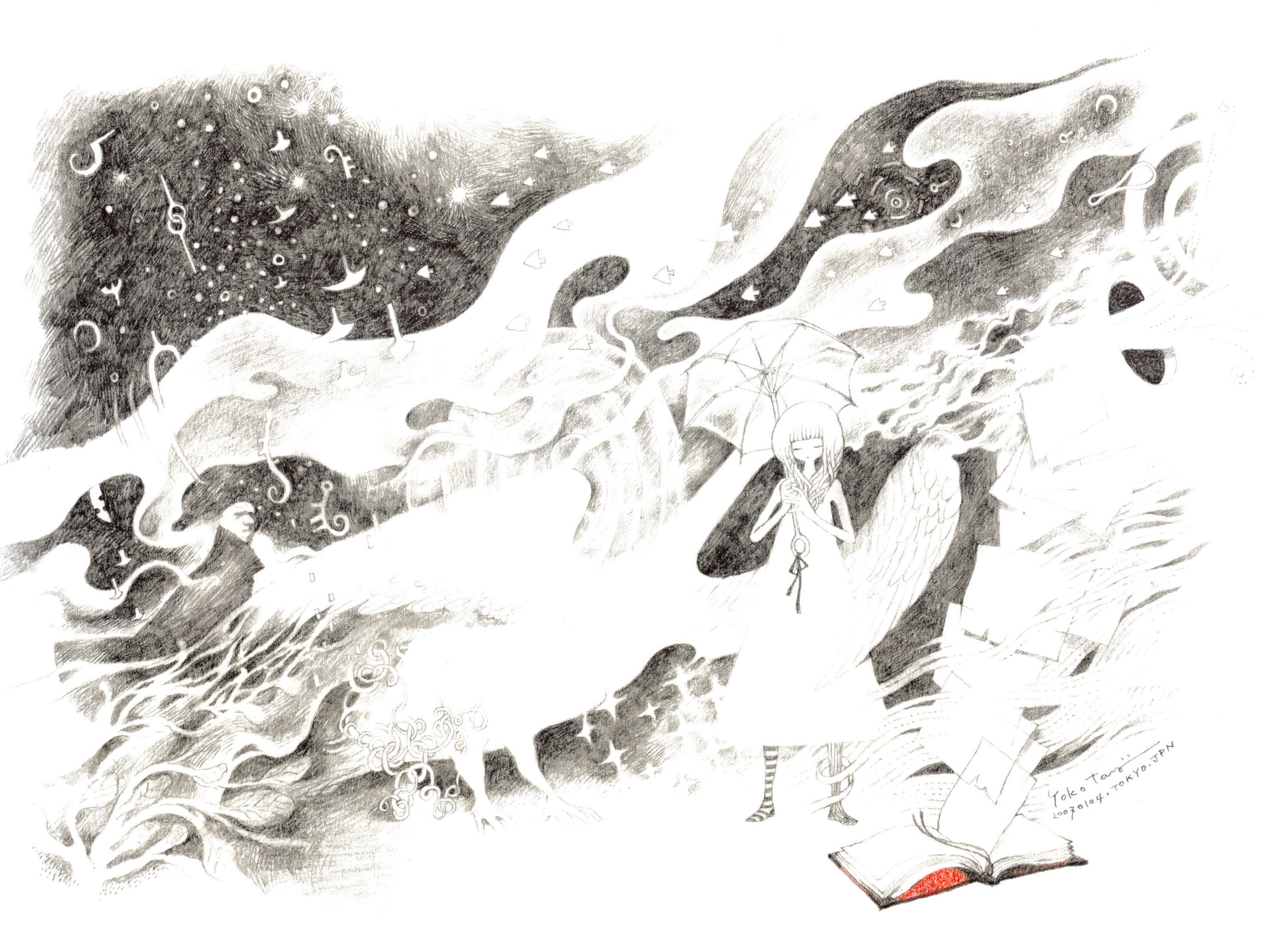
Yoko Tanji
20070104. TOKYO. JPN

Nash Dunnigan

Nash Dunnigan

"Child, I loved to find this notebook, fallen from the sky, full of visual treasures, that would have convinced me to follow this path."

Jan 16, 07
New York

?

Nash Dunnigan received *Sketchtravel* from the hands of **Andrea Blasich** on January 15, 2007, in New York and gave it to **Sang Jun Lee** on January 19, 2007, in New York.

Stop 10 Stop 11 Stop 12

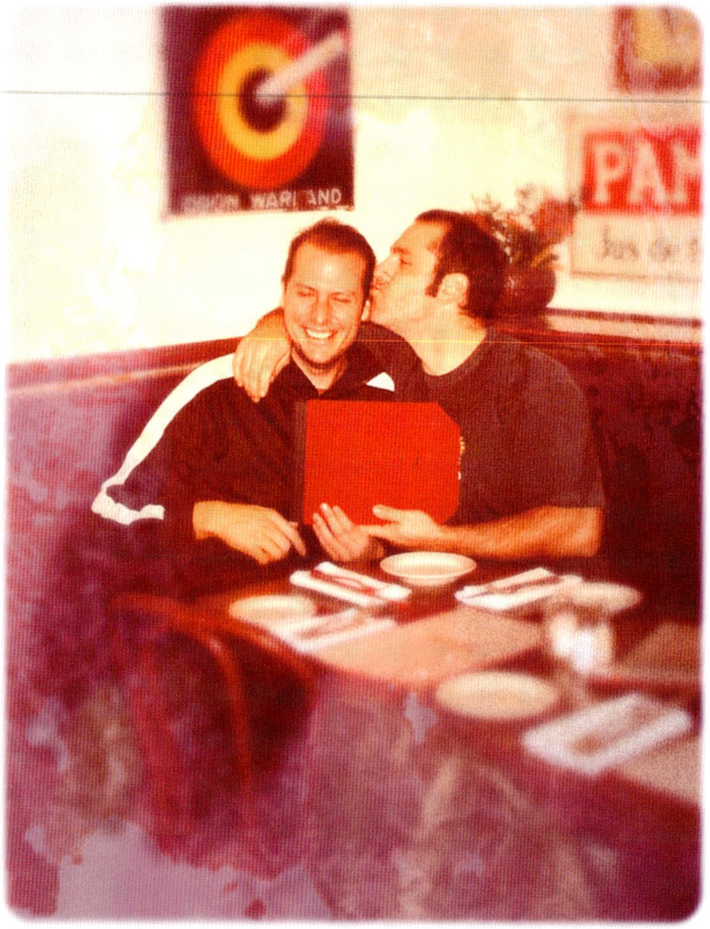
Nash Dunnigan and Andrea Blasich

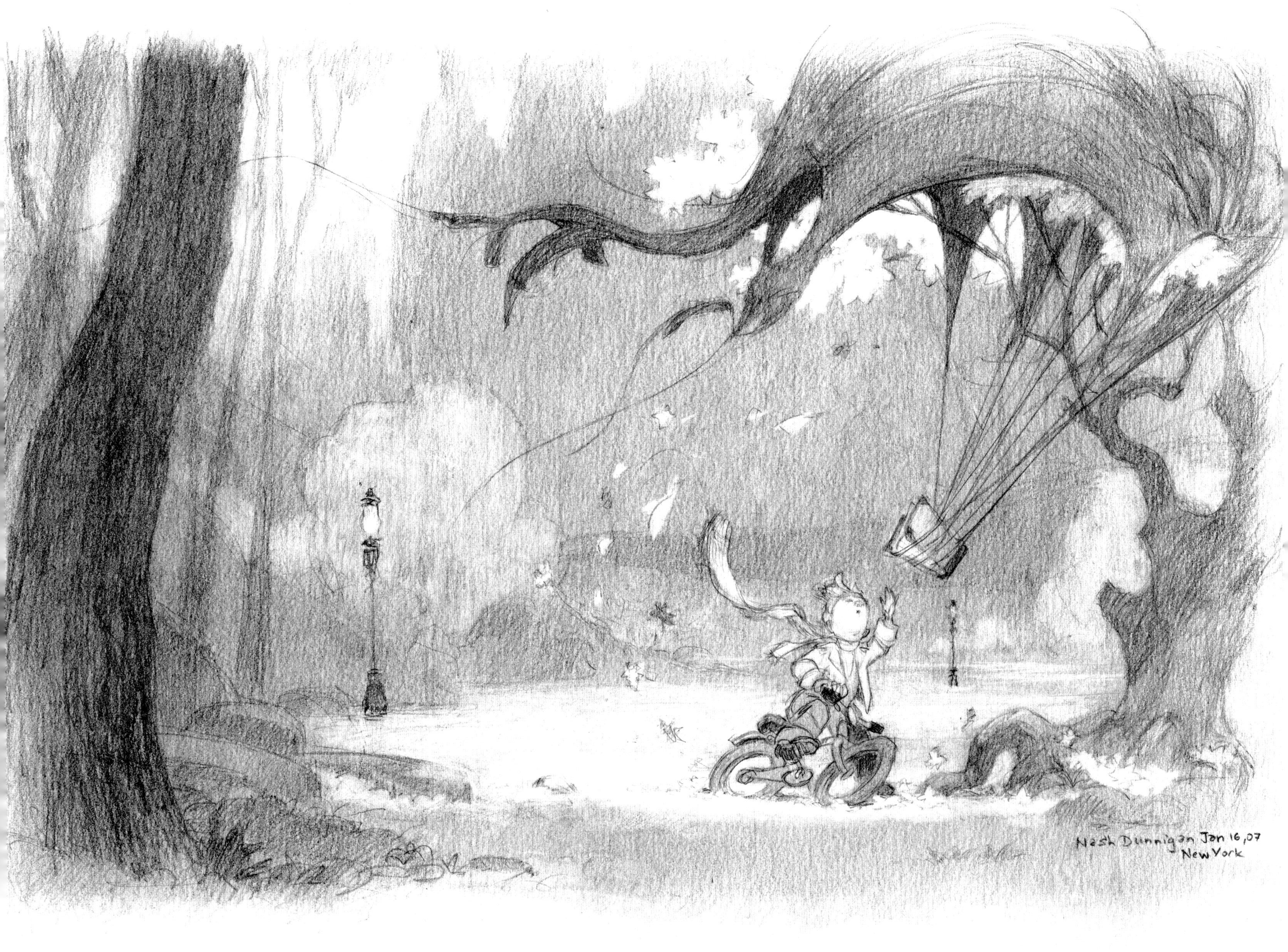
Nash Dunnigan Jan 16,07
New York

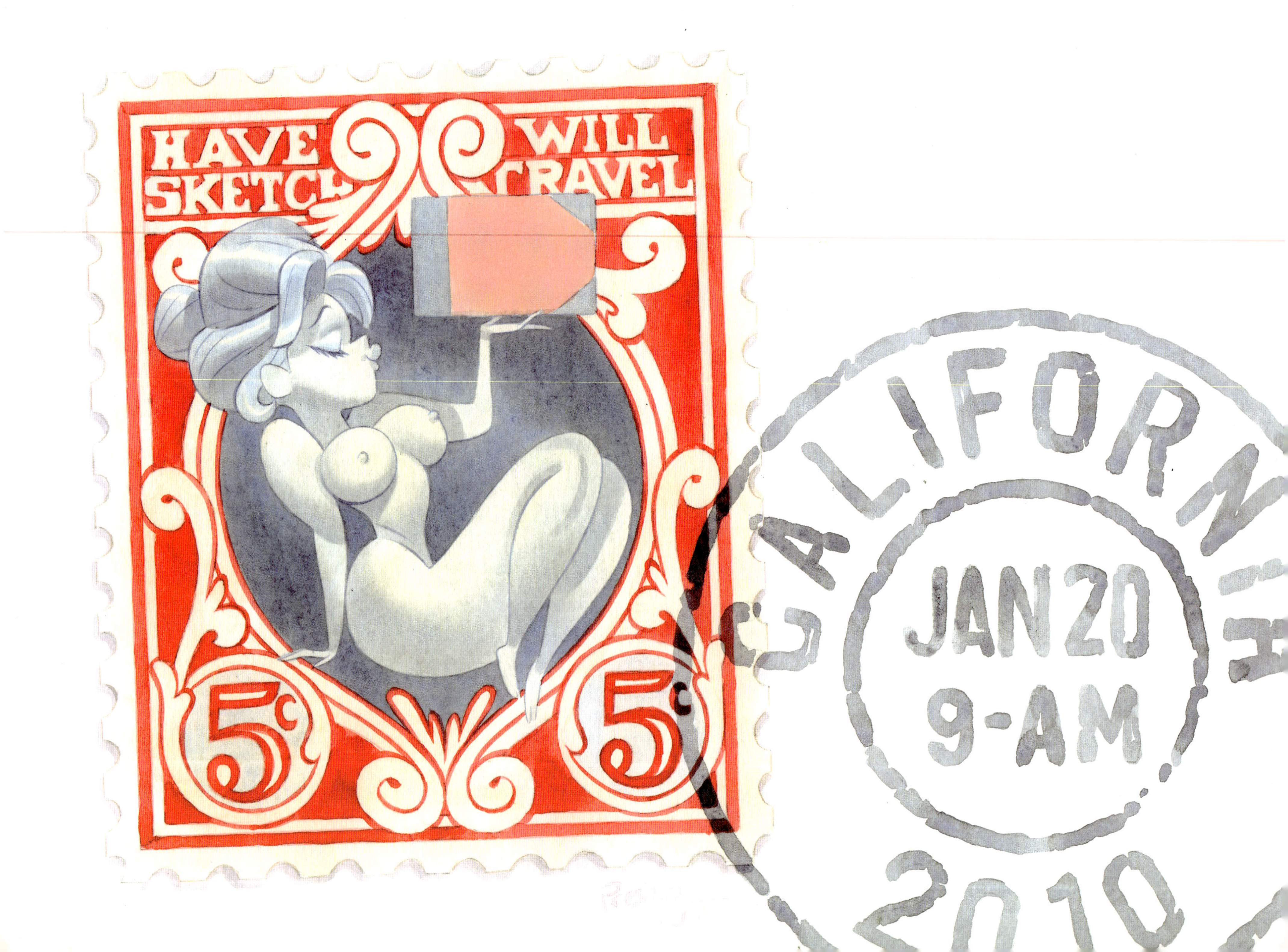
HAVE SKETCH
WILL CRAVEL
5¢
5¢
CALIFORN
JAN 20
9-AM
2010

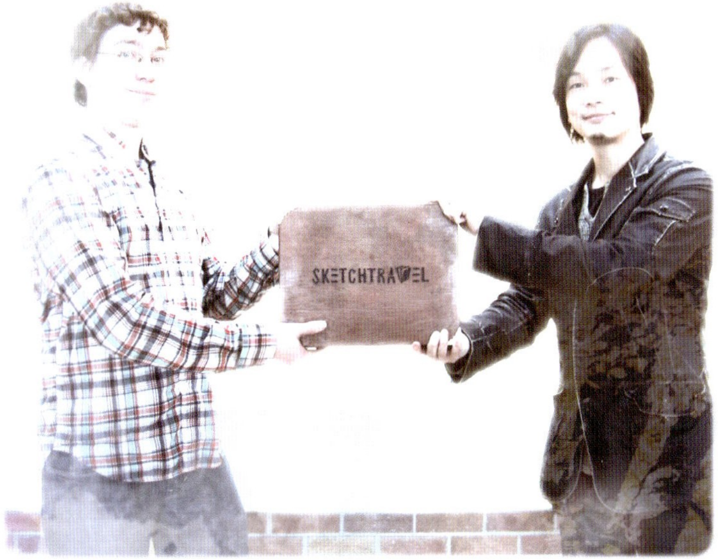

Bill Presing and Daisuke Tsutsumi

Bill Presing

"I discovered some excellent artists thanks to this notebook and had the chance to meet some old friends again. Thanks for including me in the project."

?

Bill Presing received *Sketchtravel* from the hands of **Daisuke Tsutsumi** on January 19, 2010, in San Francisco and gave it to **Carter Goodrich** on January 22, 2010, in San Francisco.

Stop 52 Stop 53 Stop 54

Sang Jun. Lee

Sang Jun Lee

"The idea is simply perfect: a book in which you can taste the talents of artists from all four corners of the world. I sincerely hope that this book completes its tour of the globe.

When I found myself face-to-face with the white page, I didn't have any idea what I would draw. I have to say that looking at all the magnificent drawings on the previous pages, I was a little afraid. But at the same time, I was inspired.

Then, the word *dream* came to me, and I started to draw, and everything went well!"

2007
Jan/20.

Sang Jun Lee received *Sketchtravel* from the hands of **Daisuke Tsutsumi** on January 19, 2007, in New York and gave it to **Vincent Di Nguyen** on January 25, 2007, in New York.

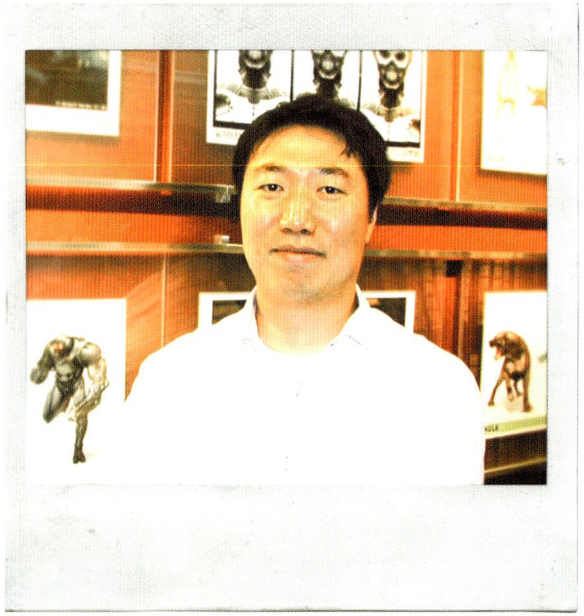

Sang Jun Lee

Stop 11 Stop 12 Stop 13

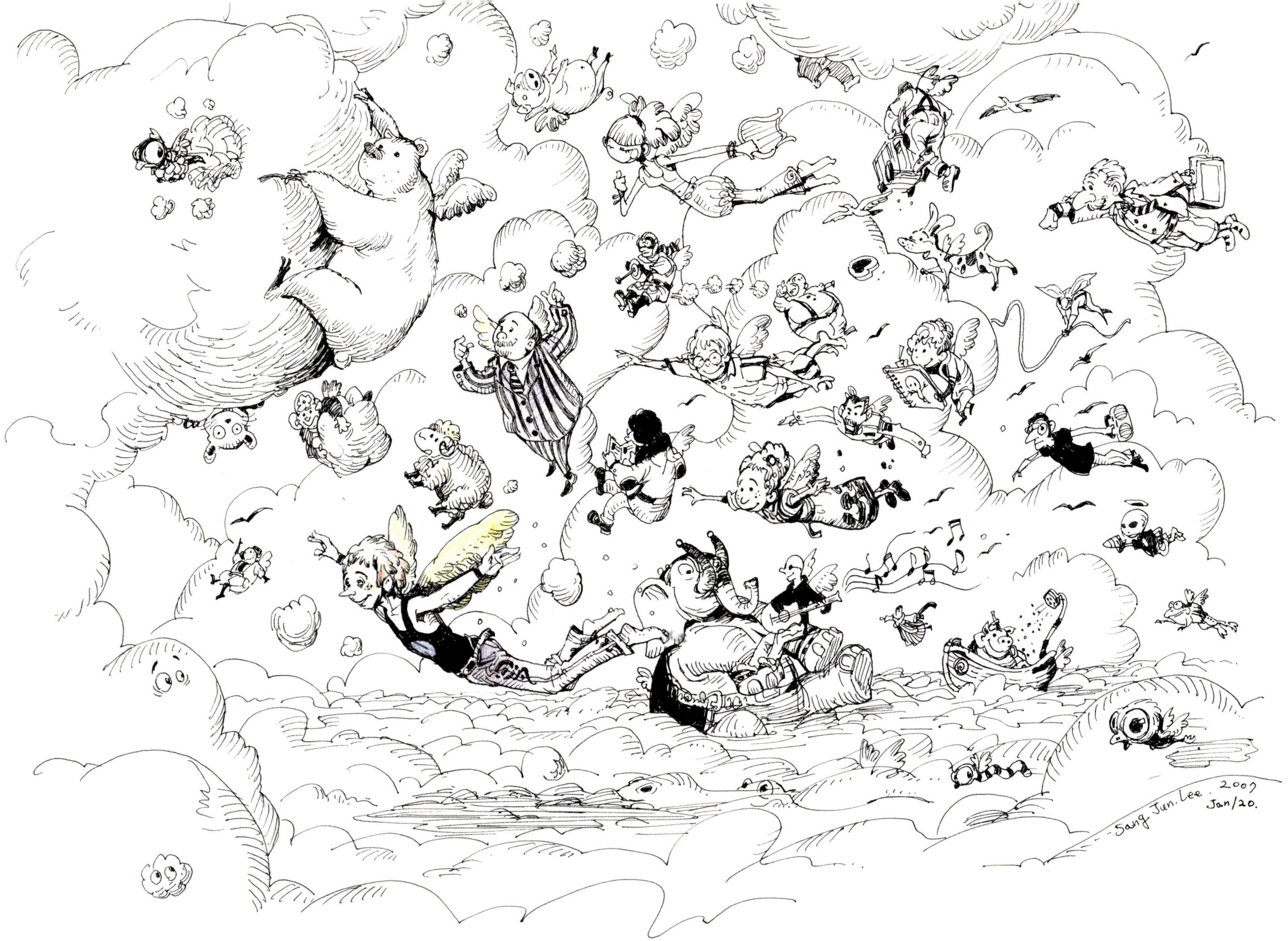
Sang Jun. Lee. 2007
Jan/20.

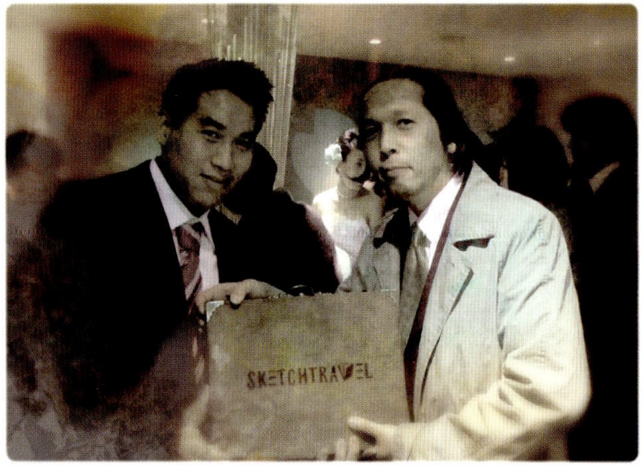

Vincent Di Nguyen and Katsuya Terada

· Vincent Di Nguyen ·

Vincent Di Nguyen

"This project is an excellent way to display the talents coming from different creative domains.

The only thing I regret is that there wasn't enough space for even more artists. I was one of the first to get the book, and I made a very simple drawing.

Now I'd like to get it back so that I could do a little more!"

January 27 2007.

Vincent Di Nguyen received *Sketchtravel* from the hands of **Sang Jun Lee** on January 25, 2010, in New York and gave it to **Michael Knapp** on January 28, 2007, in New York.

Stop 12 Stop 13 Stop 14

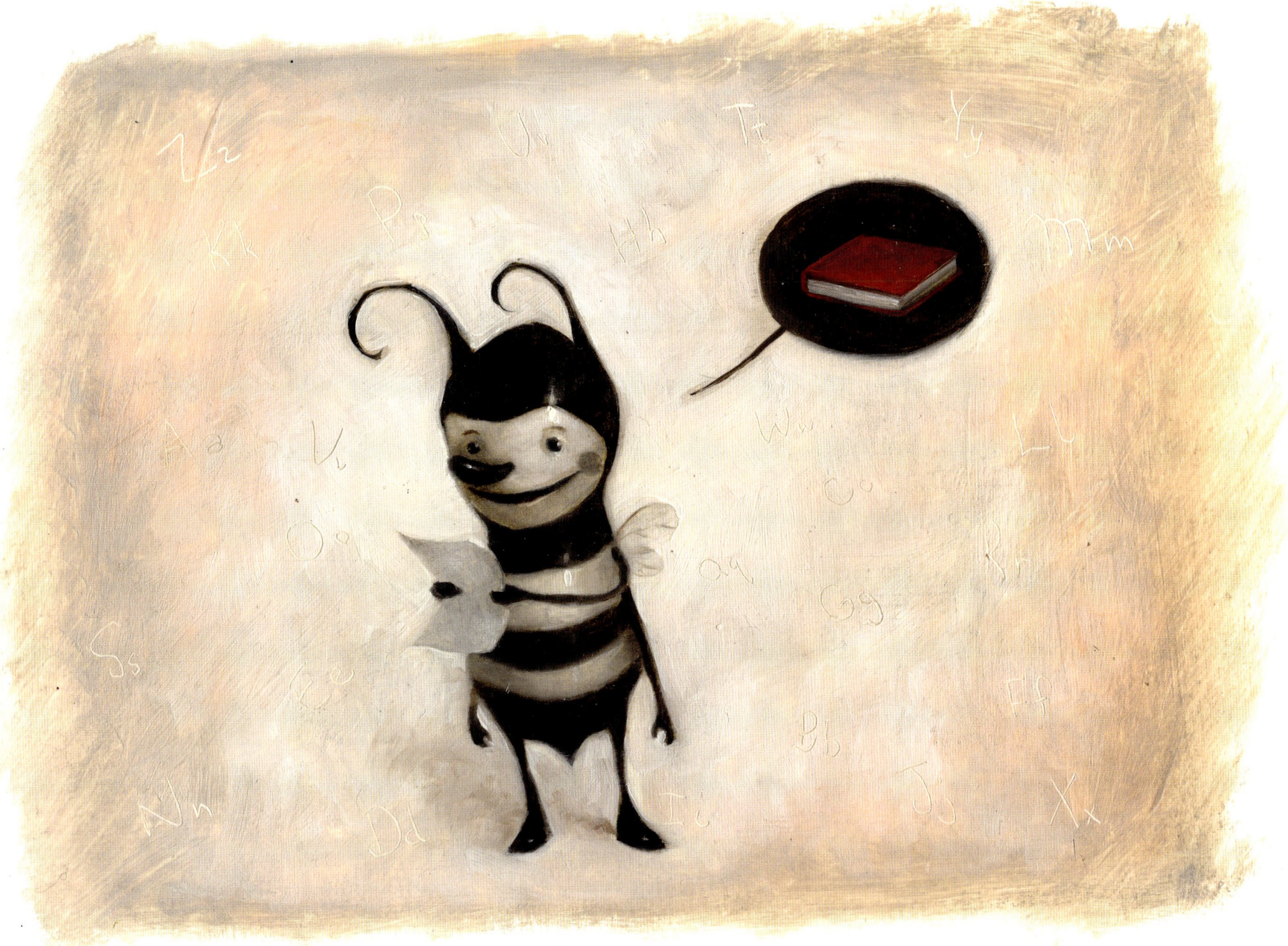

· Vincent Di Nguyen · January 27 2007 ·

Michael Knapp

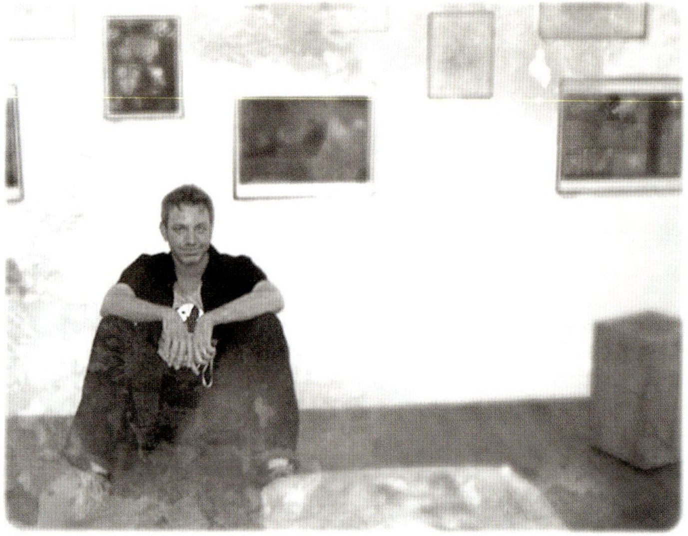

Michael Knapp

"I've never seen such a collection of drawings by so many talented artists. It is completely incredible. I spent several days admiring the work of others to give myself an idea of what I would do.

I loved the idea of a book that would travel around the world, a work of art that passed from hand to hand. For me, it evoked old spy movies and stories of the Cold War. Once I made this link, I knew that I was on my way.

Twelve or so artists had already had the book before me, and you could say that it was stressful."

January 29, 2006 • NYC • USA

Michael Knapp received *Sketchtravel* from the hands of **Vincent Di Nguyen** on January 28, 2007, in New York and gave it to **Daisuke Tsutsumi** on February 4, 2007, in New York.

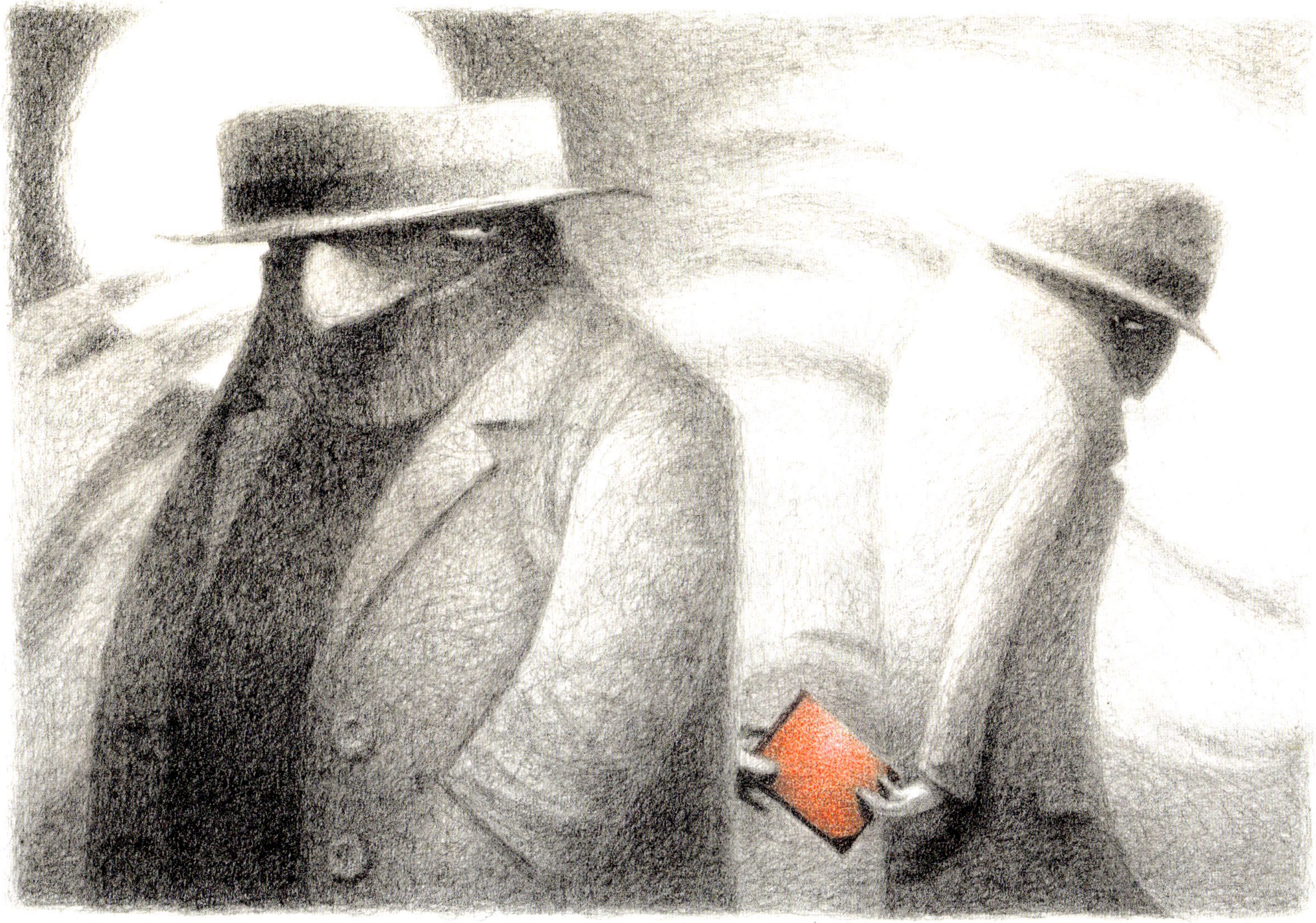

"The Handoff"

January 29, 2006 • NYC • USA

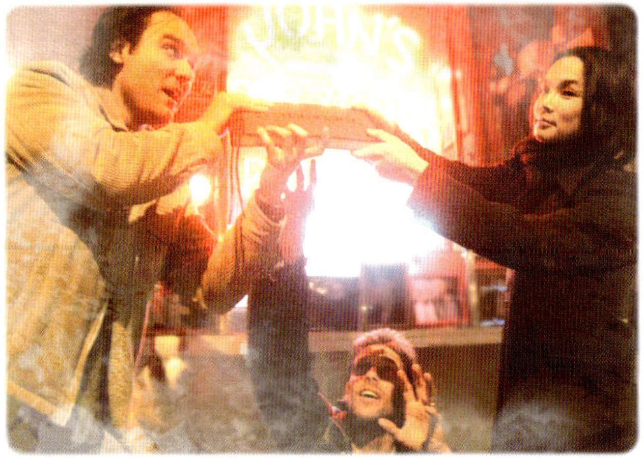

Daniel López Muñoz, Peter de Sève, and Daisuke Tsutsumi

DANIEL LÓPEZ MUÑOZ

Daniel López Muñoz

"For me, *Sketchtravel* is among the most important collective artistic projects of our generation. It crossed borders, joining artists from the four corners of the world around their common passion.

After its humble beginnings, it aroused the interest of the great masters of animation, including the younger generation. But I wasn't sure that a book that fragile would be able to endure such a long and difficult journey; so I made it a box, to protect it.

S.F. BAY MARZO 25 · 2007

Daniel López Muñoz received *Sketchtravel* from the hands of **Daisuke Tsutsumi** on February 4, 2007, in New York and gave it to **Lou Romano** on March 26, 2007, in San Francisco.

Stop 14 Stop 15 Stop 16

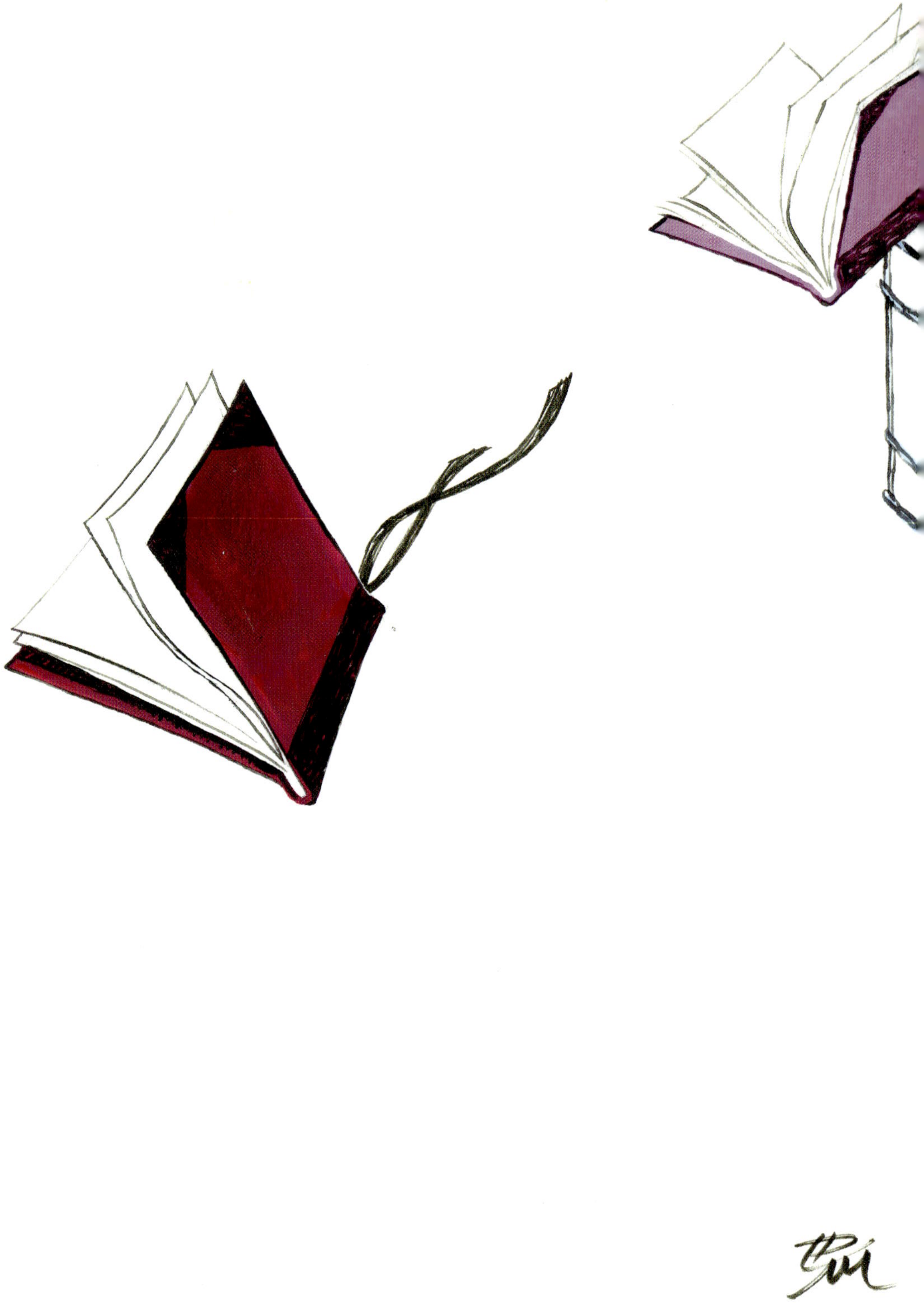

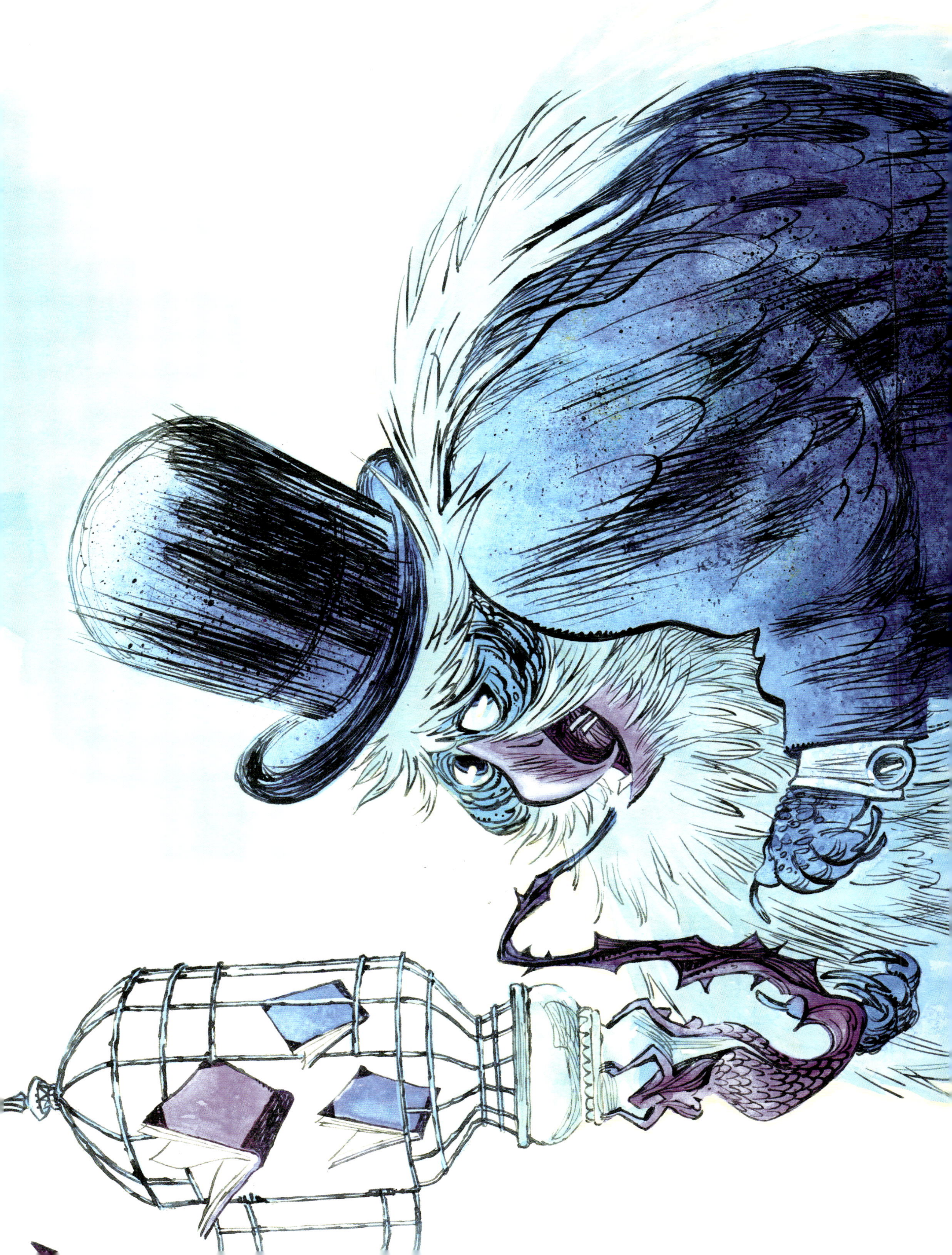

Lou Romano 07

Lou Romano

"I'm happy to be part of such a project. I think that it's a great idea!"

Lou Romano received *Sketchtravel* from the hands of **Daniel López Muñoz** on March 26, 2007, in San Francisco and gave it to **Enrico Casarosa** on May 7, 2007, in San Francisco.

Stop 15 · Stop 16 · Stop 17

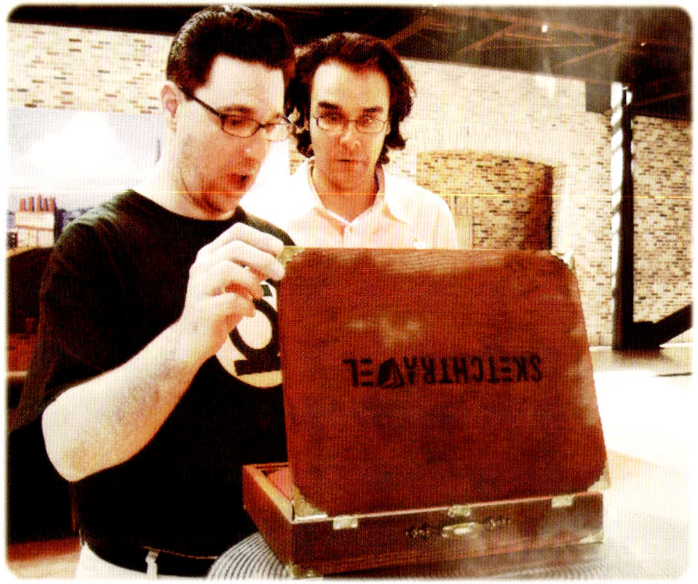

Lou Romano and Daniel López Muñoz

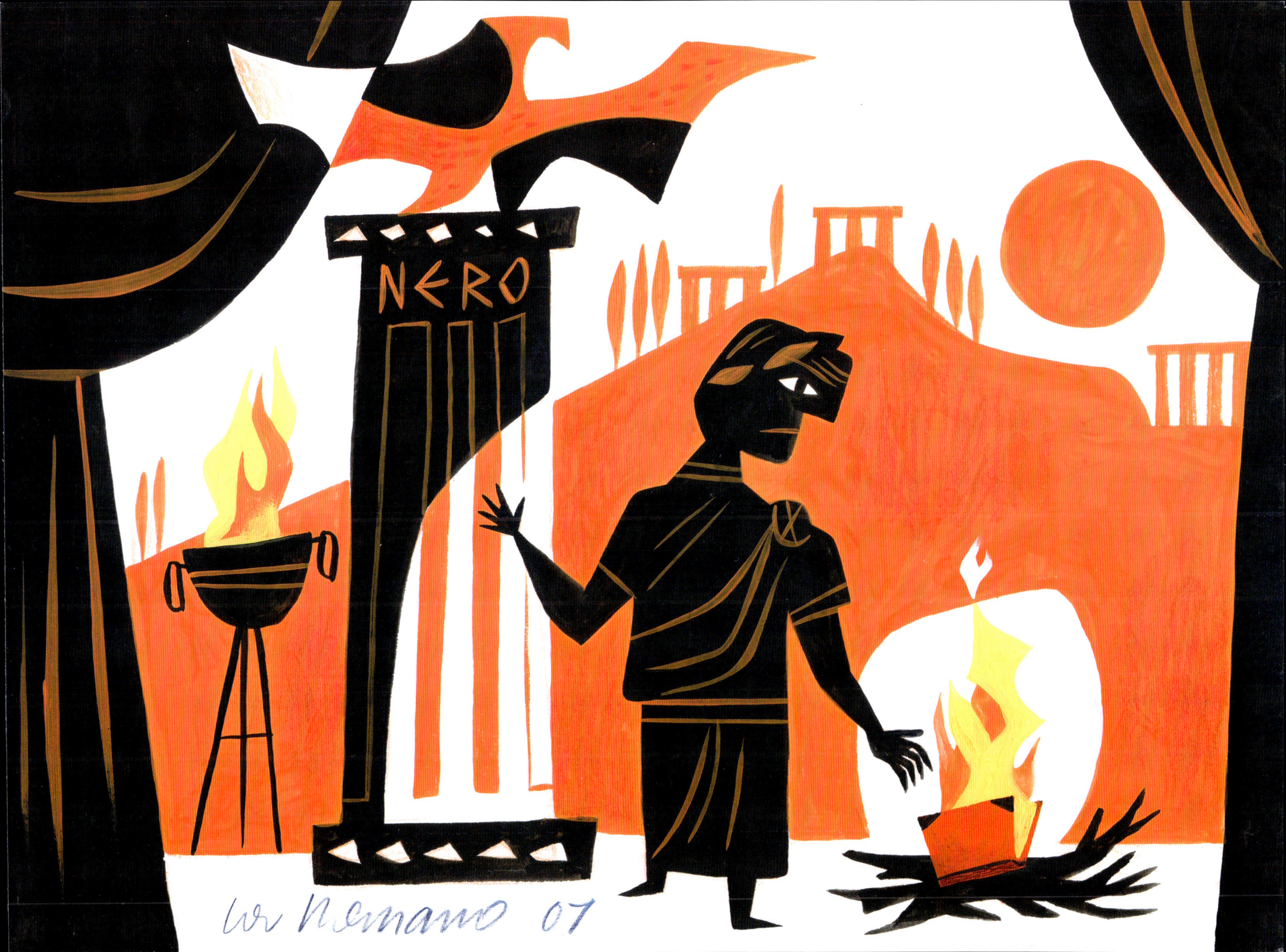
NERO

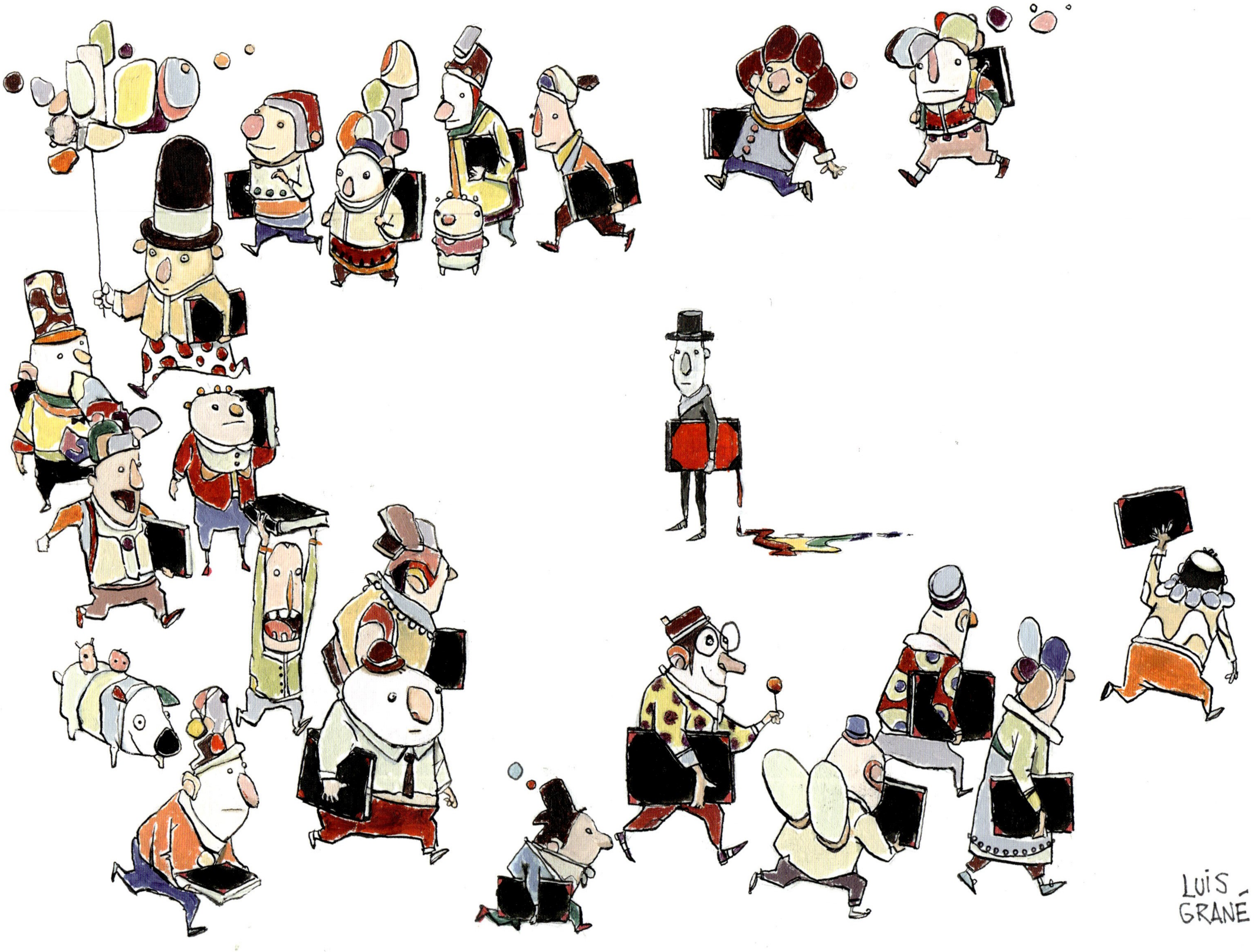
LUIS GRANÉ

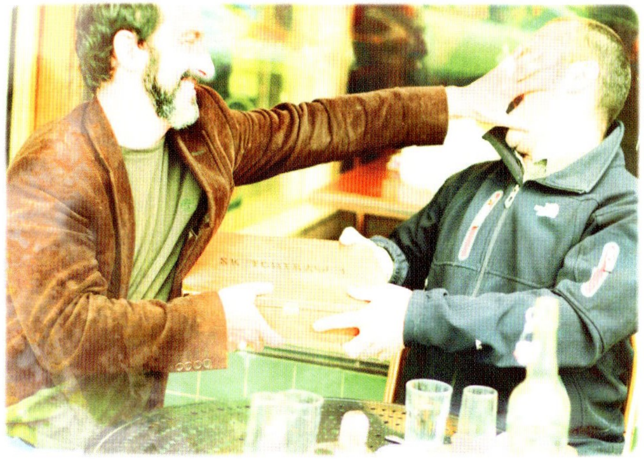

Andrea Blasich and Luis Grané

LUIS GRANÉ

Luis Grané

“To persuade artists from the four corners of the world to make drawings for a worthwhile cause is an excellent idea.

I knew that we were supposed to include the book in our drawing, so I already had a vague idea of what I would do, but I did not want to lose the basic spontaneity of a sketch. So I did my best to add touches of improvisation as I was drawing.”

Luis Grané received *Sketchtravel* from the hands of **Andrea Blasich** in November of 2010 in San Francisco and gave it to **Daisuke Tsutsumi** in November of 2010 in San Francisco.

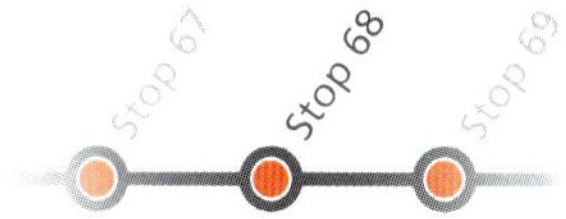

"*Sketchtravel* has a very special place in my heart because it brought together an extraordinary community of artists from all around the world. Even more importantly, it brought us all together with a meaningful purpose. I can't think of a better use for our art than to allow it to help raise money to fund programs that cultivate creativity and literacy and to build libraries for children in need. Thank you so much to Dice and Gérald for giving us the opportunity to be a positive force in the world."

ENRICO CASAROSA E 07

Enrico Casarosa

Enrico Casarosa received *Sketchtravel* from the hands of **Lou Romano** on May 7, 2007, in San Francisco and gave it to **Ronnie del Carmen** on June 2, 2007, in San Francisco.

Stop 16 Stop 17 Stop 18

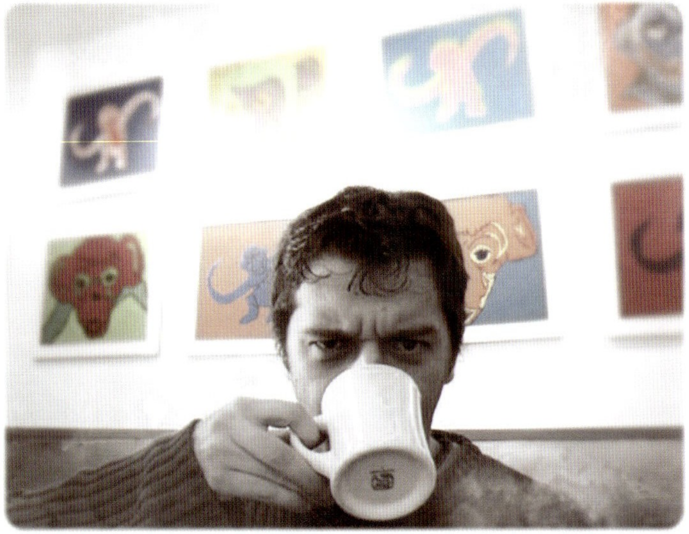

Enrico Casarosa

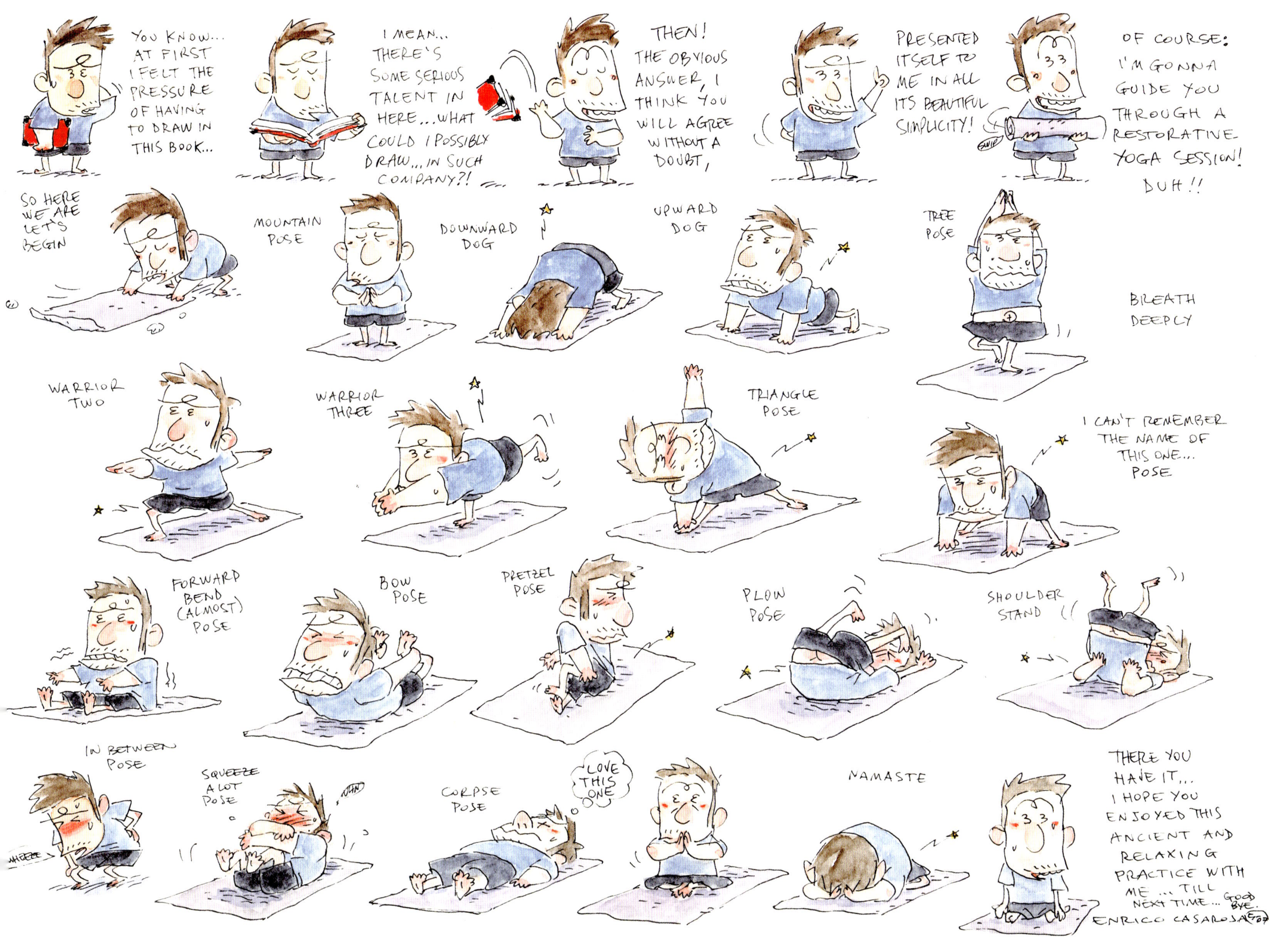

YOU KNOW... AT FIRST I FELT THE PRESSURE OF HAVING TO DRAW IN THIS BOOK...
I MEAN... THERE'S SOME SERIOUS TALENT IN HERE... WHAT COULD I POSSIBLY DRAW... IN SUCH COMPANY?!
THEN! THE OBVIOUS ANSWER, I THINK YOU WILL AGREE WITHOUT A DOUBT,
PRESENTED ITSELF TO ME IN ALL ITS BEAUTIFUL SIMPLICITY!
SWIP
OF COURSE: I'M GONNA GUIDE YOU THROUGH A RESTORATIVE YOGA SESSION! DUH!!
SO HERE WE ARE LET'S BEGIN
MOUNTAIN POSE
DOWNWARD DOG
UPWARD DOG
TREE POSE
BREATH DEEPLY
WARRIOR TWO
WARRIOR THREE
TRIANGLE POSE
I CAN'T REMEMBER THE NAME OF THIS ONE... POSE
FORWARD BEND (ALMOST) POSE
BOW POSE
PRETZEL POSE
PLOW POSE
SHOULDER STAND
IN BETWEEN POSE
WHEEEE
SQUEEZE A LOT POSE
CORPSE POSE
LOVE THIS ONE
NAMASTE
THERE YOU HAVE IT... I HOPE YOU ENJOYED THIS ANCIENT AND RELAXING PRACTICE WITH ME... TILL NEXT TIME... GOOD BYE.
ENRICO CASAROSA

Ronnie del Carmen

"We all know that art gains value with time.

An image that has survived the ravages of time is necessarily taken seriously; it gains importance as well as dignity. You could almost say that it is owed respect. This book joined an impressive cast of artists. It's overwhelming that each of them has painted and drawn on these pages. How is such a thing possible?

Joining these holy and talented beings is a superhuman effort, of which the result is a book that has crossed space and time, passing from one creator to the next."

Ronnie del Carmen received *Sketchtravel* from the hands of **Enrico Casarosa** on June 2, 2007, in San Francisco and gave it to **Daisuke Tsutsumi** on June 25, 2007, in San Francisco.

Stop 17 Stop 18 Stop 19

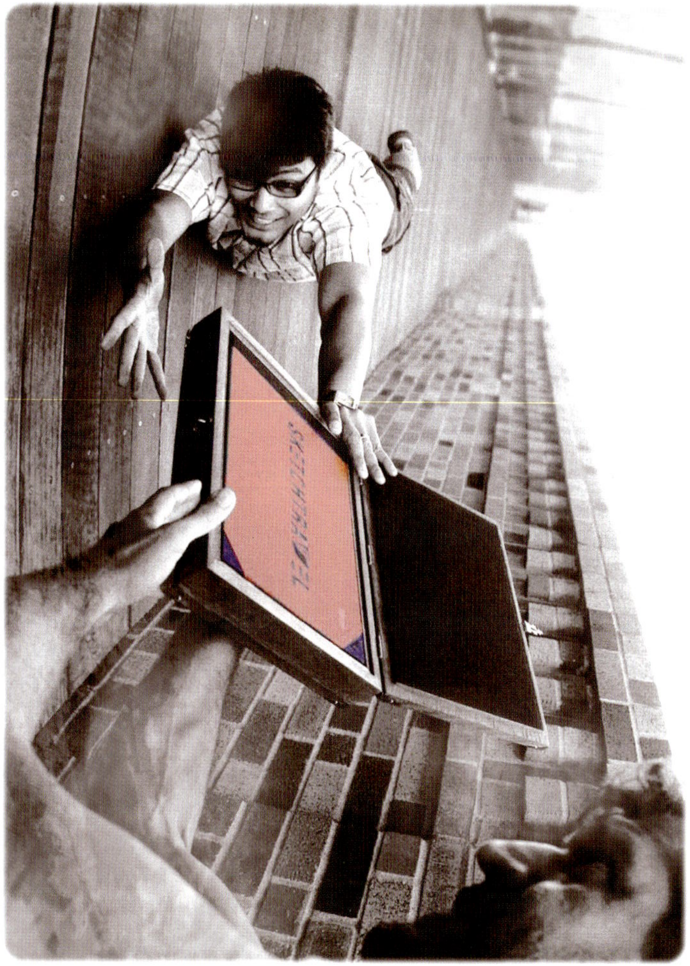

Ronnie del Carmen and Enrico Casarosa

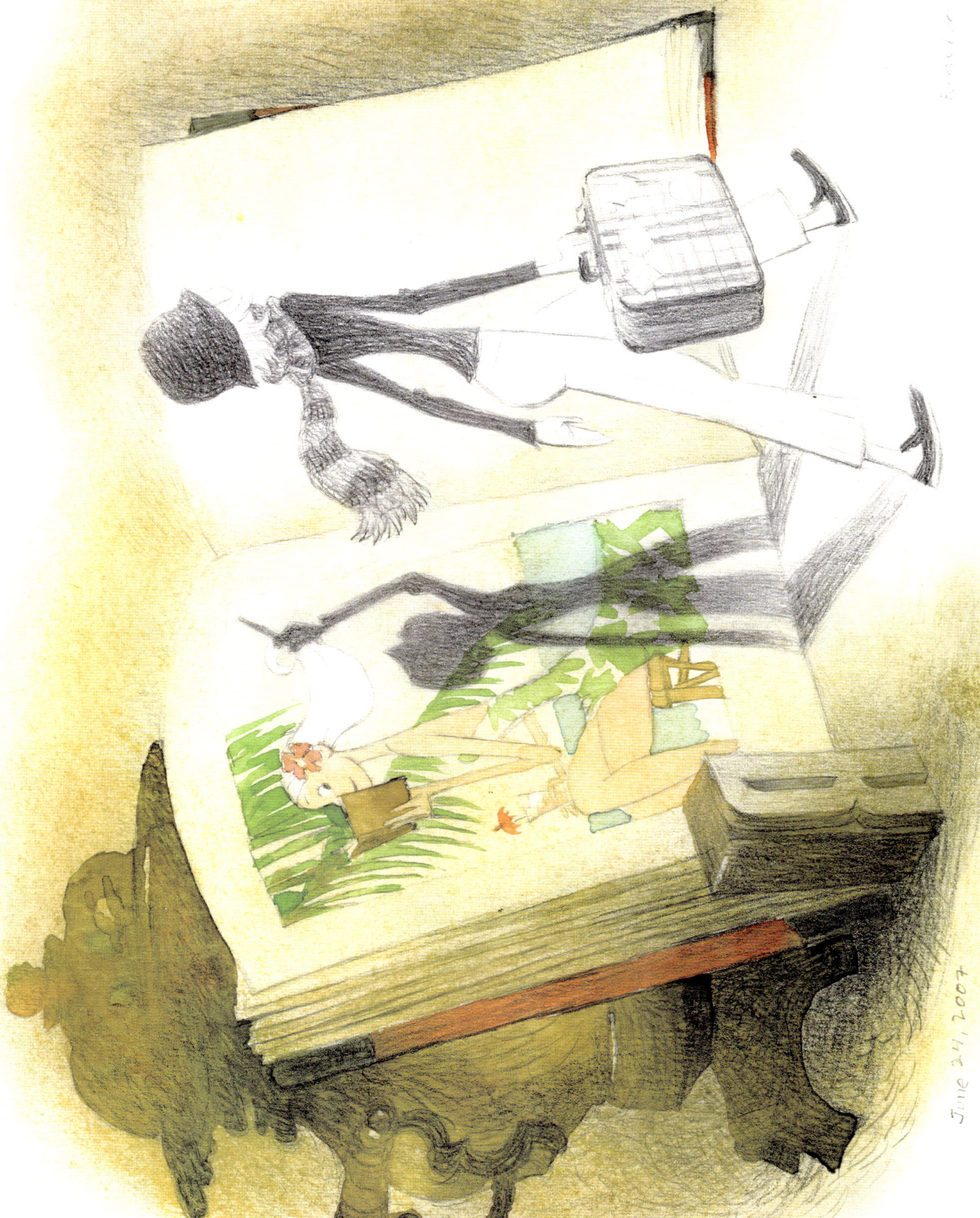
June 24, 2007

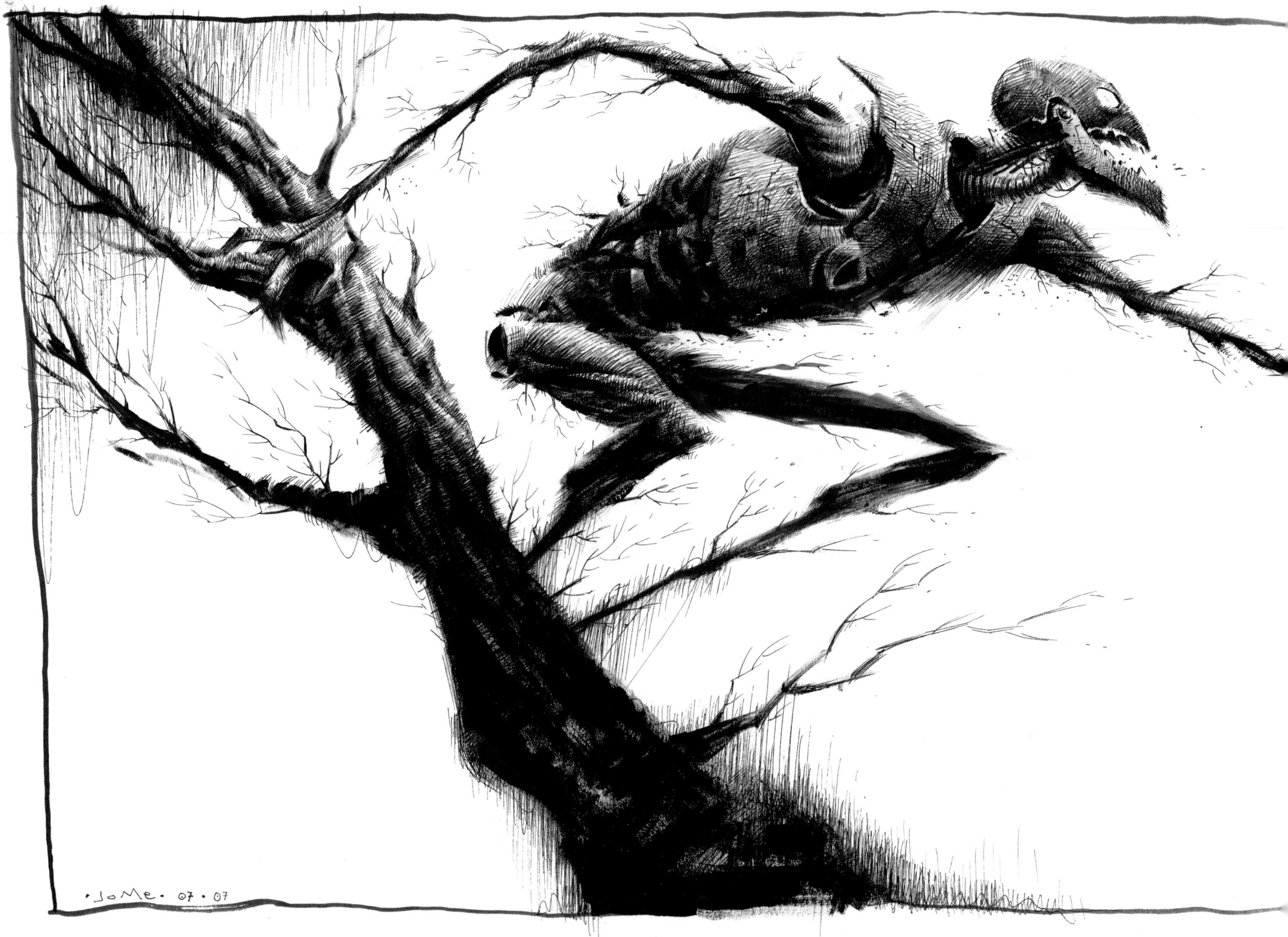
JoMe · 07 · 07

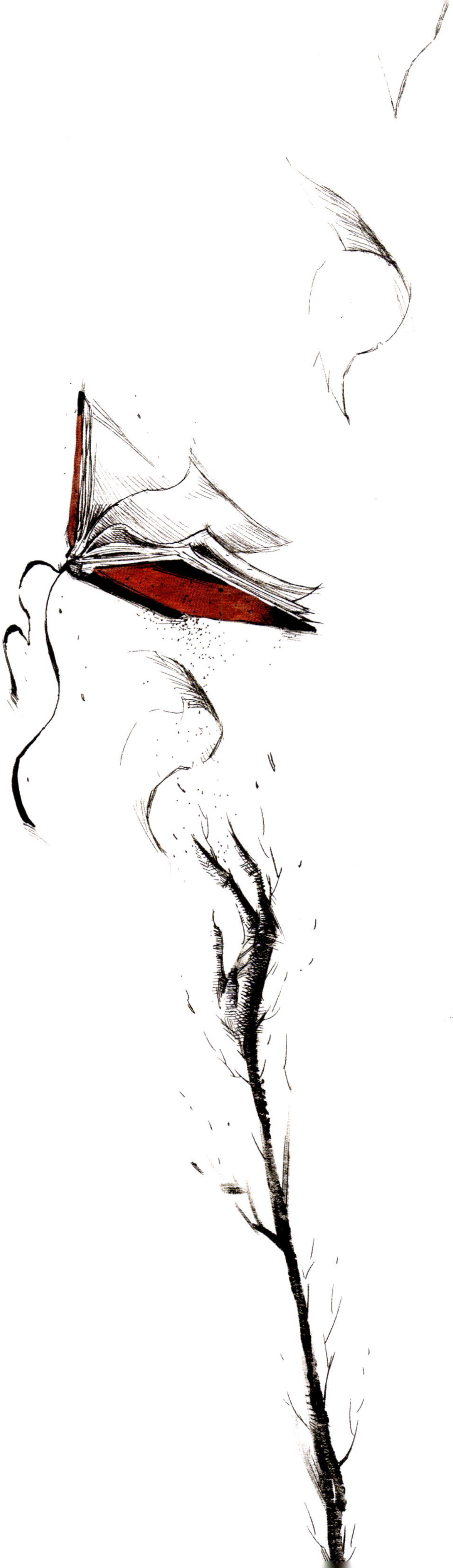

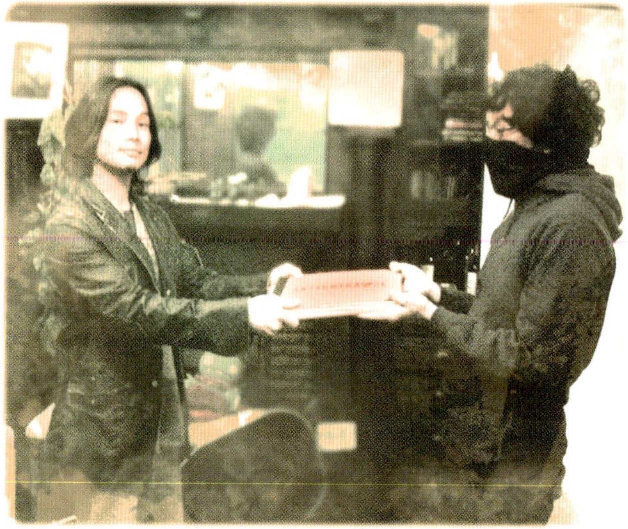

Daisuke Tsutsumi and Jerome Opeña

·JoMe·

Jerome Opeña

"It's a great idea and I can't believe that it's over after all this time. I did my drawing four years ago! I have always loved to draw robots and that's why I chose this theme. But I was afraid that my drawing wouldn't be worthy of the great artists who would come after me—and those who were already there."

07 · 07

?

Jerome Opeña received *Sketchtravel* from the hands of **Daisuke Tsutsumi** on July 5, 2007, in Los Angeles and gave it to **Daisuke Tsutsumi** on July 26, 2007, in San Diego.

Stop 18 Stop 19 Stop 20

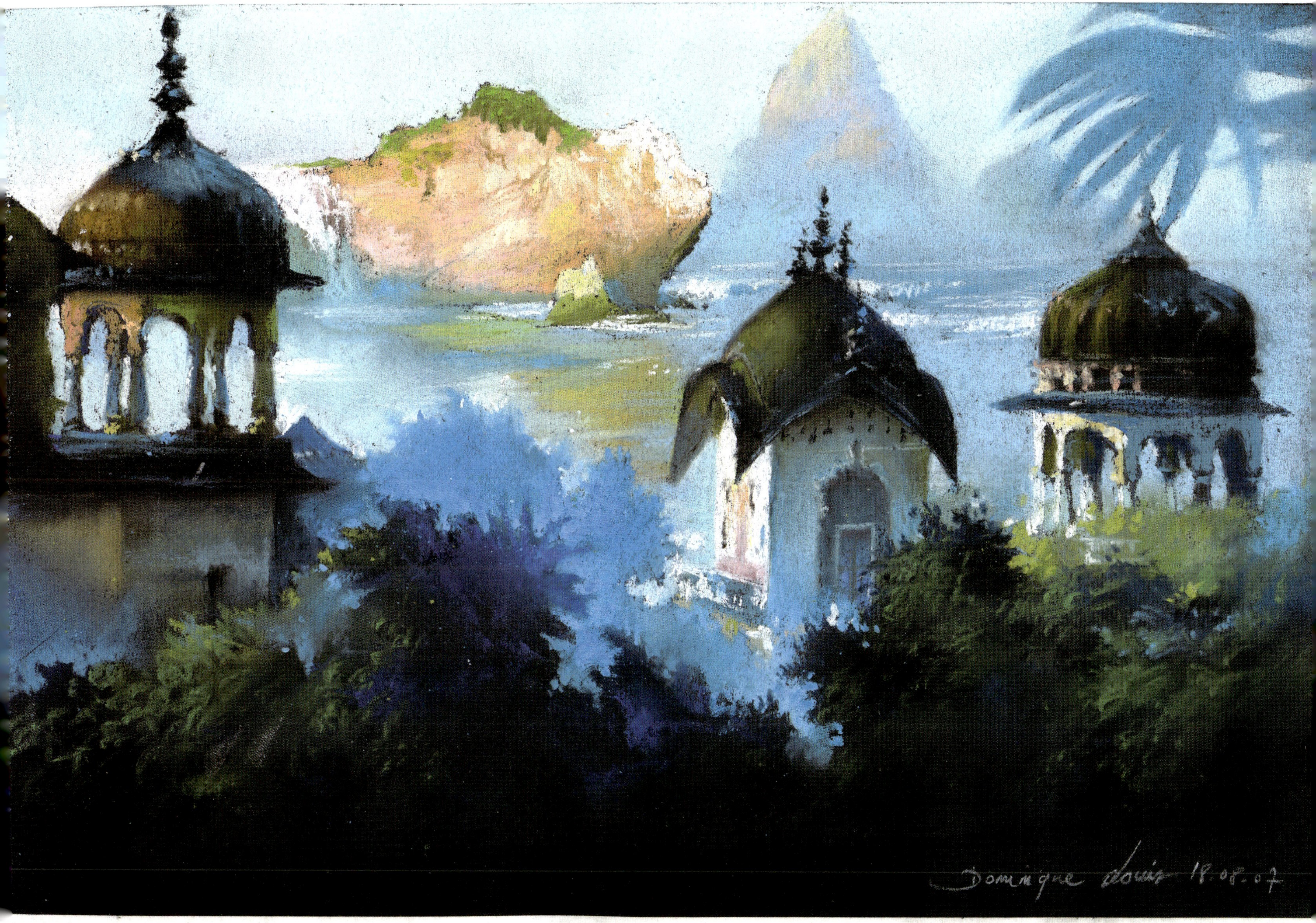

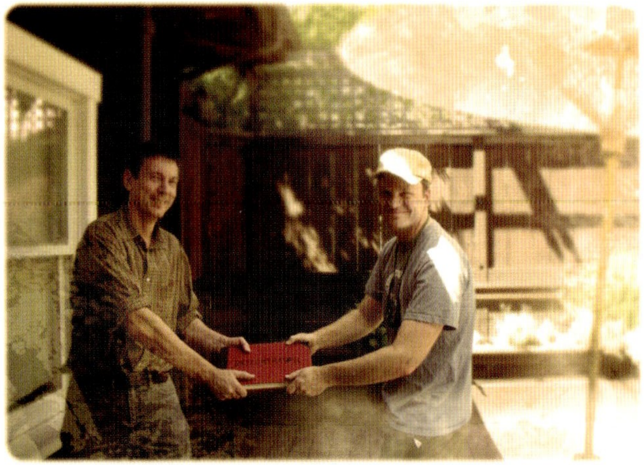

Dominique Louis and Erik Tiemens

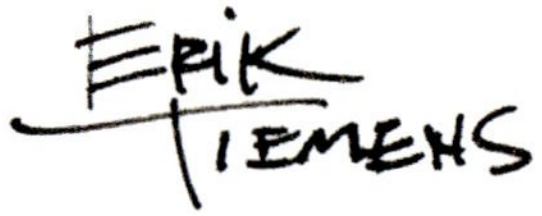

Erik Tiemens

"It's fantastic: the concept of a living book that grows with each artist, mixing cultures and nationalities. And each participant demonstrated remarkable inventiveness in expressing their ideas."

9·22·2007
SAUSALITO, CA

Erik Tiemens received *Sketchtravel* from the hands of **Dominique Louis** on August 31, 2007, in San Francisco and gave it to **Daisuke Tsutsumi** on September 22, 2007, in Sausalito.

Stop 22 Stop 23 Stop 24

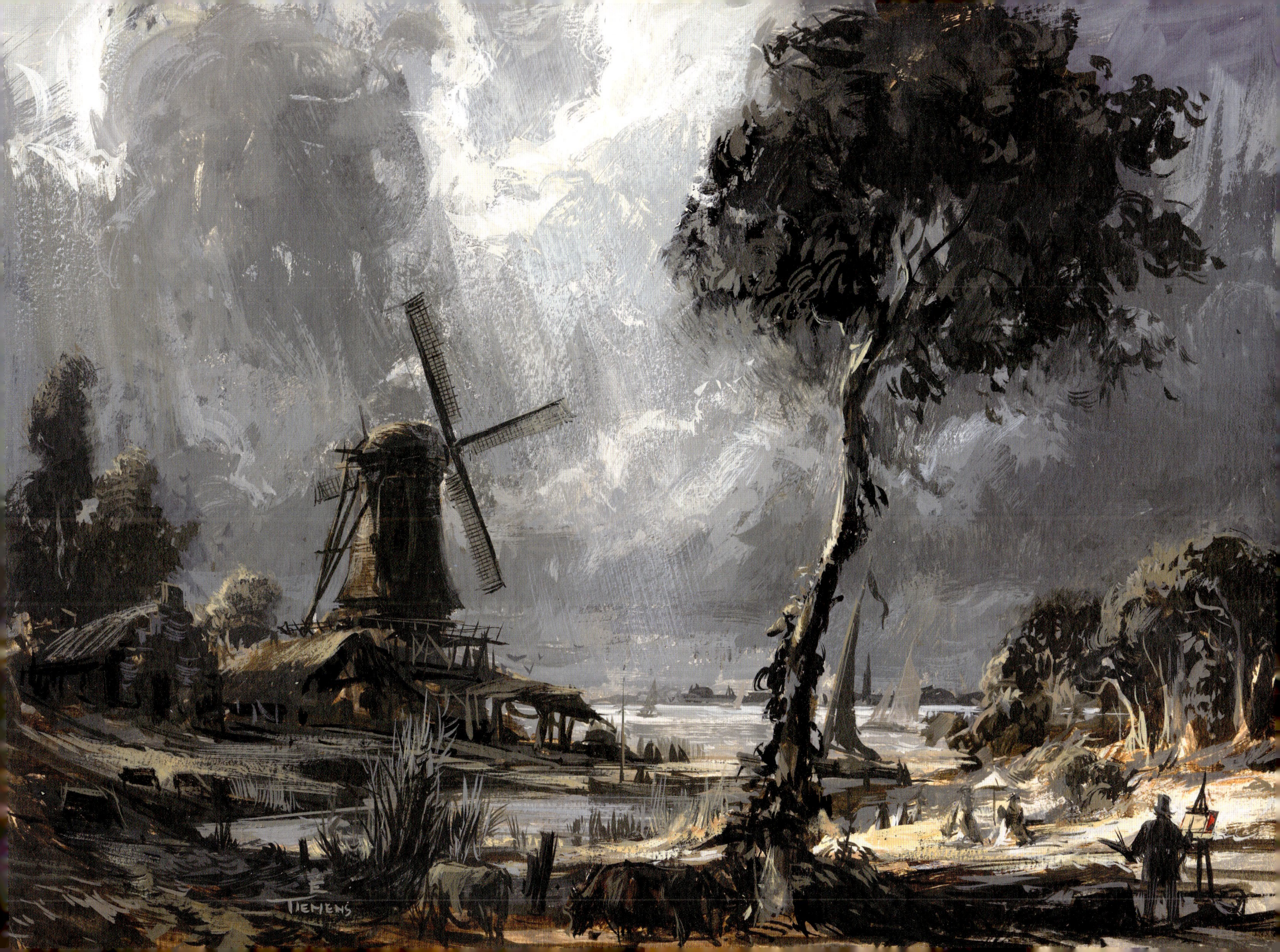
TIEMENS

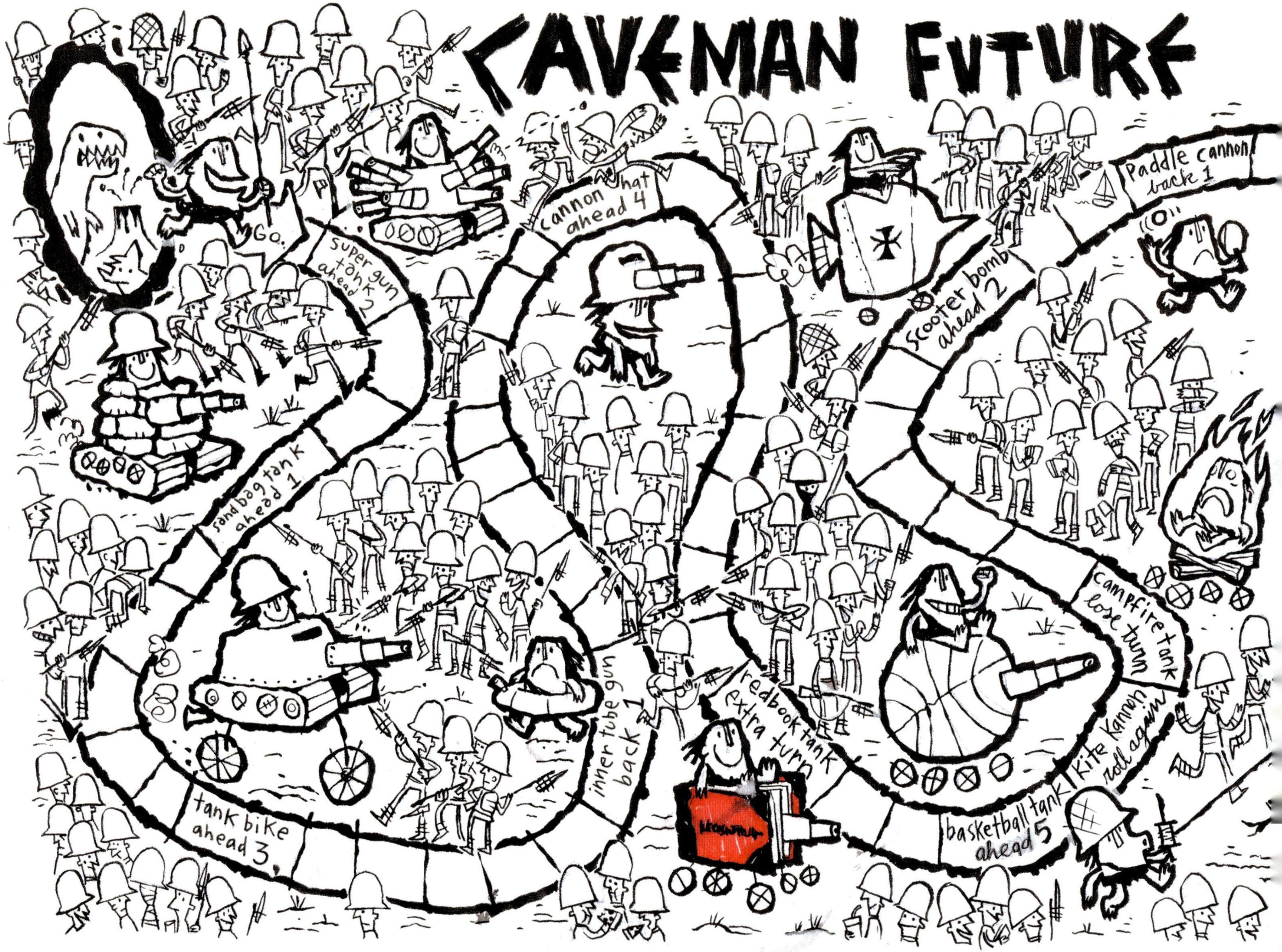
CAVEMAN FUTURE
Go.
super gun tank ahead 2
cannon hat ahead 4
Paddle cannon back 1
scooter bomb ahead 2
sandbag tank ahead 1
campfire tank lose turn
inner tube gun back 1
redbook tank extra turn
kite kannon roll again
basketball tank ahead 5
tank bike ahead 3

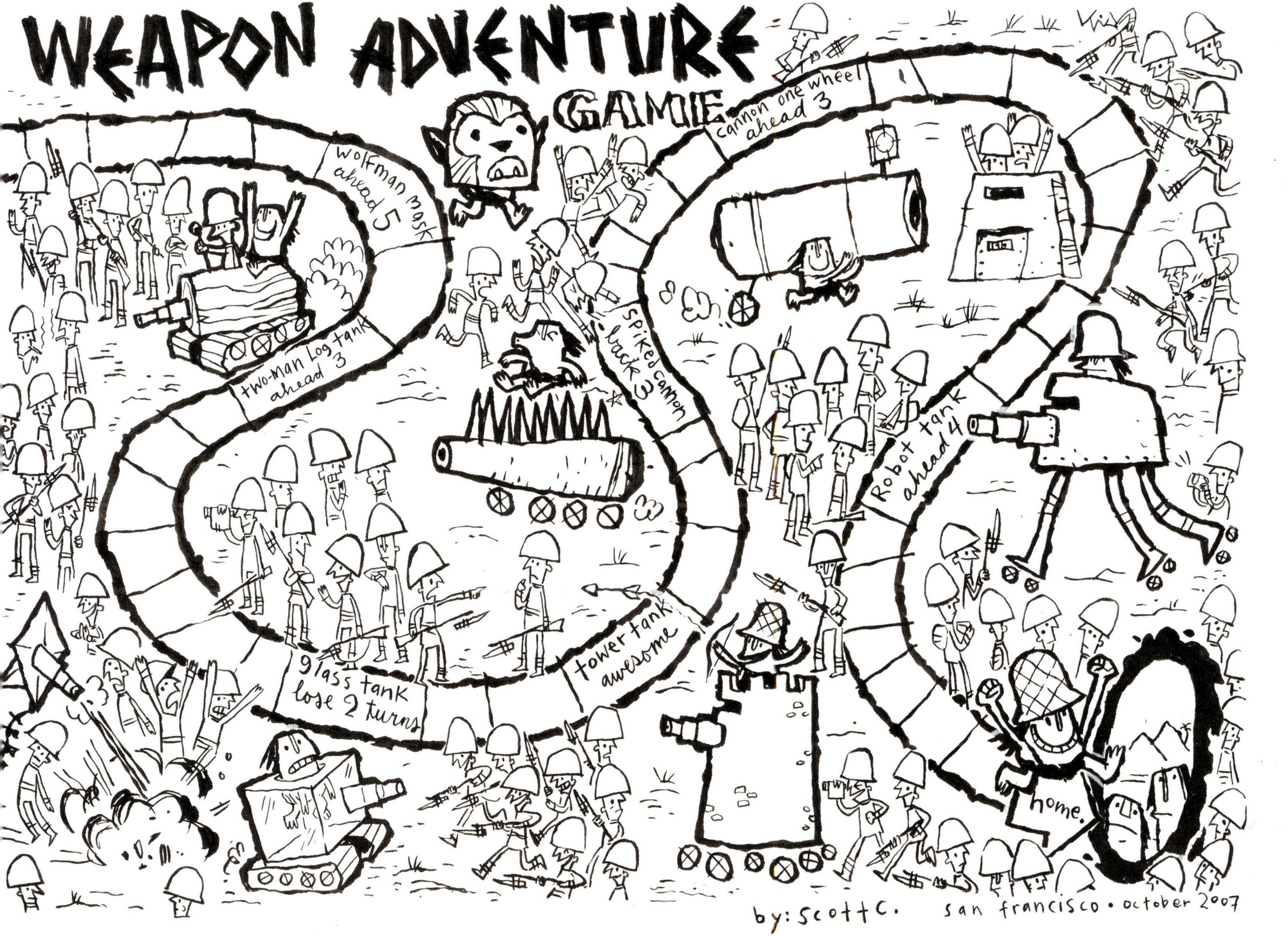
WEAPON ADVENTURE
GAME
wolfman mask ahead 5
cannon one wheel ahead 3
two-man log tank ahead 3
spiked cannon back 3
Robot tank ahead 4
glass tank lose 2 turns
tower tank awesome
home.
by: scott c.
san francisco • october 2007

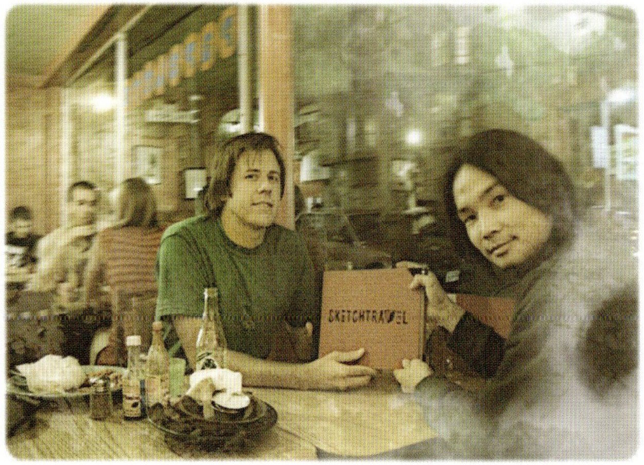

Scott Campbell and Daisuke Tsutsumi

scott c.

Scott Campbell

"I like to think that *Sketchtravel* is a kind of person who travels from country to country, meeting artists: a protagonist who feels an intense pleasure each time new hands embellish its pages in their unique style.

It is an enormous honor for me to have been chosen to be part of the project. I was anxious that my drawing would not be up to the level of the others. That said, it was in looking at what the others had done before me that I was inspired."

san francisco • october 2007

?

Scott Campbell received *Sketchtravel* from the hands of **Daisuke Tsutsumi** on October 6, 2007, in San Francisco and gave it back to **Daisuke Tsutsumi** on October 10, 2007, in San Francisco.

Stop 23 Stop 24 Stop 25

James Jean

"As artists, we are all linked and influenced by the culture that surrounds us. I cannot imagine a better way to represent this bond than with a book that travels around the world, passing from one artist to the next.

When it comes to drawing a sketch, I try never to have preconceived ideas. I was afraid—this book is such a precious object.

A treasure, moreover, that I had to debase . . ."

James Jean received *Sketchtravel* from the hands of **Daisuke Tsutsumi** on October 13, 2007, in Los Angeles and gave it to **Yuko Shimizu** in February 2008 in California.

Stop 24 Stop 25 Stop 26

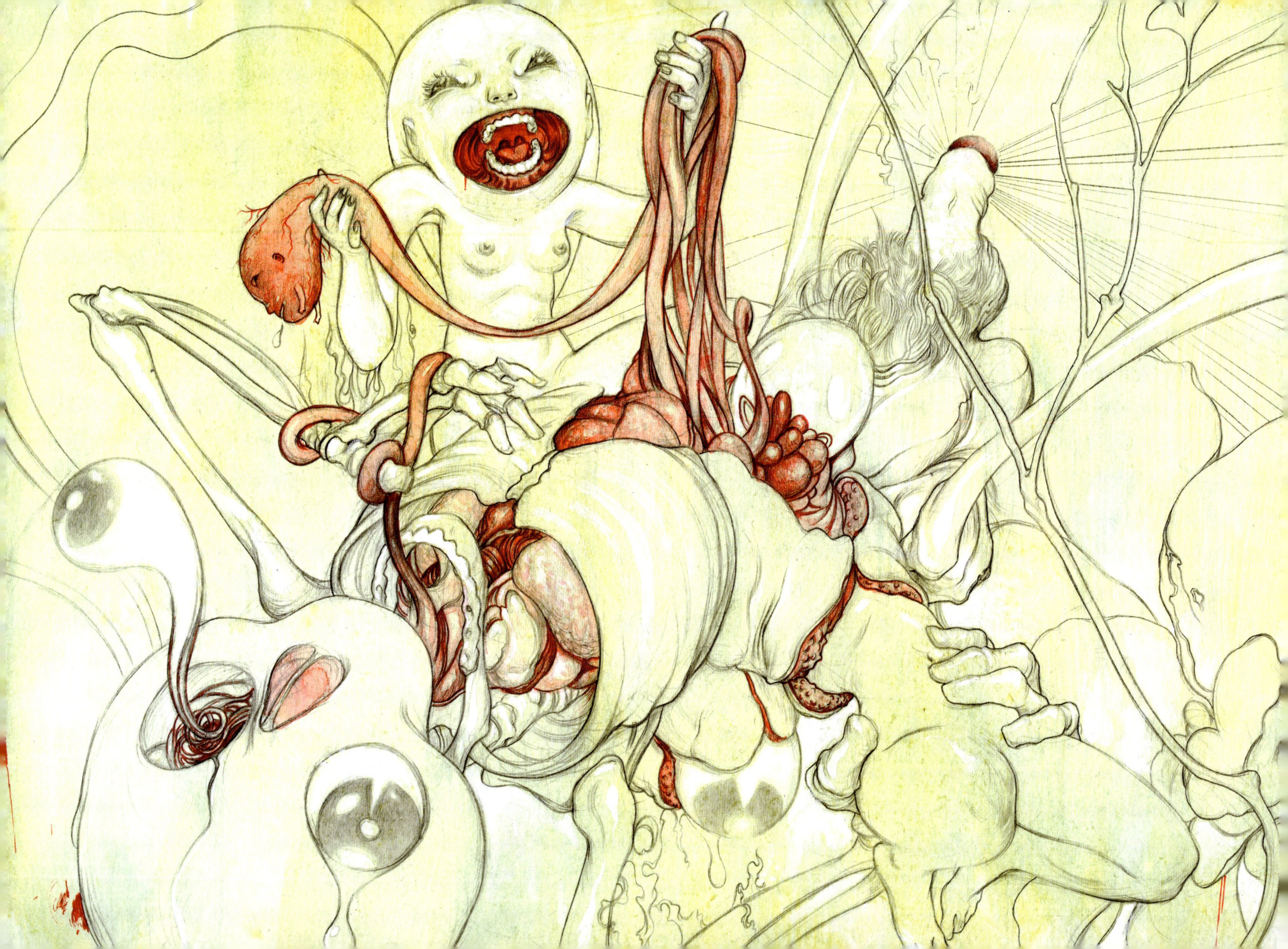

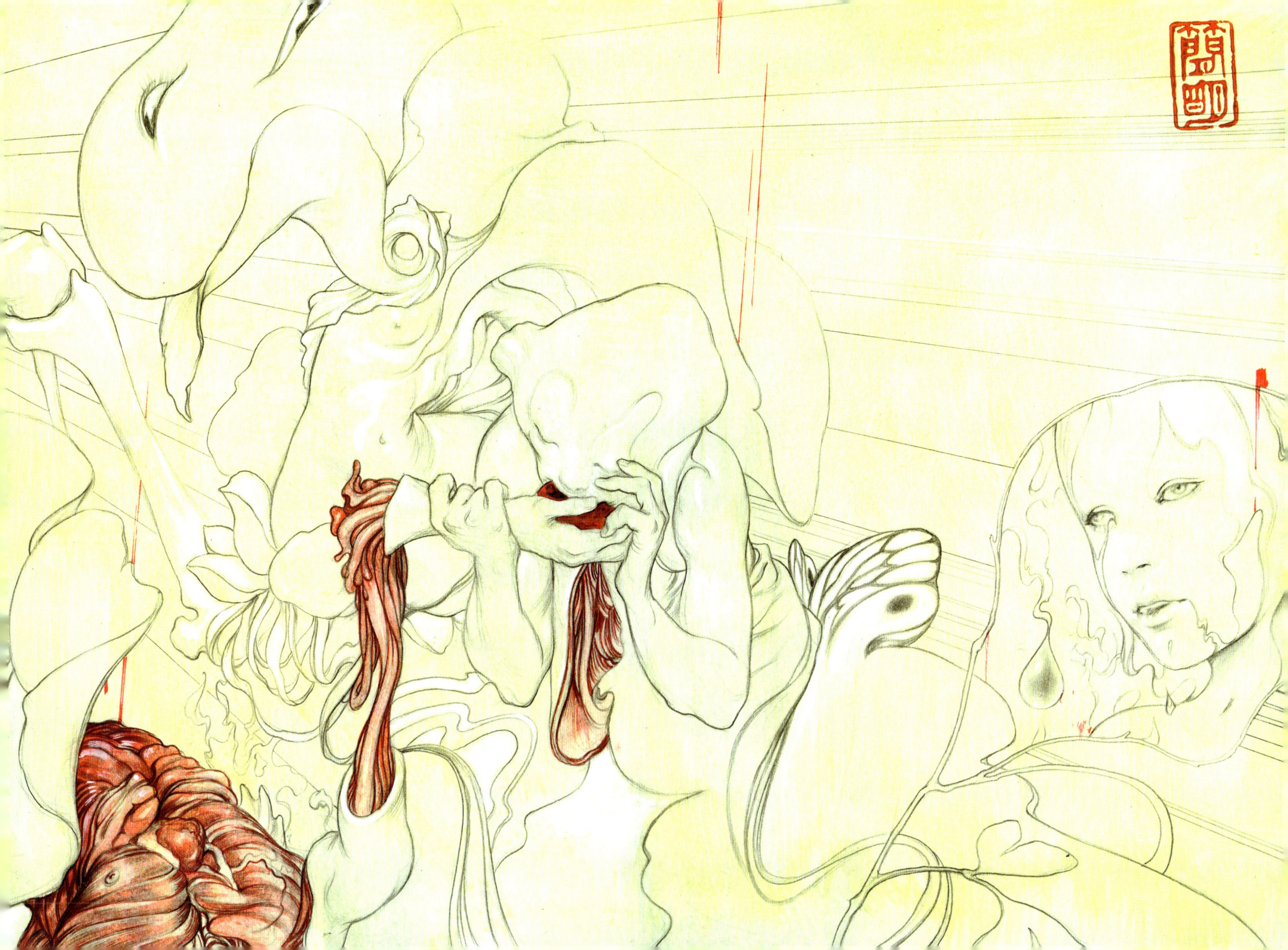

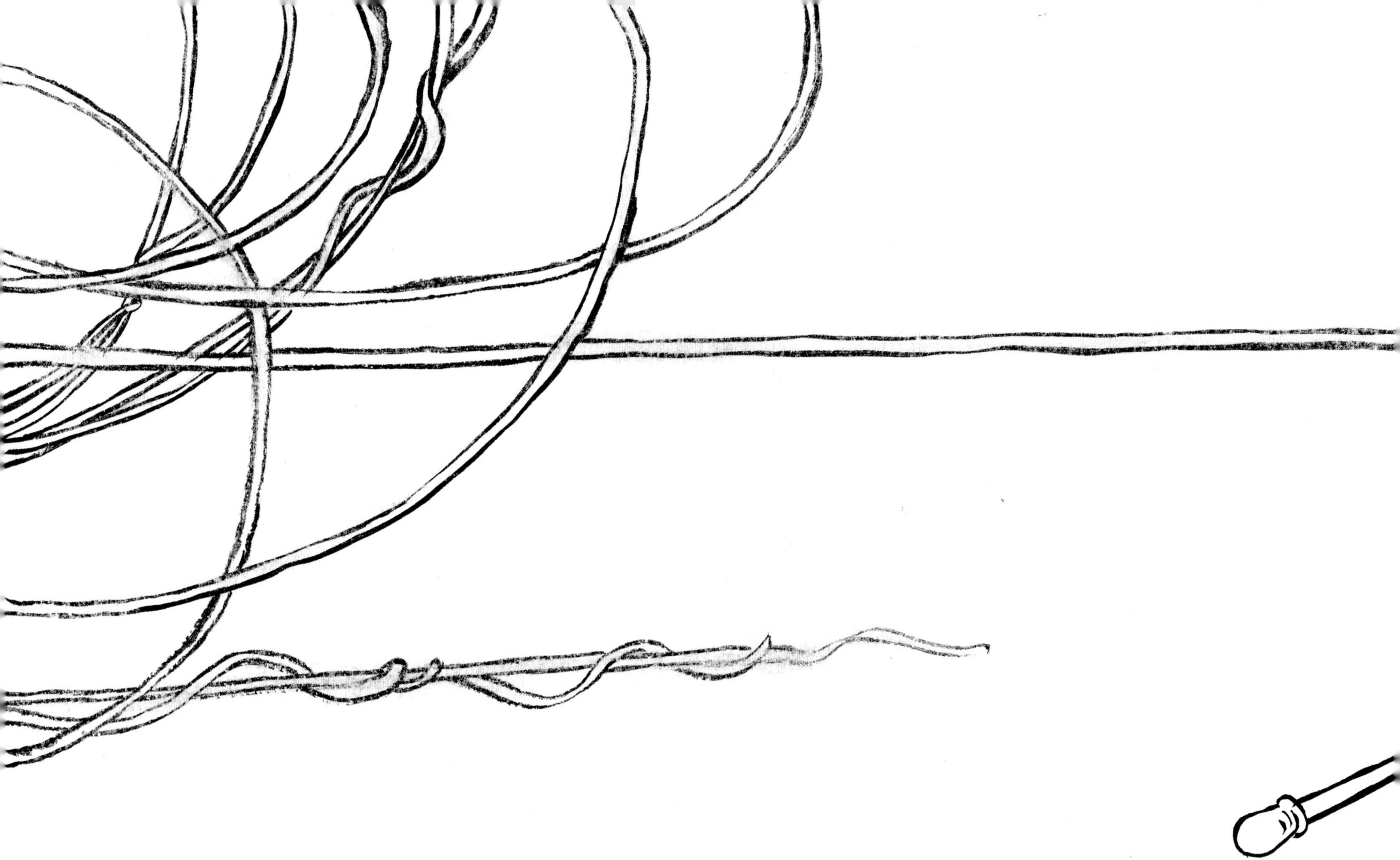

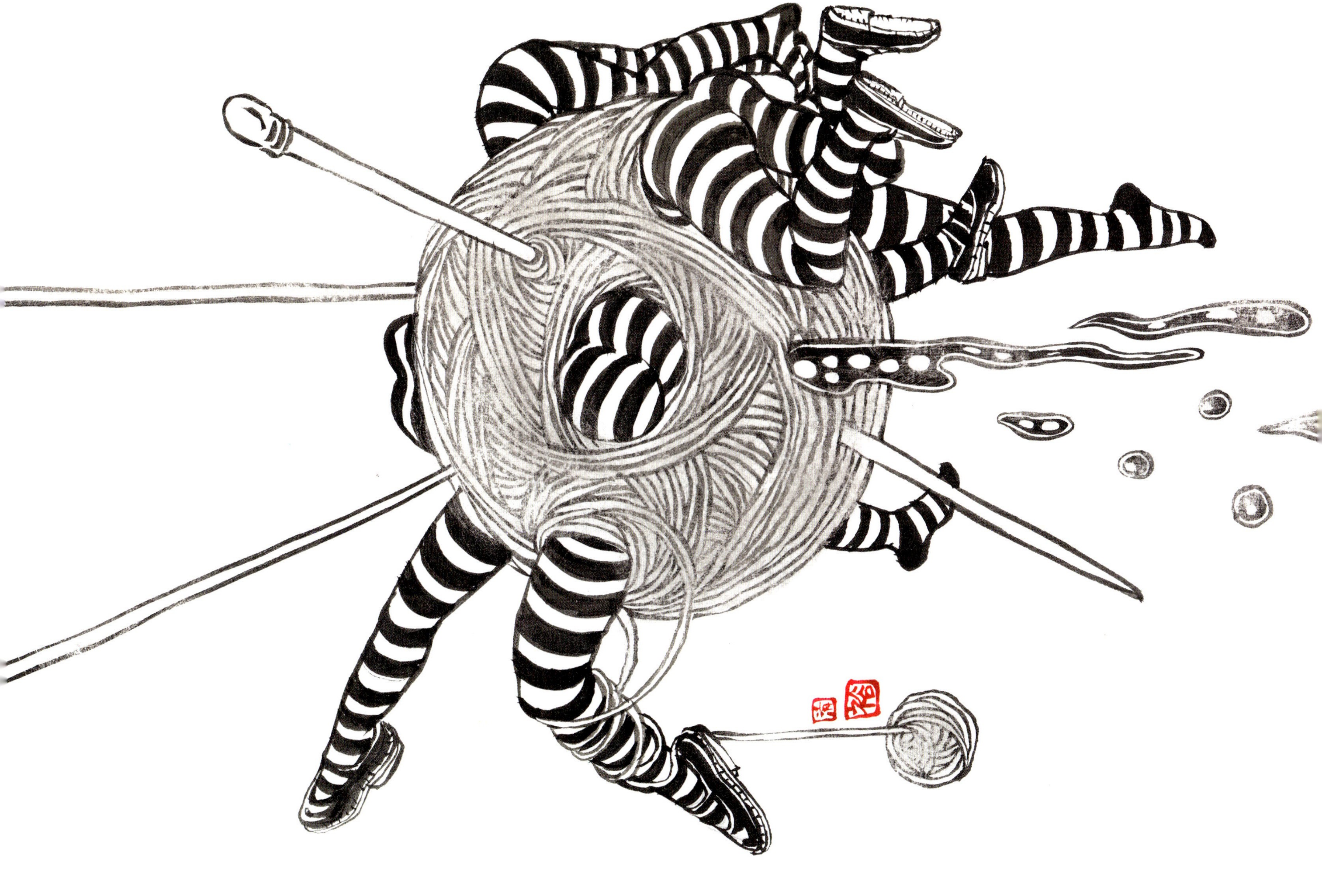

Yuko Shimizu

"It was only after having seen what the others had done before me that I knew what I would draw. An artist has to be creative and original, and I wanted a new idea, different from the others.

It is for this reason, for example, that I chose to hold the book vertically rather than horizontally, as most people had done. I wanted something simple and minimalist.

I loved the other drawings, not always knowing where they had come from. They were almost always signed, but sometimes I didn't know the artist, and sometimes I couldn't decipher the signature."

Yuko Shimizu received *Sketchtravel* from the hands of **James Jean** in February 2008 in California and gave it to **Daisuke Tsutsumi** in March 2008 in San Francisco

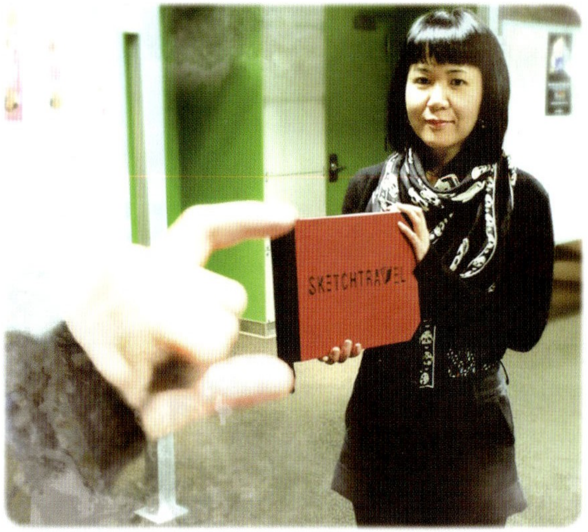

Yuko Shimizu

Stop 25
Stop 26
Stop 27

Dominique Bertail

"Moments of pure recreation like this are more and more rare, even more when you are surrounded by such talented and honored playmates . . .

My idea came to me while I was looking at the previous drawings. I wanted to do a spread, but with a constraint; not too much watercolor on the left-hand page so I wouldn't spoil Bill Plympton's drawing on the other side. Then a white wall. Then a villa. Then a pool . . . a pretty girl . . . polo players . . . and a Lou Romano on the wall.

I just tried to think of pleasant things."

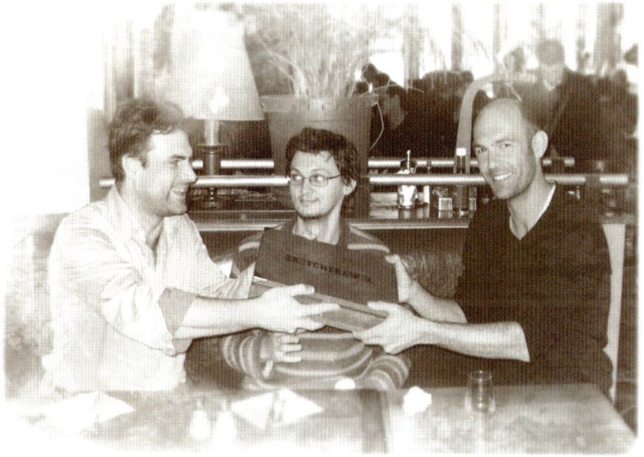

Dominique Bertail, Sébastien Cosset of Kerascoët, and Nicolas de Crécy

Stop 28
Stop 29
Stop 30

Dominique Bertail received *Sketchtravel* from the hands of **Gérald Guerlais** on September 16, 2008, in Paris and gave it to **Pierre Alary** on September 20, 2008, in Paris.

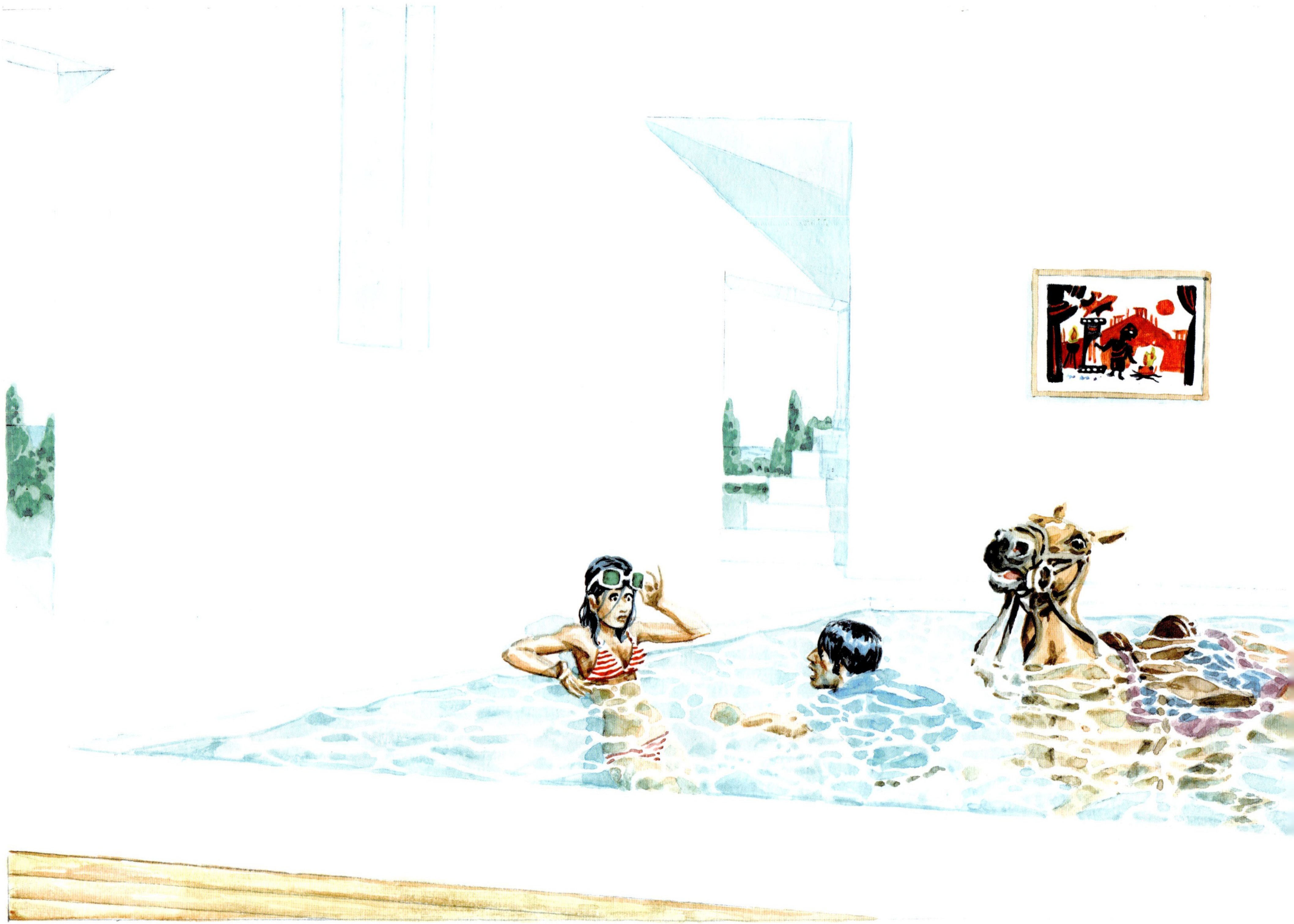

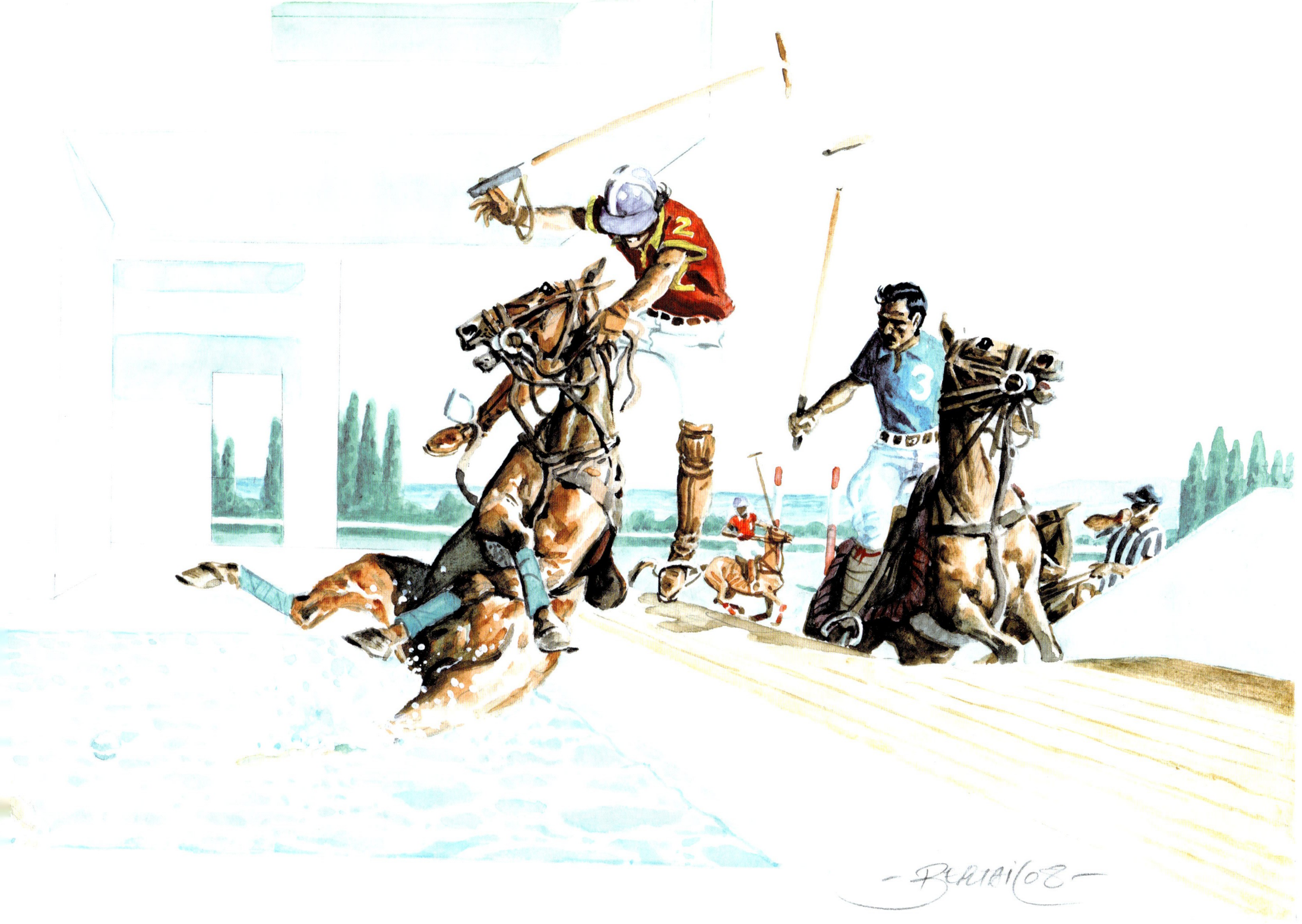

David Gordon

"One of the most interesting and meaningful projects I've had the chance to participate in. I have to admit that I was guilty of a little procrastination when it was my turn. I was truly intimidated by the work of the other artists.

I am unbelievably proud to have played a role in making this magnificent book."

- NYC 2008 -

David Gordon received *Sketchtravel* from the hands of **Daisuke Tsutsumi** in August 2008 in California and gave it back to **Daisuke Tsutsumi** in August 2008 in California.

Stop 26 Stop 27 Stop 28

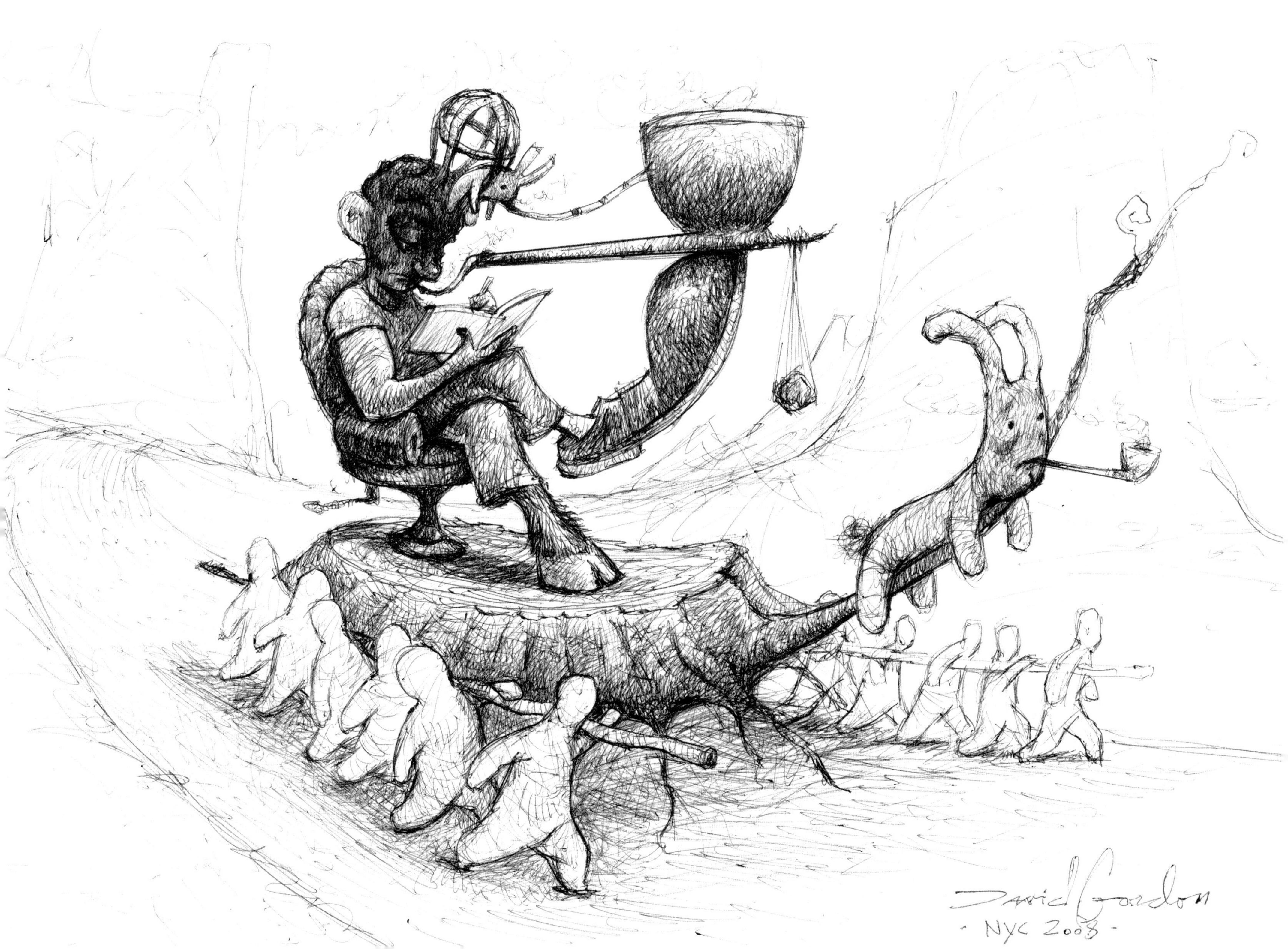
David Gordon
· NYC 2008 ·

Bill Plympton

Bill Plympton

"I am going to have problems with feminists."

Sept 2 2008

?

Bill Plympton received *Sketchtravel* from the hands of **Catherine Bonvalot** on September 2, 2008, in New York and gave it back to **Catherine Bonvalot** on September 2, 2008, in New York.

Stop 27 Stop 28 Stop 29

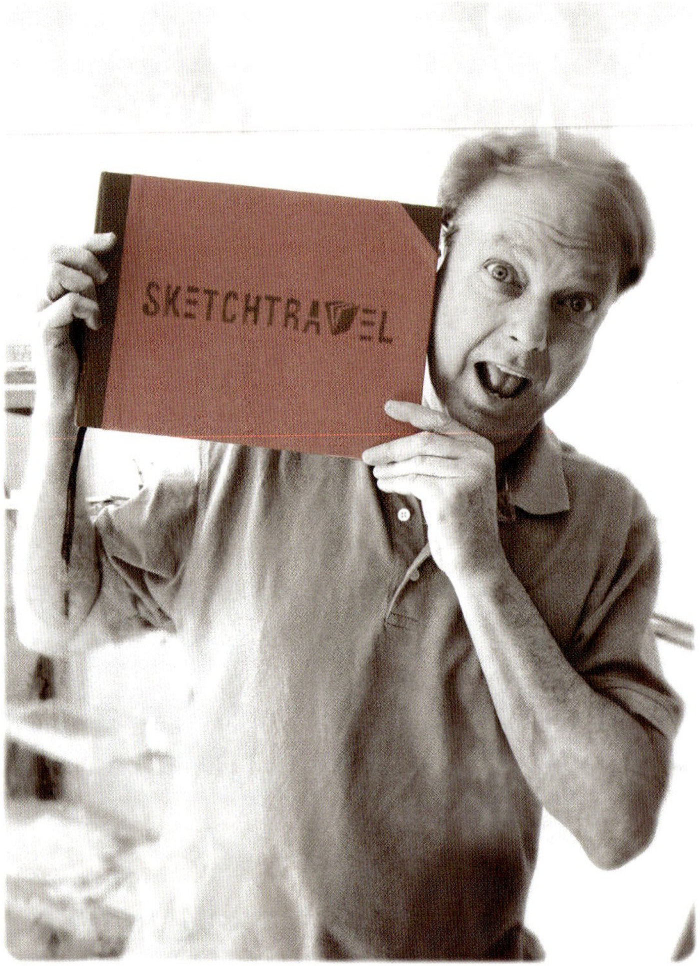

Bill Plympton

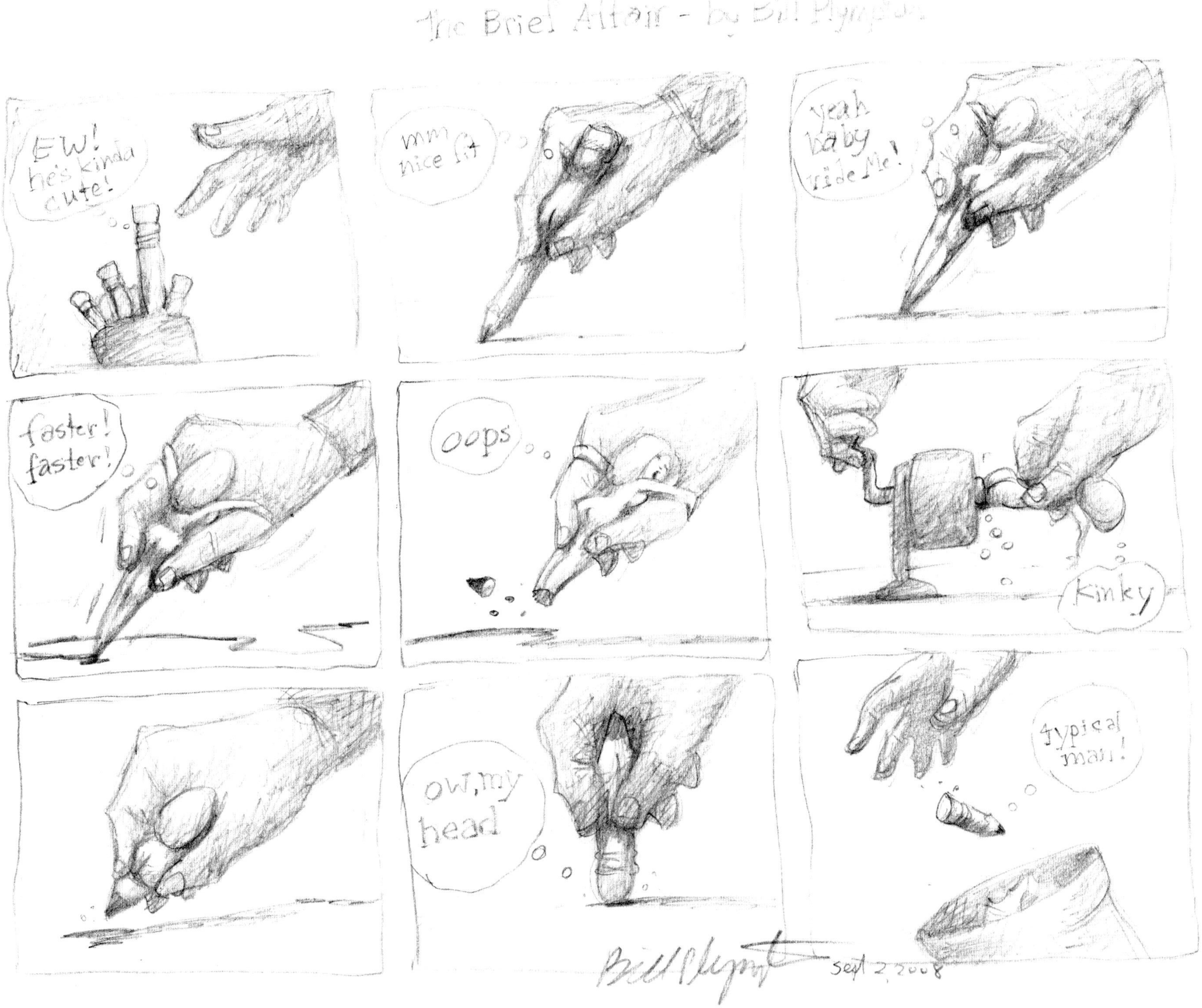
The Brief Affair - by Bill Plympton
EW! he's kinda cute!
mm nice fit
yeah baby ride Me!
faster! faster!
oops
kinky
ow, my head
typical man!
Bill Plympton
Sept 2, 2008

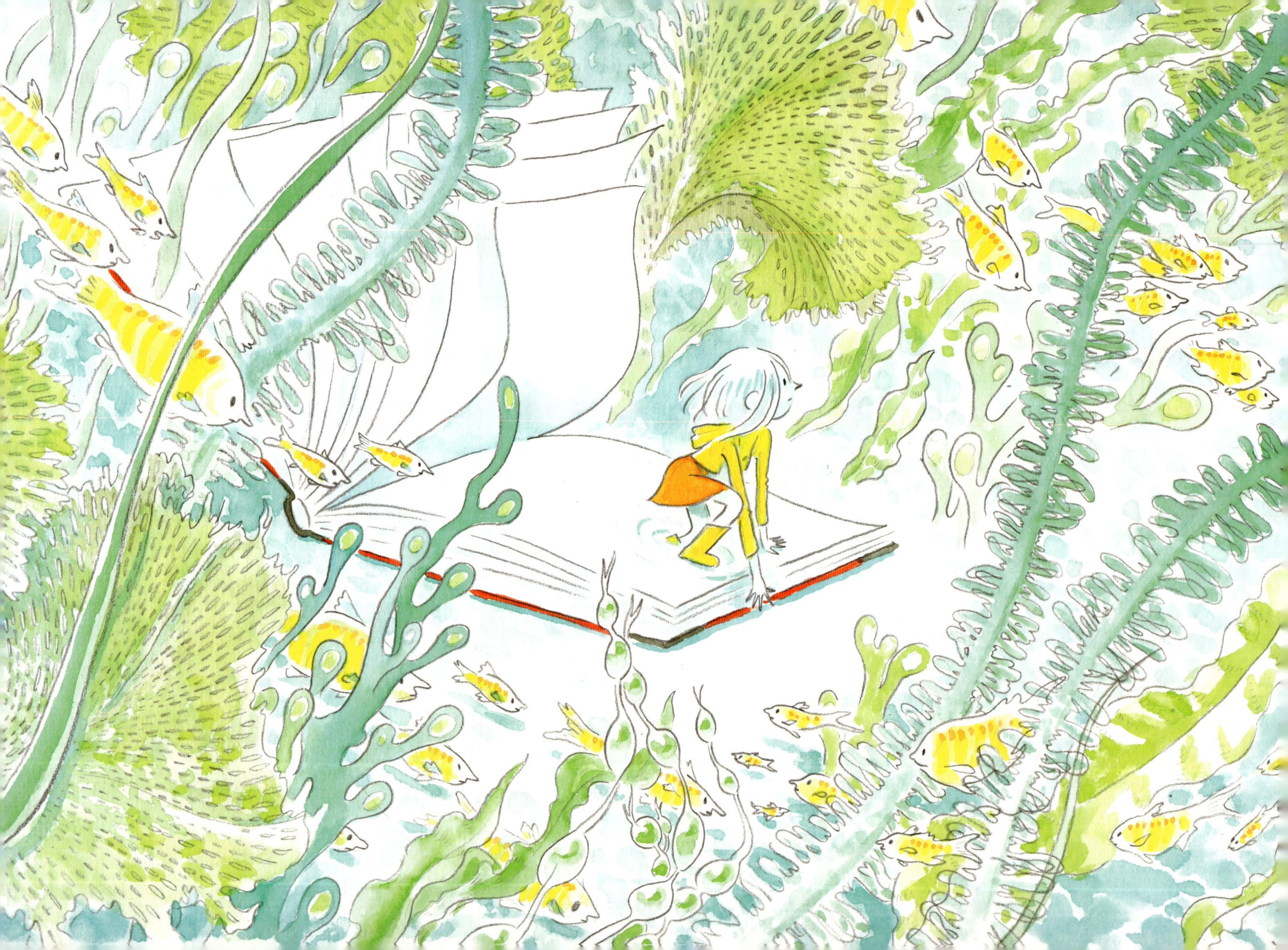

Kerascoët

Sébastien Cosset and Marie Pommepuy of Kerascoët

"It was both a challenge and a pleasure, more exciting because it was shared with many great artists. To crown everything, it is a selfless act and a real sharing of talents . . . In brief, it's a really great idea!

We had to make a drawing just after Quentin Blake (on the same page!). We couldn't do it, too much stress. We decided to react to the drawing of our friend Dominique, who himself had winked at the participation of Lou Romano."

Paris mars 2009

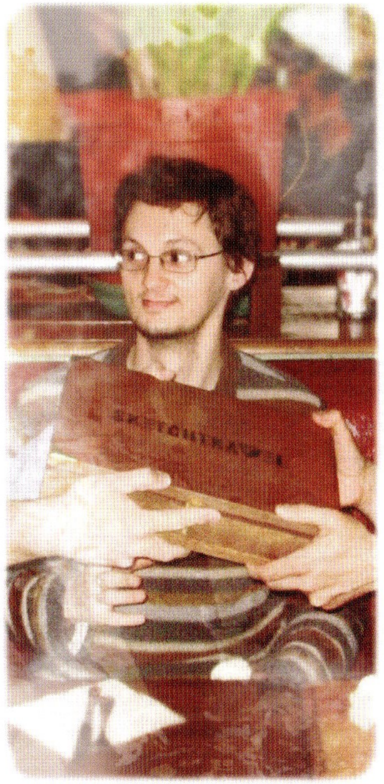

Sébastien Cosset

?

Sébastien Cosset and Marie Pommepuy of Kerascoët received *Sketchtravel* from the hands of **Gérald Guerlais** on March 15, 2009, in Paris and gave it back to **Gérald Guerlais** on March 16, 2009, in Paris.

Stop 36 — Stop 37 — Stop 38

Pierre Alary

"This collective project is a superb idea that only got better.

I tried watercolor to stay in the spirit, but I found myself a little disoriented by the quality of my predecessors . . . In the end, the drawing was made in fear and doubt. I thought I would have time to find an idea. I had the time to think about it, and when the kiss came, poof, nothing . . . Then, leafing through the work of my comrades, it became even worse. I wanted to learn and study with many of these artists."

- 10.2008 -

?

Pierre Alary received *Sketchtravel* from the hands of **Dominique Bertail** on September 20, 2008, in Paris and gave it to **Grégoire Villermaux** on October 15, 2008, in Brussels.

Stop 29 Stop 30 Stop 31

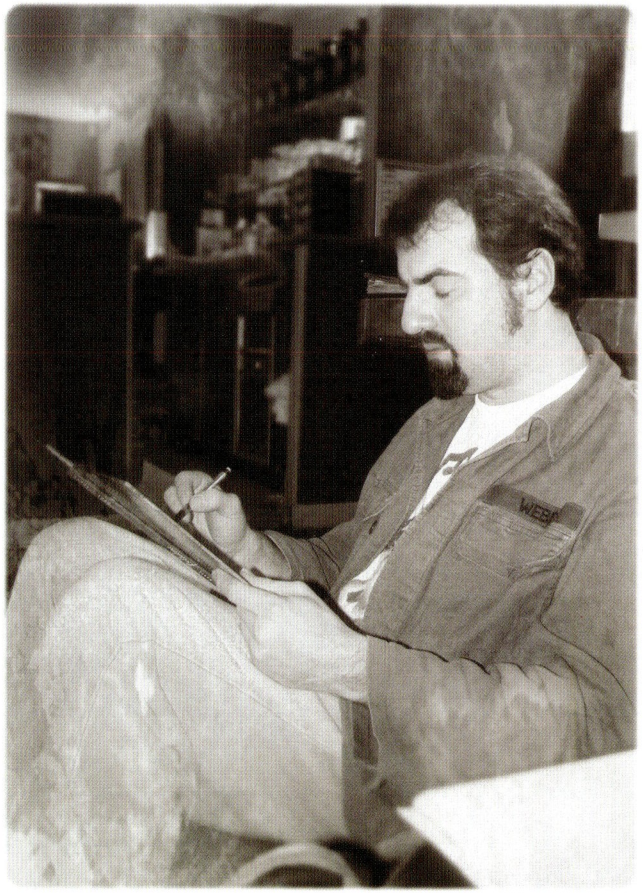

Pierre Alary

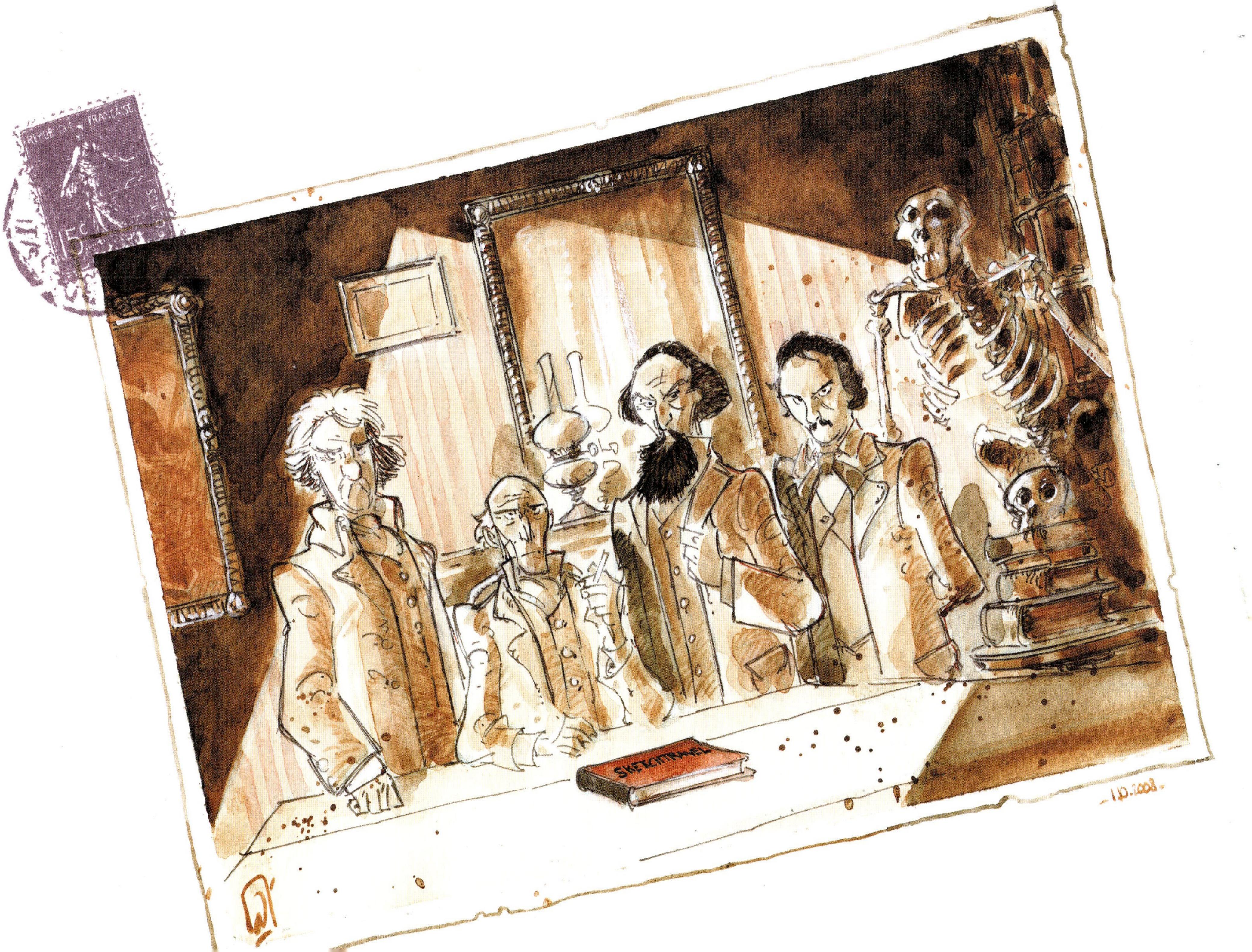
SKETCHTRAVEL
- 10.2008 -

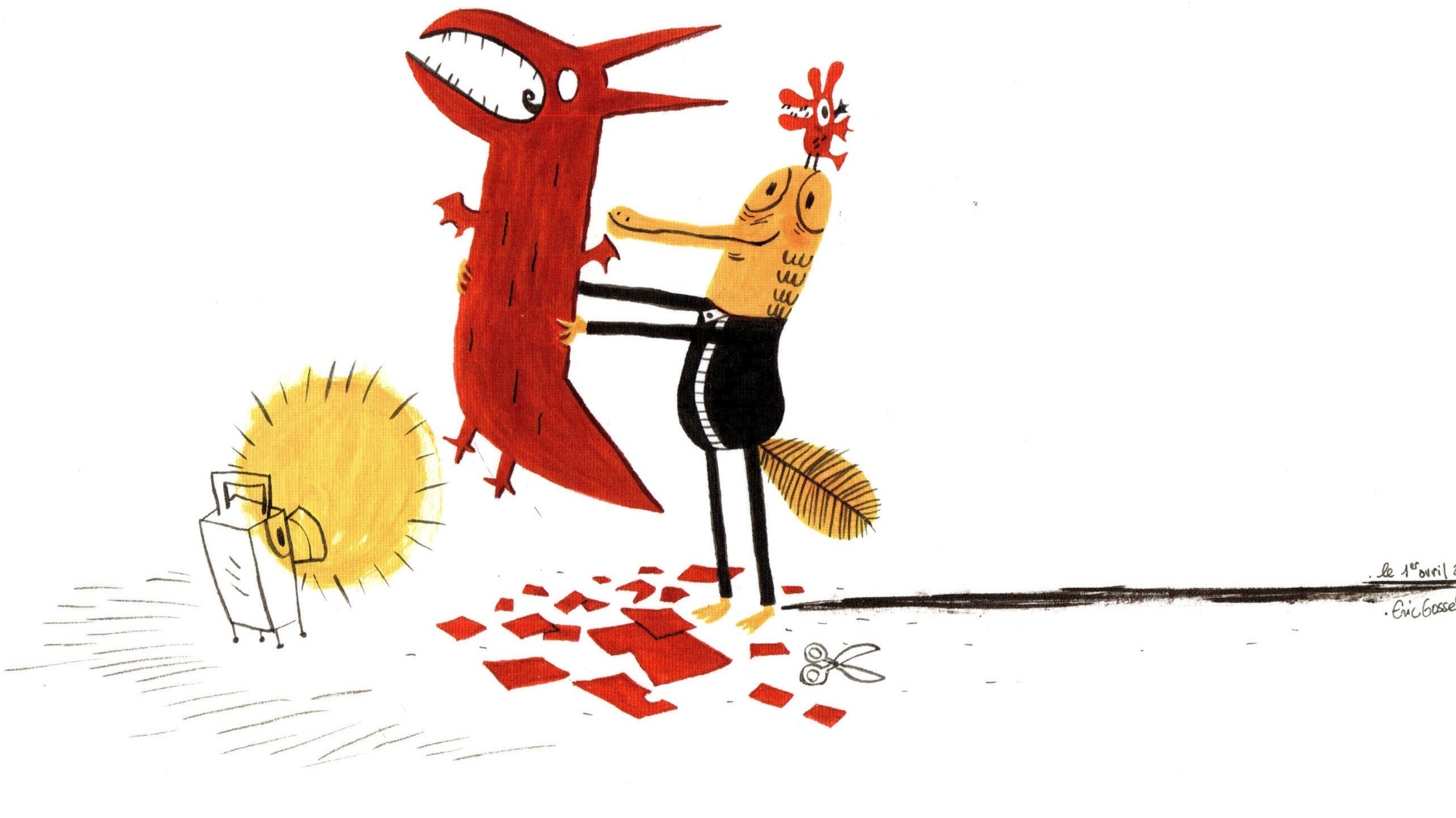
. le 1er avril 2009.
. Eric Gosselet.

·Éric Gosselet.

Éric Gosselet

"This collective walk is to be repeated without moderation.

Thanks to the notebook, I discovered Michael Knapp, Jerome Opeña, Robert MacKenzie, and Vincent Di Nguyen. When I found myself with the notebook in my hands, I was nervous. Because the object was truly impressive, and I am not talking about the content. Lou Romano's contribution gave me goose bumps. I love his work."

le 1er avril 2009.

Éric Gosselet received *Sketchtravel* from the hands of **Nicolas de Crécy** on April 1, 2009, in Paris and gave it to **Gérald Guerlais** on April 2, 2009, in Paris.

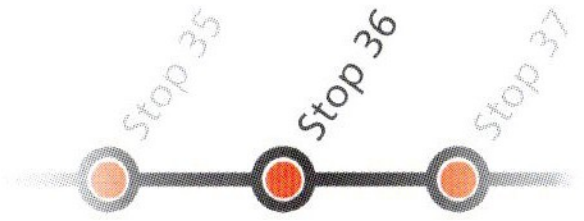

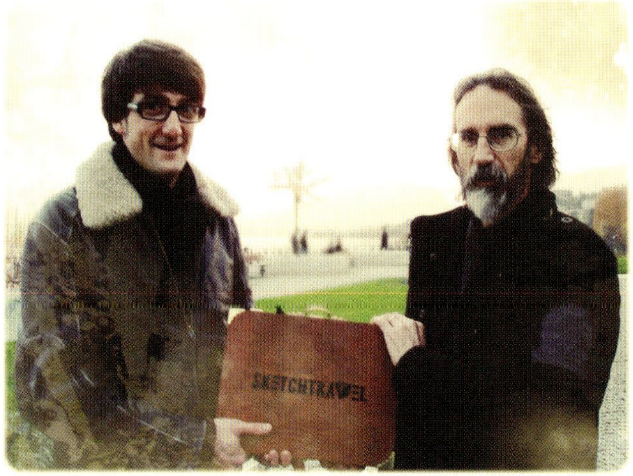

Grégoire Villermaux and John Howe

GRÉGOIRE VILLERMAUX.

Grégoire Villermaux

"I asked as a personal favor to be able to give the notebook to John Howe. Because after all, it is what makes the essence of this adventure: to be able to shake the hand of the man who made you want to do this work. All things considered, Mr. Howe is not at all the dragon that I represented in my drawing. He looked at the drawings already in the notebook with real pleasure and humility.

I had the chance to meet one of these role models who inspires us to be artists."

À LILLE, LE 19 OCTOBRE 2008.

Grégoire Villermaux received *Sketchtravel* from the hands of **Pierre Alary** on September 17, 2008, in Brussels and gave it to **John Howe** on November 9, 2008, in Neuchâtel.

Stop 30 Stop 31 Stop 32

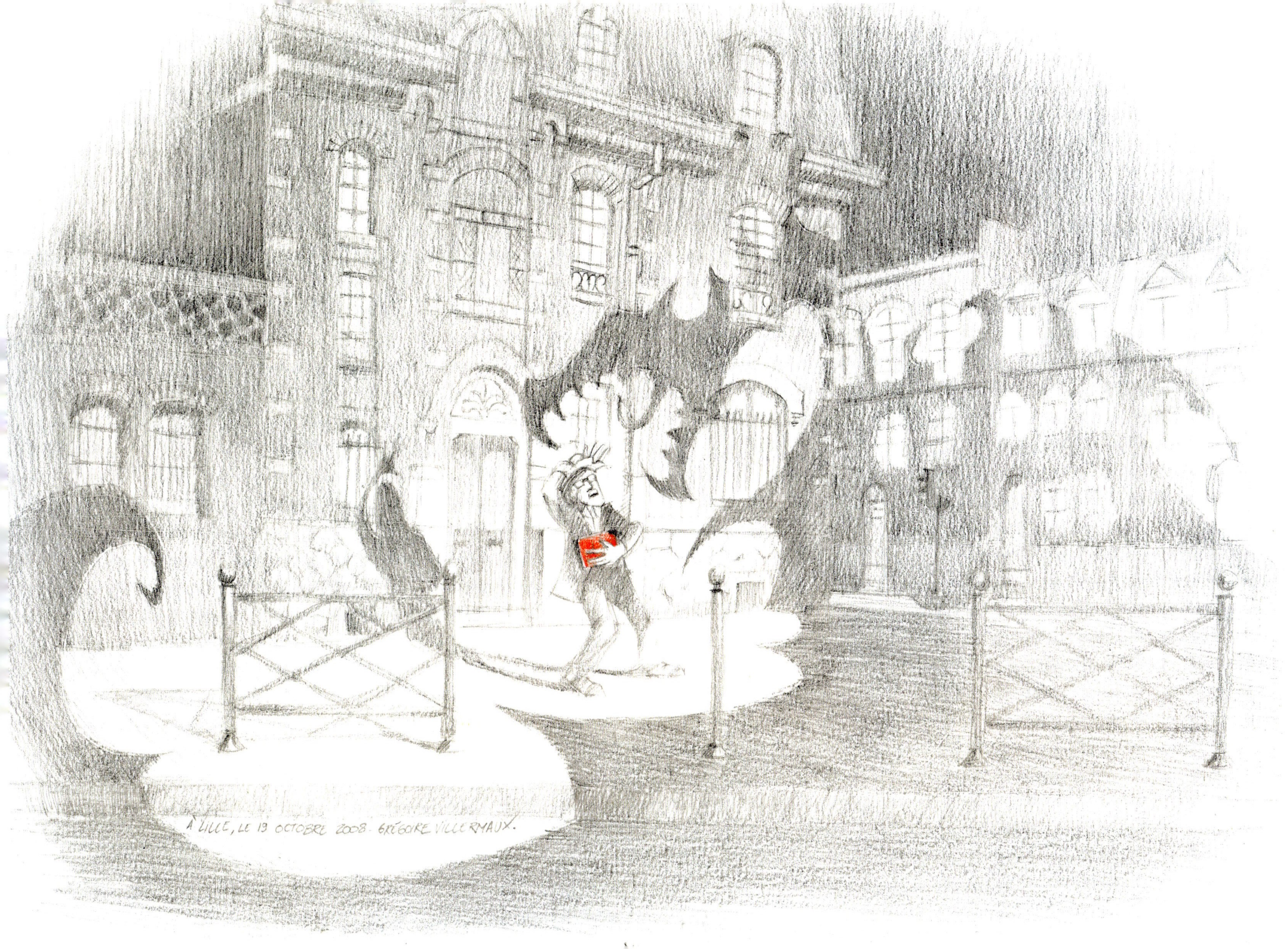
À LILLE, LE 13 OCTOBRE 2008. GRÉGOIRE VILLERMAUX.

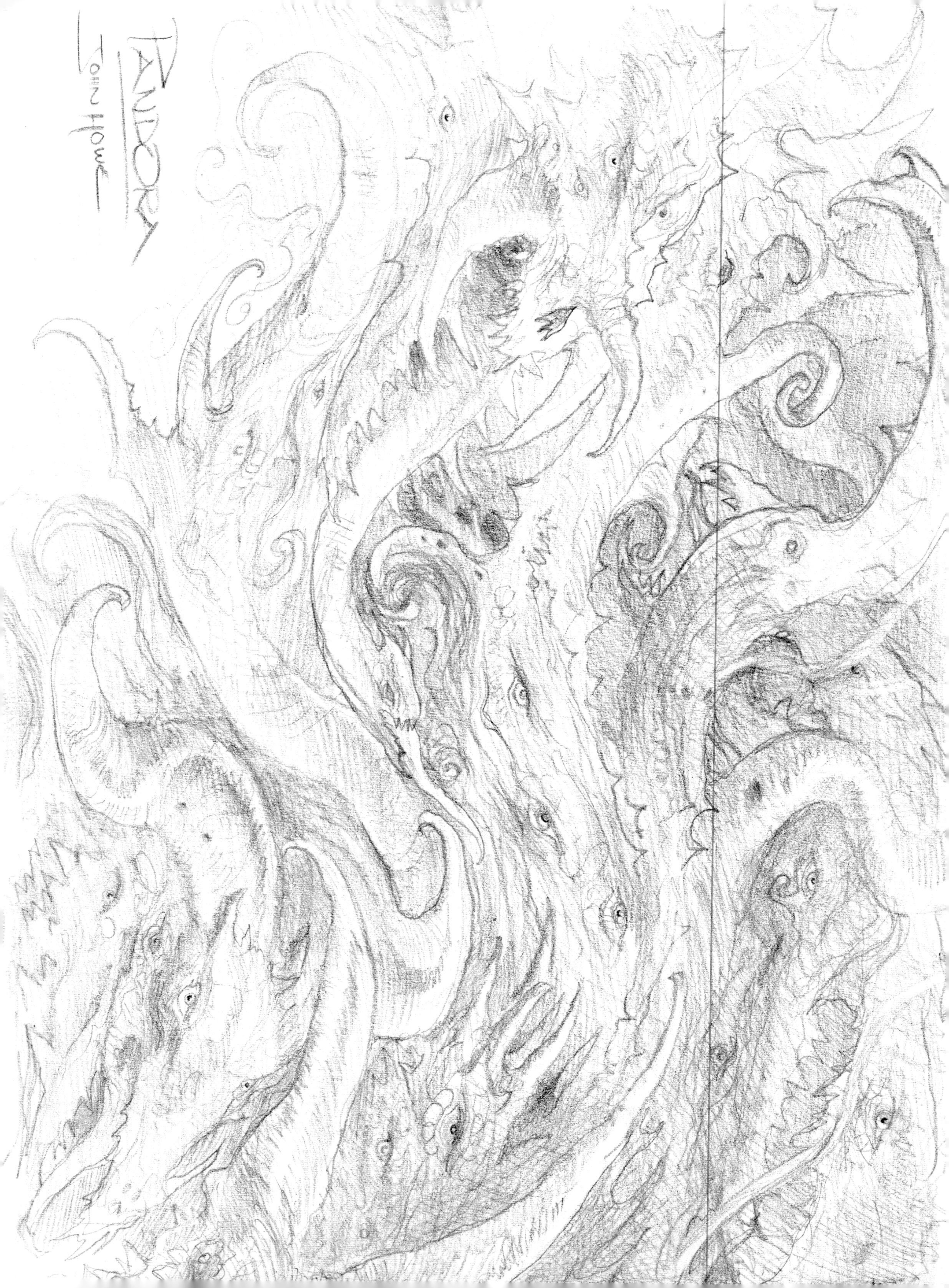
PANDORA
JOHN HOWE

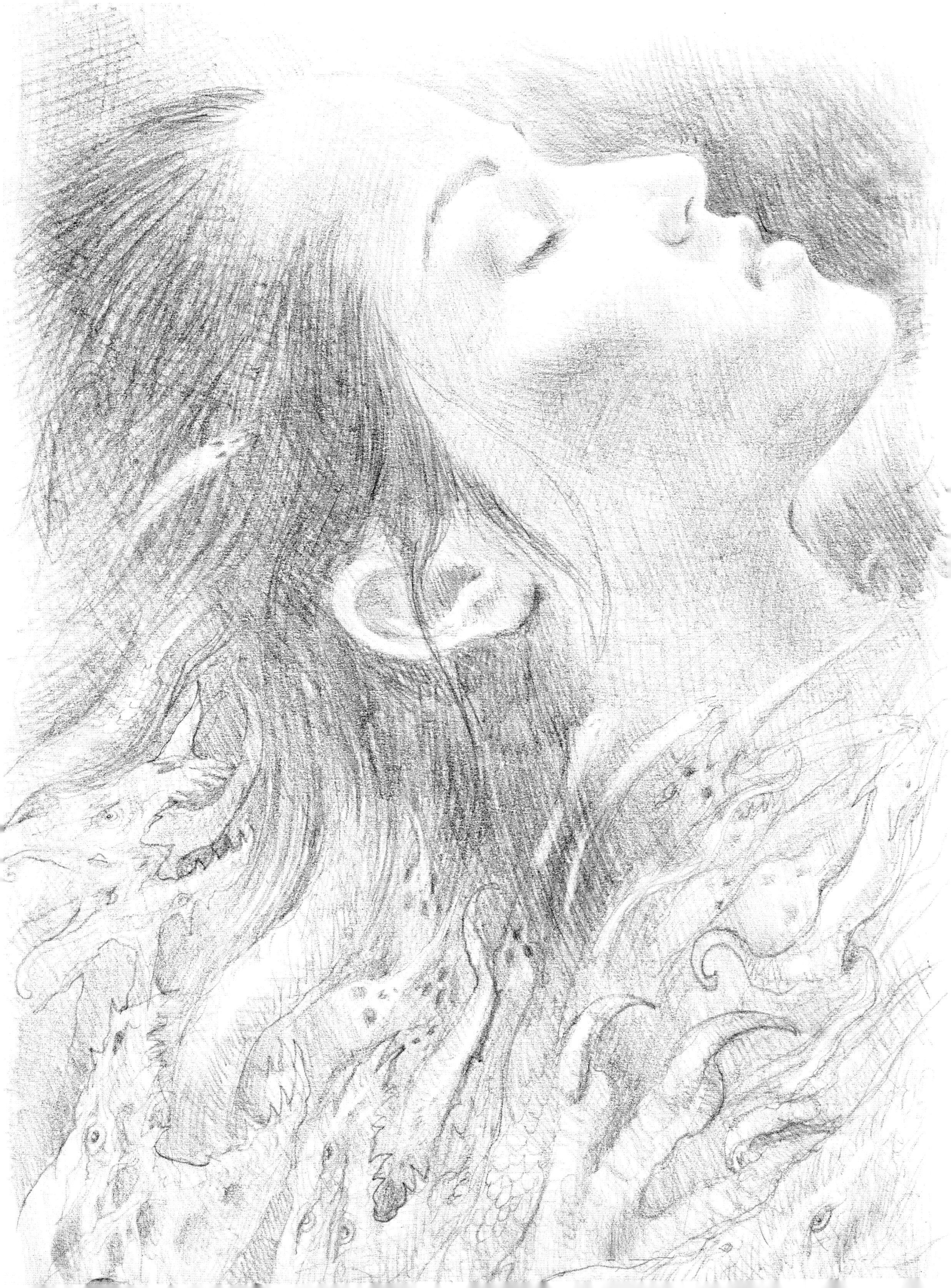

John Howe

John Howe received *Sketchtravel* from the hands of **Grégoire Villermaux** on November 9, 2008, in Neuchâtel and gave it back to **Grégoire Villermaux** on November 10, 2008, in Neuchâtel.

Stop 31 · **Stop 32** · Stop 33

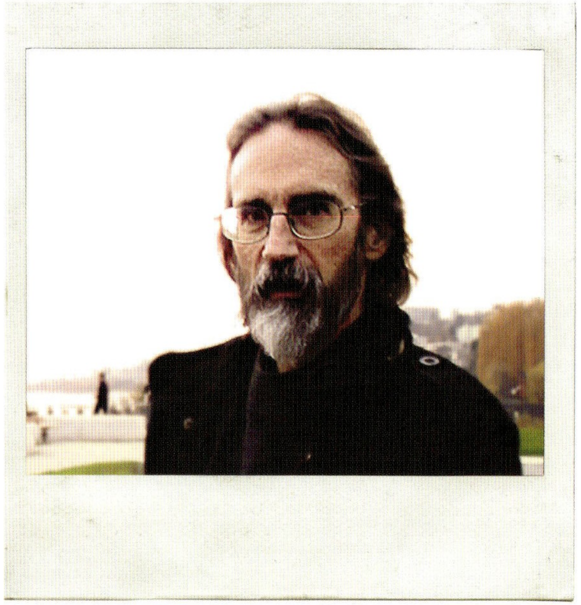

John Howe

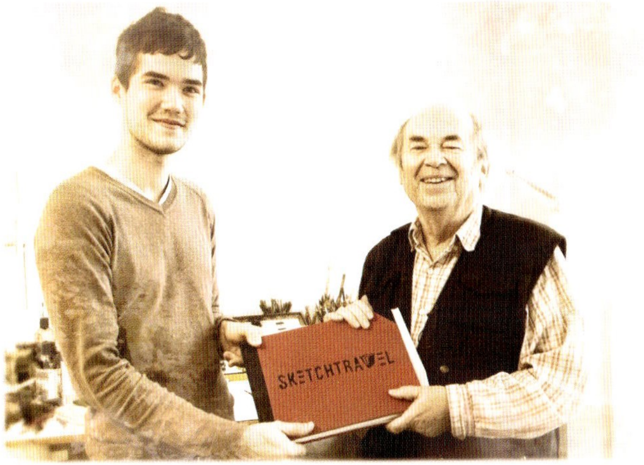

Sylvain Marc and Quentin Blake

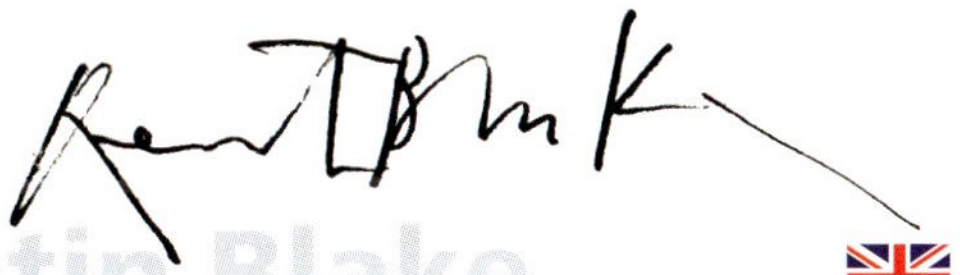

Quentin Blake

London
3 Nov 2008

Quentin Blake received *Sketchtravel* from the hands of **Sylvain Marc** on November 3, 2008, in London and gave it to **Catherine Bonvalot** on November 3, 2008, in London.

Stop 32 — Stop 33 — Stop 34

London
3 Nov 2008

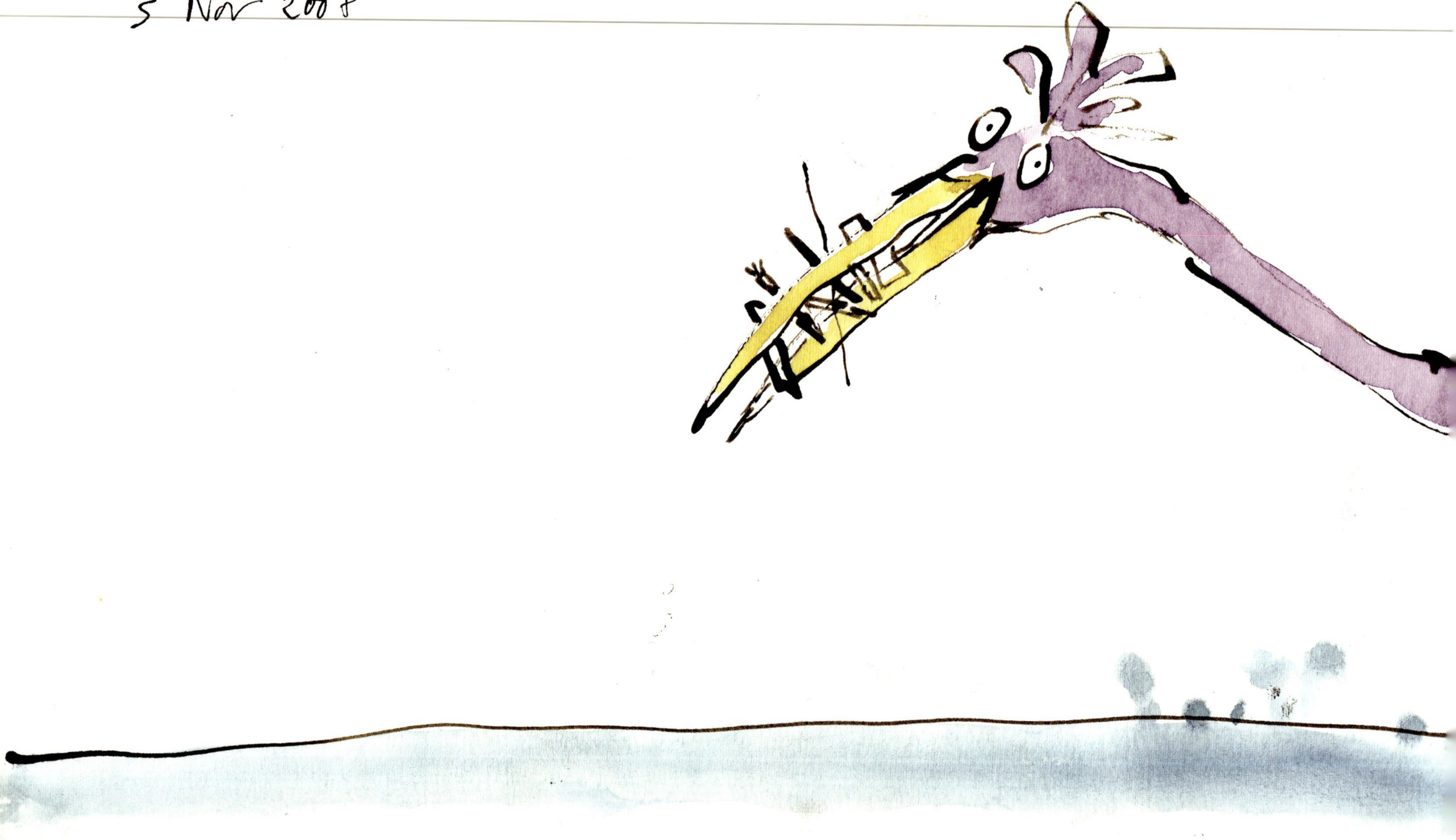

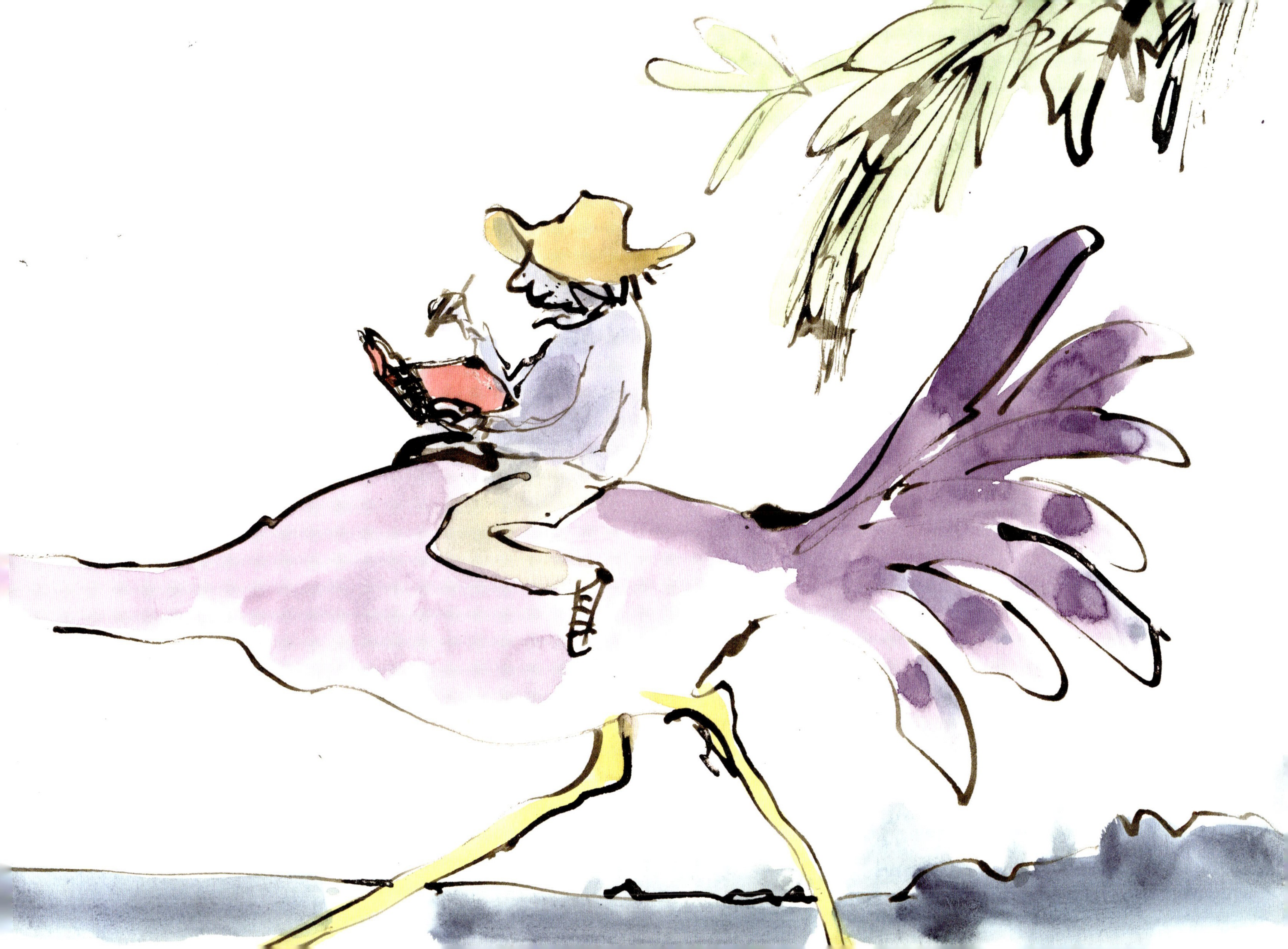

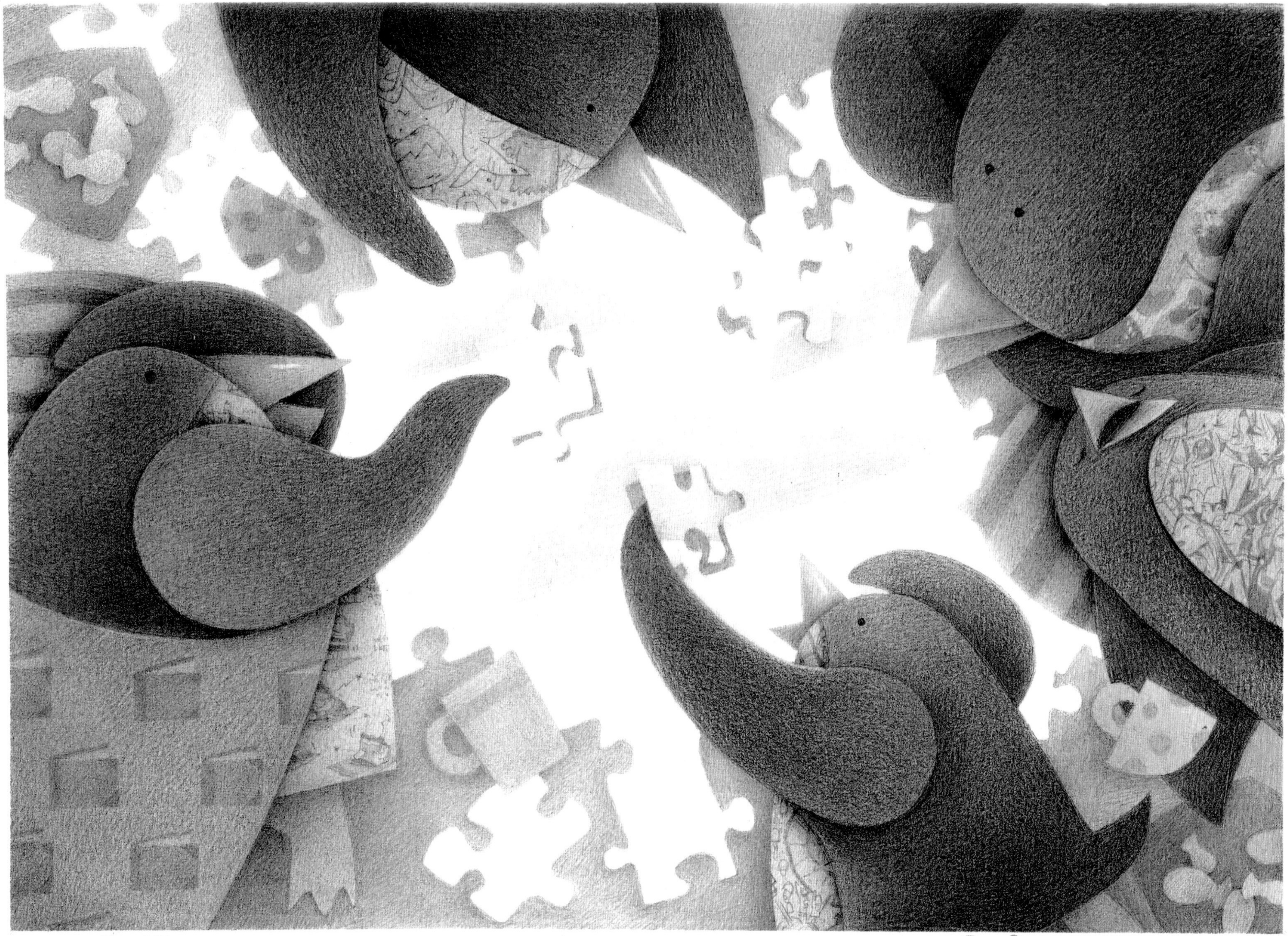

NEW YORK, NY

MIKE LEE . OCTOBER 18, 2009

MIKE LEE

Mike Lee

"This book holds so many inspiring and positive ideas. For me, its beauty resides in the moments of life that each of us gave to its creation. Each image hidden in these pages gives a hint of the artists we are, and of the amount of ourselves that we are able to give.

Honestly, at the beginning, I was very afraid. But once I was home with all these marvelous drawings, I couldn't help but be inspired and the ideas started pouring out."

OCTOBER 18, 2009
NEW YORK, NY

Stop 48 Stop 49 Stop 50

Mike Lee received *Sketchtravel* from the hands of **Peter Nguyen** on October 18, 2009, in New York and gave it to **Daisuke Tsutsumi** on October 19, 2009, in New York.

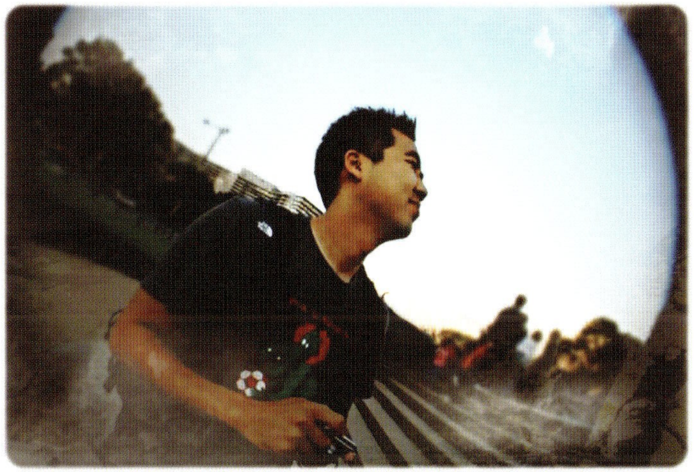

Mike Lee

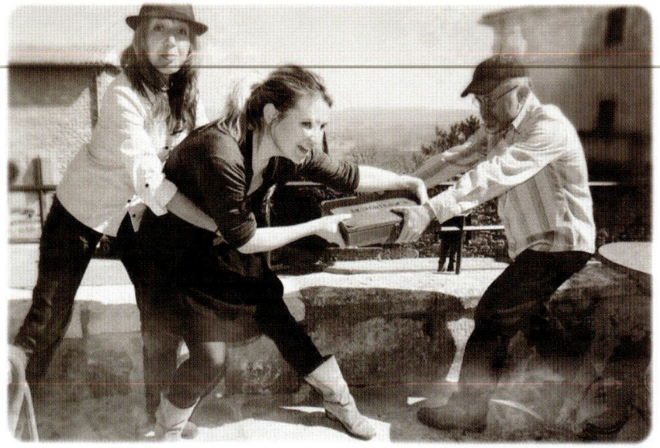

Caroline Charles, Nathalie Saint-Oyant, and Daniel Adel

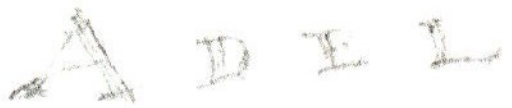

Daniel Adel

"This was a very agreeable experience. I thank Dice and Gérald for inviting me to participate."

?

Daniel Adel received *Sketchtravel* from the hands of **Caroline Charles** and **Nathalie Saint-Oyant** on January 19, 2009, in Lacoste and gave it to **Catherine Bonvalot** on March 19, 2009, in Lacoste.

Stop 33 Stop 34 Stop 35

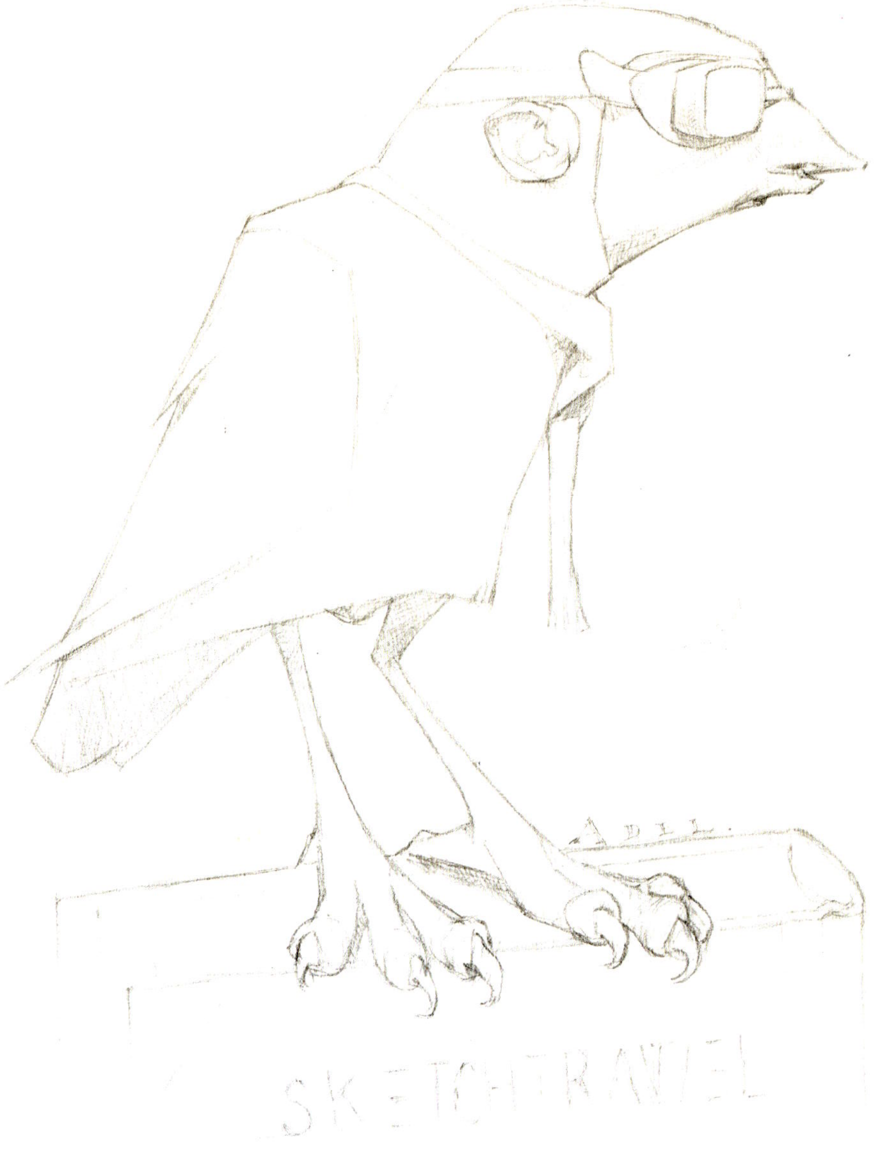
SKETCHTRAVEL

Nicolas de Crécy

“This idea of traveling ideas was original and contributing to making it real was motivating.

I was able to converse at a distance with people I admire. Drawing is a universal language, evidence that it is always agreeable to remember participating with your little pen in a project like this one, a free and spontaneous spirit.”

Nicolas de Crécy received *Sketchtravel* from the hands of **Dominique Bertail** on March 22, 2009, in Paris and gave it to Éric Gosselet on April 1, 2009, in Paris.

Stop 34 **Stop 35** Stop 36

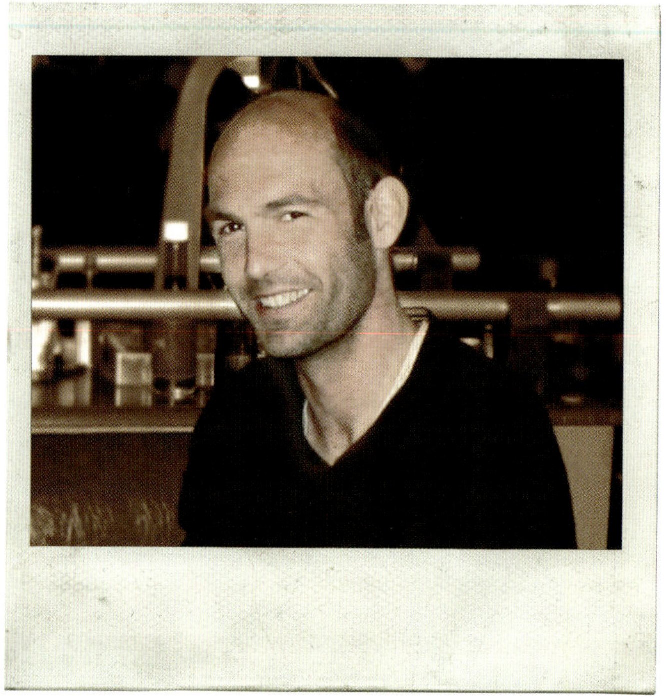

Nicolas de Crécy

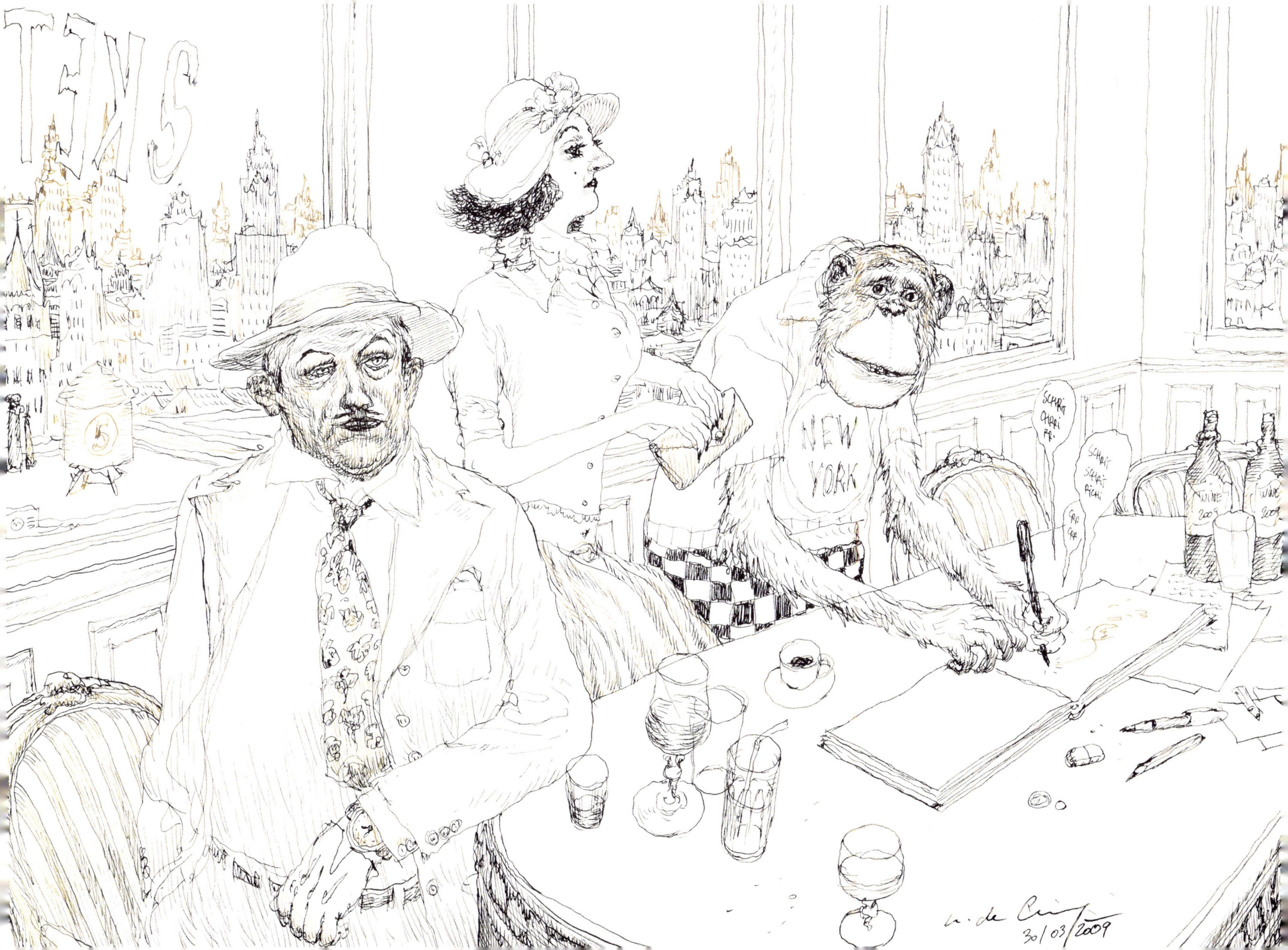
TENS
NEW YORK
SCHRIT CHRRI FR.
SCHRIT SCHRIT RICHI
GRR GRR
WINE 2009
WINE 2009
30/03/2009

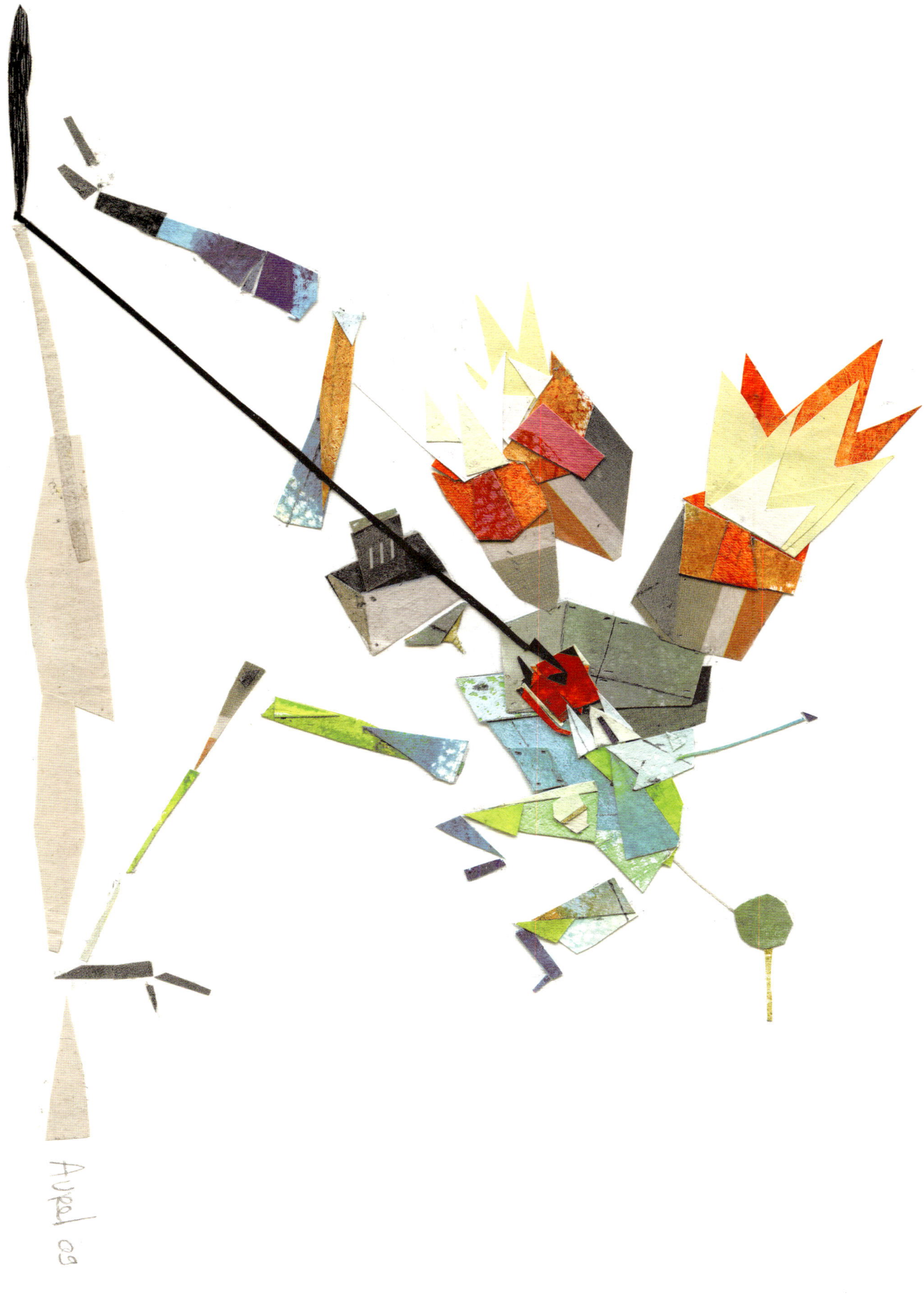

12/05/09

" à la pêche au sketchtravel" par Auréliem Prédal & Maïlys Vallade ...

Aurel 09

Aurélien Predal

"Like any collective work, for me it was a question of being included in a communal process while proposing something of my own.

Nevertheless, the intimidating character of the number of works made before mine, as well as the responsibility of possessing the original notebook for a certain amount of time, made me keep a certain distance; don't look too closely so as not to be discouraged by the comparison."

Aurélien Predal received *Sketchtravel* from the hands of **Gérald Guerlais** on May 7, 2009, in Paris and gave it to **Maïlys Vallade** on May 12, 2009, in Plessis-Robinson.

Stop 37 Stop 38 Stop 39

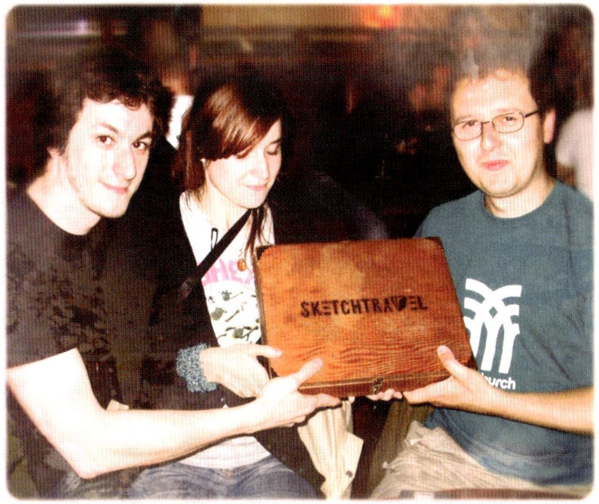

Aurélien Predal, Maïlys Vallade, and Enrique Fernández

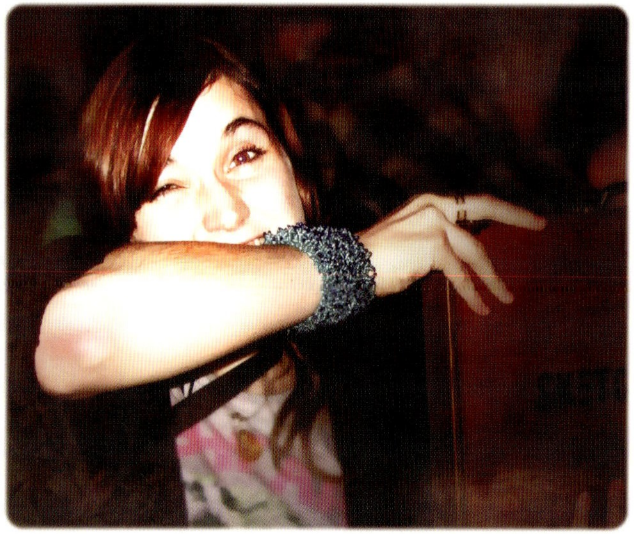

Maïlys Vallade

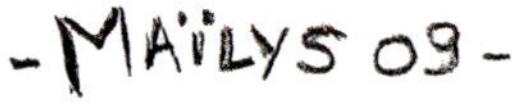

Maïlys Vallade

"There is nothing more captivating than sharing creativity and sensitivity for a humanitarian cause.

When I had the notebook in my hands, I devoured each page, all these artists who put so much heart into their work. I adored the burlesque of Carlos Nine and the freedom of Quentin Blake; I was touched by their childlike souls, and every subject and feeling moved me.

I am honored to have contributed to this work with them. The universes are so different, I'd like to learn from each of them!"

Maïlys Vallade received *Sketchtravel* from the hands of **Aurélien Predal** on May 12, 2009, in Plessis-Robinson and gave it to **Enrique Fernández** on May 15, 2009, in Paris.

Stop 38 Stop 39 Stop 40

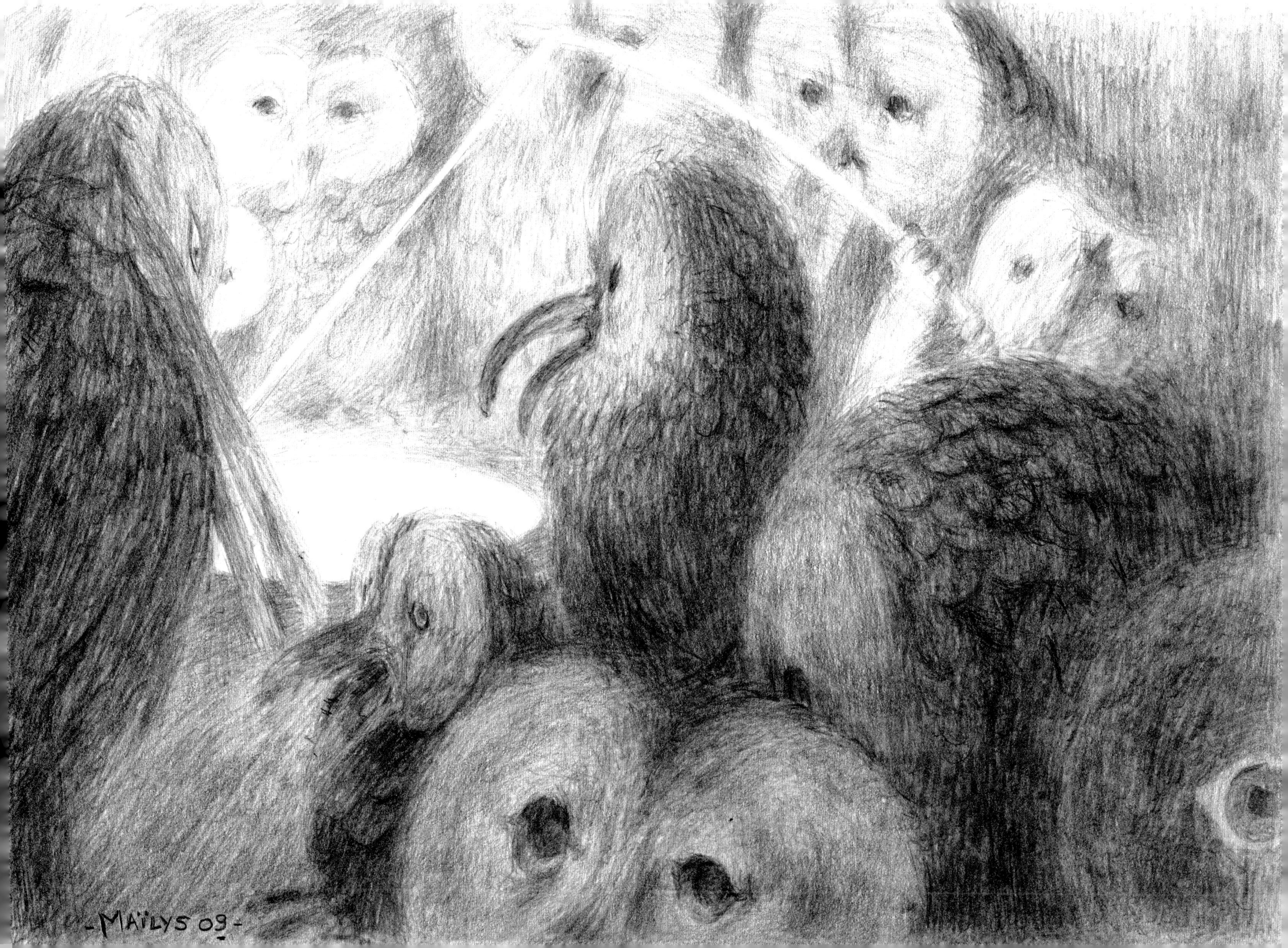
-MAÏLYS 09-

Enrique Fernández

16-MAY-2009

"It's a phenomenal idea, the kind of event that you see only once in your life. Even if you hope that it will happen again . . .

At the beginning, I was simply curious to see the book and all the unique art that it held. Once the book was open, I experienced extreme jealousy in the face of other people's talent and a very simple question: How to steal it without suffering the consequences?

For my drawing, I wanted to play with the concept of traveling art, carrying with it new ideas and objects."

Stop 39 · Stop 40 · Stop 41

Enrique Fernández received *Sketchtravel* from the hands of **Maïlys Vallade** on May 15, 2009, in Paris and gave it to **Gérald Guerlais** on May 17, 2009, in Paris.

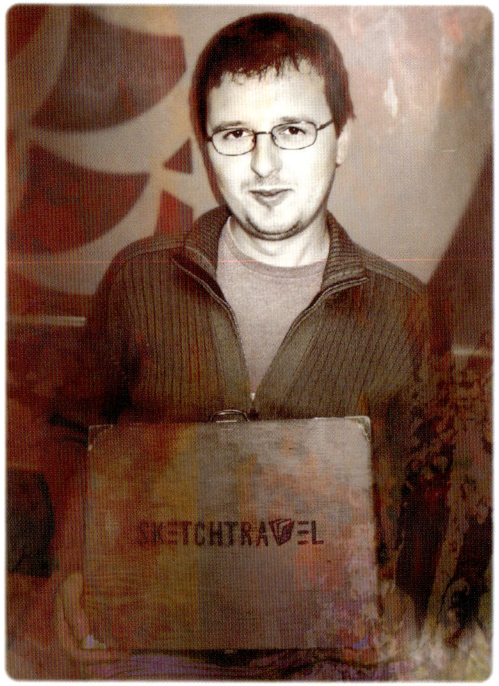

Enrique Fernández

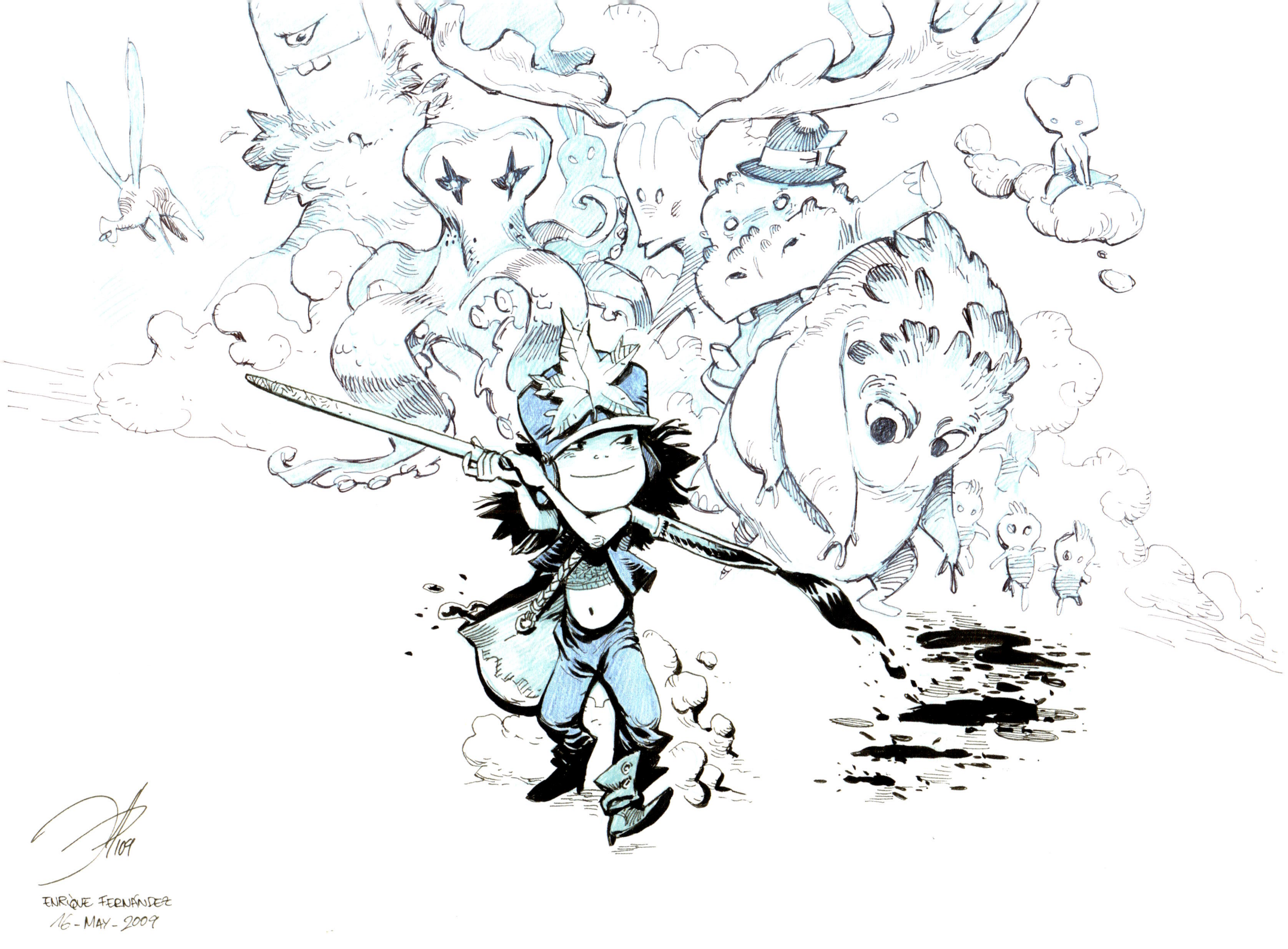
ENRIQUE FERNÁNDEZ
16-MAY-2009

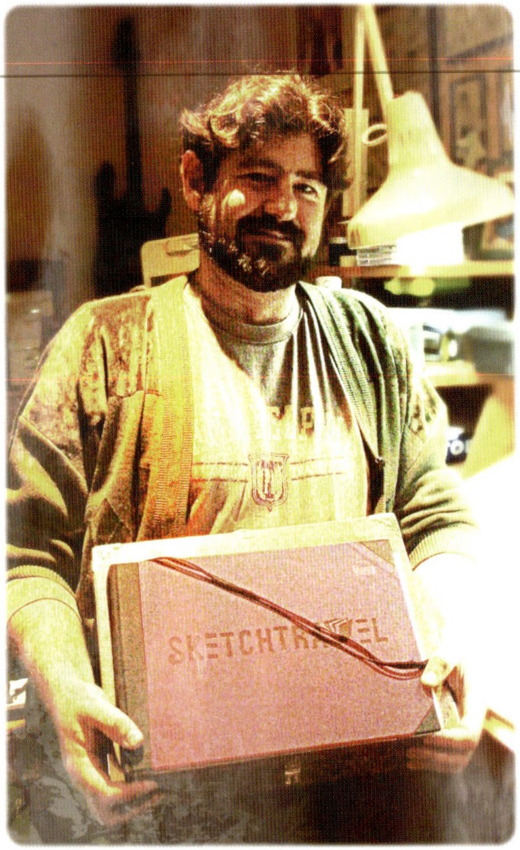

Juanjo Guarnido

J. Guarnido

JUANJO GUARNIDO

"As with so many projects that don't start with your own ideas, you begin a project like *Sketchtravel* almost as an obligation, but at a given moment, you engage with it. You say that you are going to contribute but not take too much time about it, always staying dignified and professional . . .

And in the end, as always, you join the game."

Paris,
JUNE 2009

?

Jaunjo Guarnido received *Sketchtravel* from the hands of **Gérald Guerlais** on May 18, 2009, in Nogent-sur-Marne and gave it back to **Gérald Guerlais** on June 4, 2009, in Nogent-sur-Marne.

Stop 40 Stop 41 Stop 42

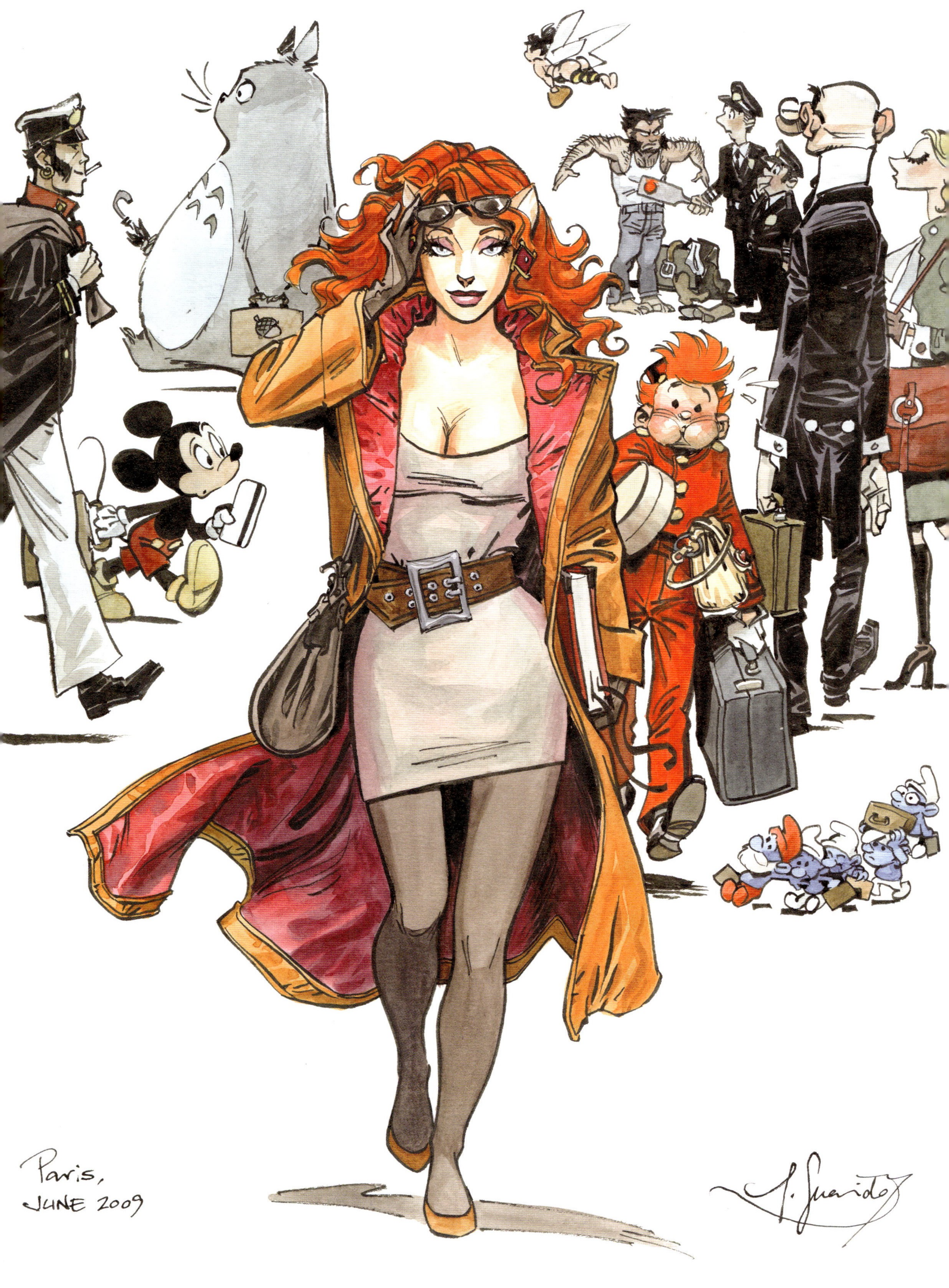
Paris,
JUNE 2009

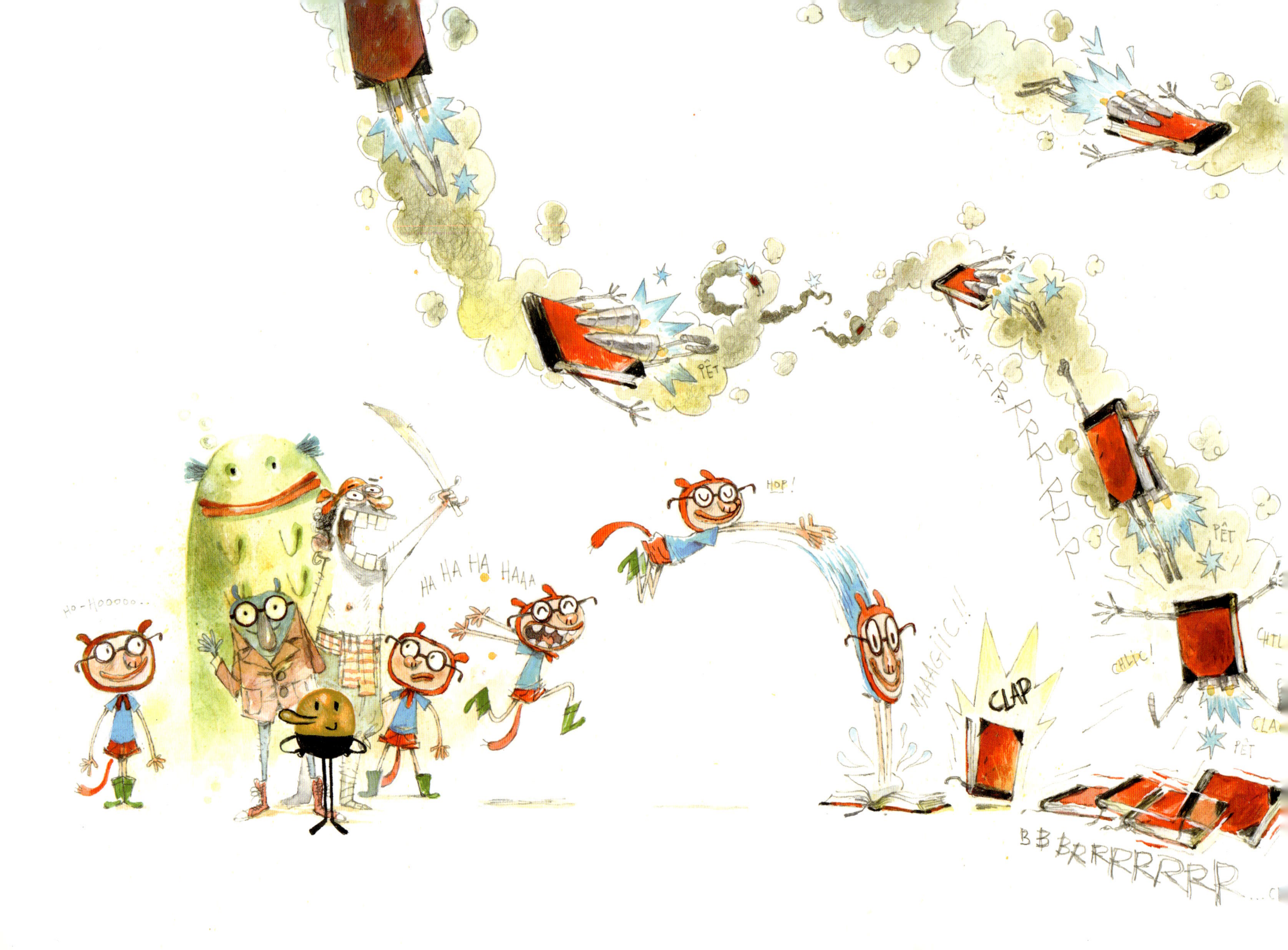

HO-HOOOOO...
HA HA HA HAAA
HOP!
MAAAGIIIC!!
CLAP
BBBRRRRRRRP...
PÊT
CHLIC!
PÊT
PÊT

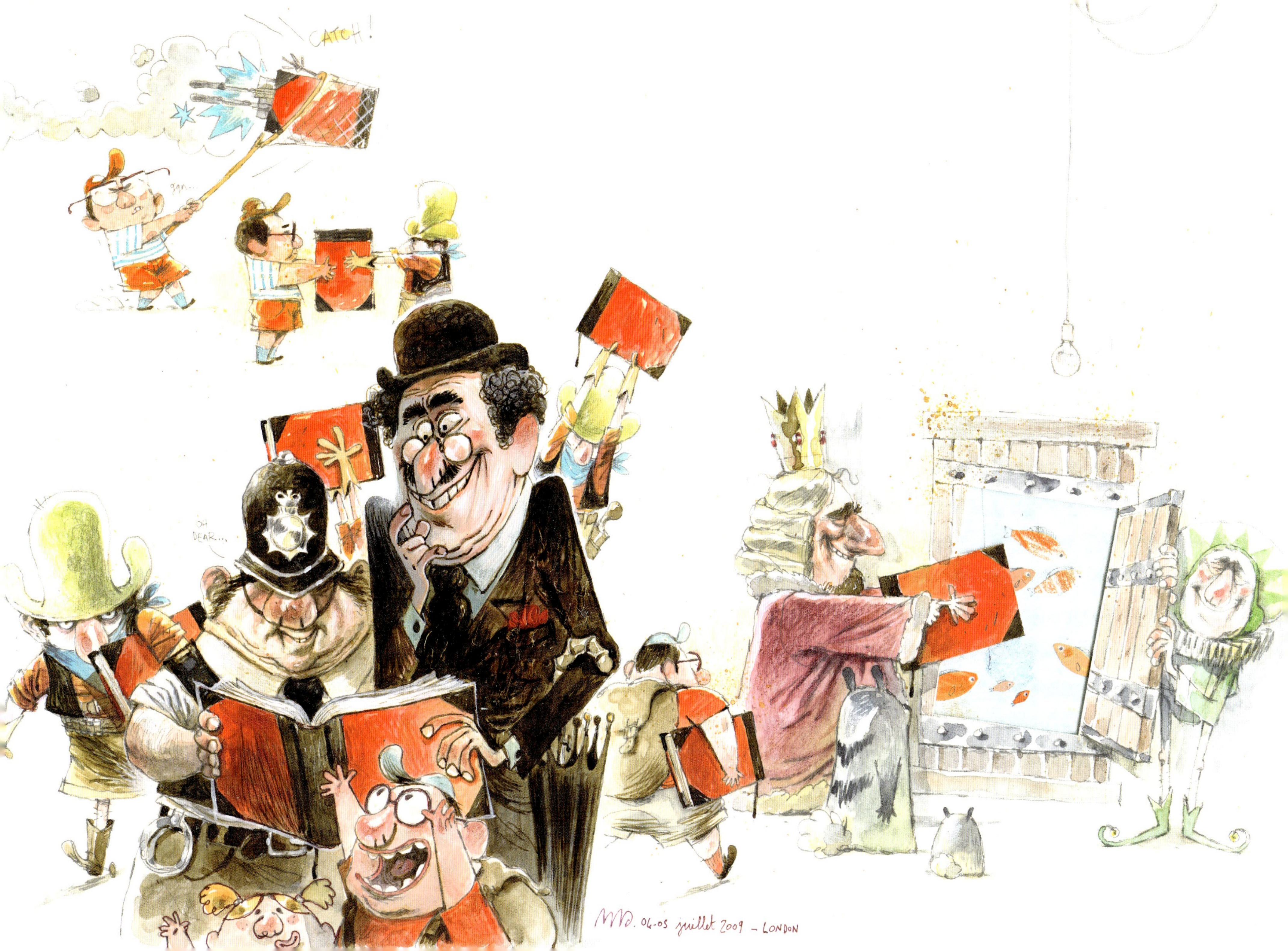
CATCH!
ggn...
OH DEAR...
04-05 juillet 2009 - LONDON

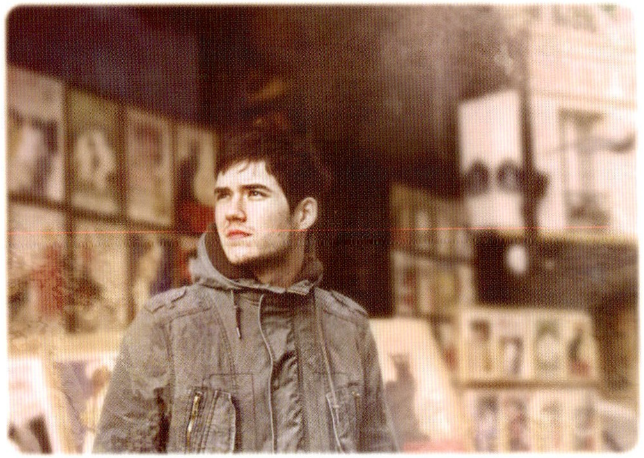

Sylvain Marc

Sylvain Marc

"I fell into this project by chance, when it was still in its idea stage, surfing the net. I immediately said that I wanted to participate.

I contacted Mr. Guerlais (who I didn't know at the time) to express my enthusiasm, and asked him if he was thinking of a second book. To my great surprise, he replied that I was already on the list for the first one!

Artists generally have asocial, slightly autistic, tendencies; this kind of project can only do them good."

04-05 juillet 2009 – LONDON

Sylvain Marc received *Sketchtravel* from the hands of **Gérald Guerlais** on June 30, 2009, in Issy-les-Moulineaux and gave it to **Véronique Joffre** on July 5, 2009, in London.

Stop 41 Stop 42 Stop 43

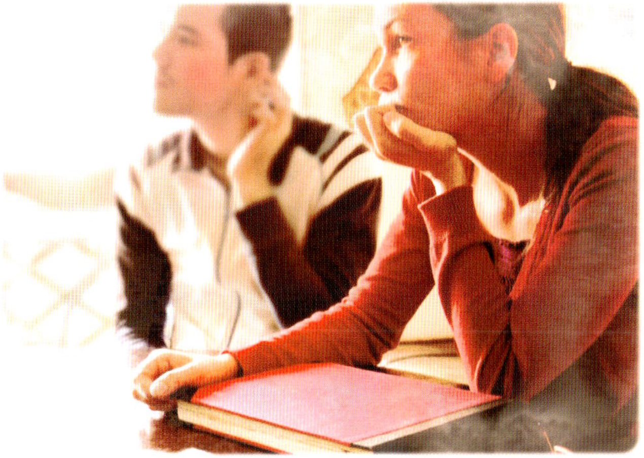

Sylvain Marc and Véronique Joffre

Véronique Joffre

"This is a marvelous and unique project. First, because its purpose is charitable. It is very agreeable to say for once that it isn't for oneself or for money that one draws, but to help other people. You do what you love to do, you enjoy it, and at the same time, you serve a good cause.

But the beauty of the work also lies in its collective nature. To be part of this team of artists who made a book together is an unbelievable experience. It makes one want to meet all together in person."

7 & 8 Juillet 2009...

Véronique Joffre received *Sketchtravel* from the hands of **Sylvain Marc** on July 5, 2009, in London and gave it to **Gérald Guerlais** on July 12, 2009, in Paris.

Stop 42 Stop 43 Stop 44

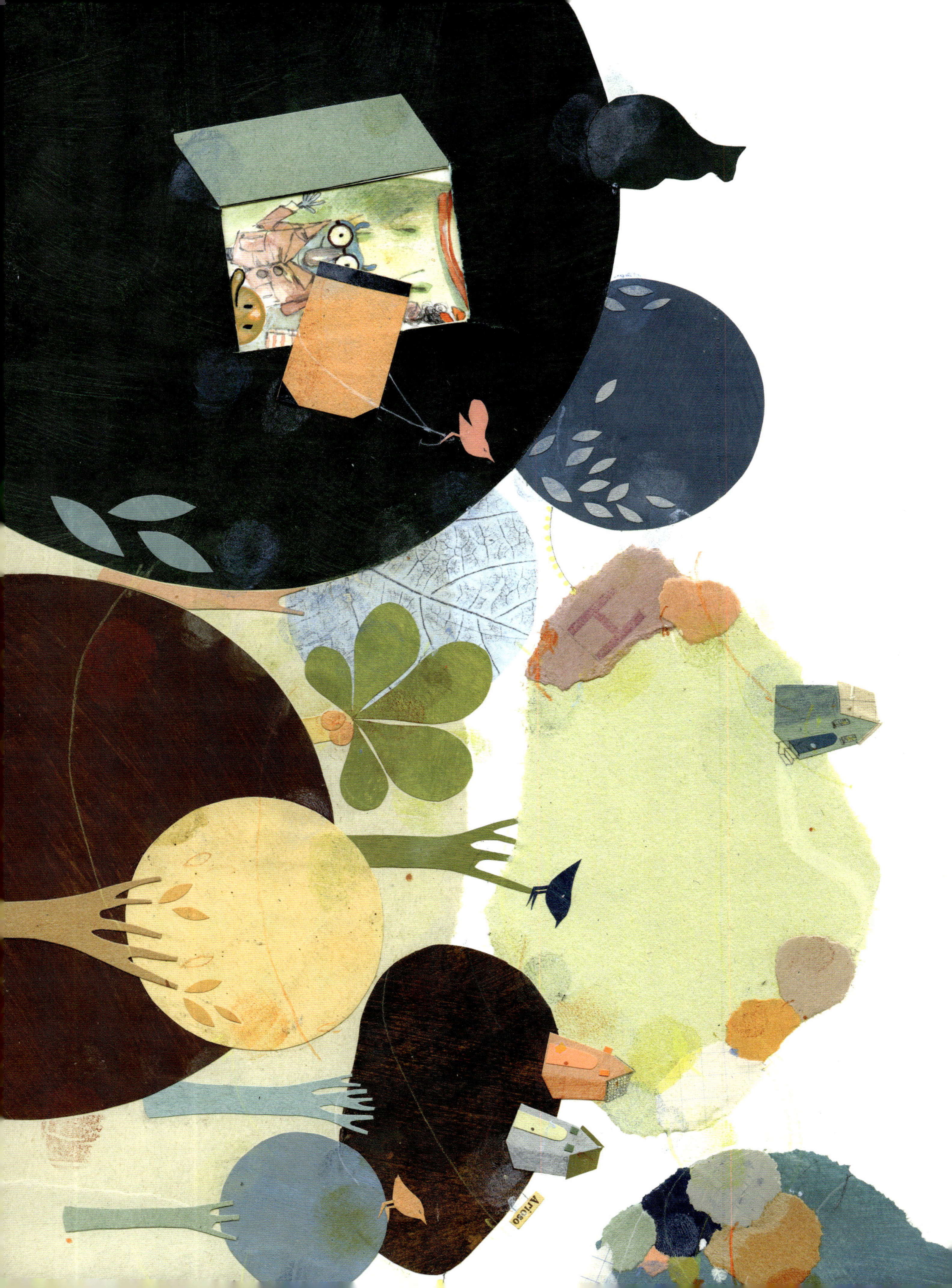
Arioso

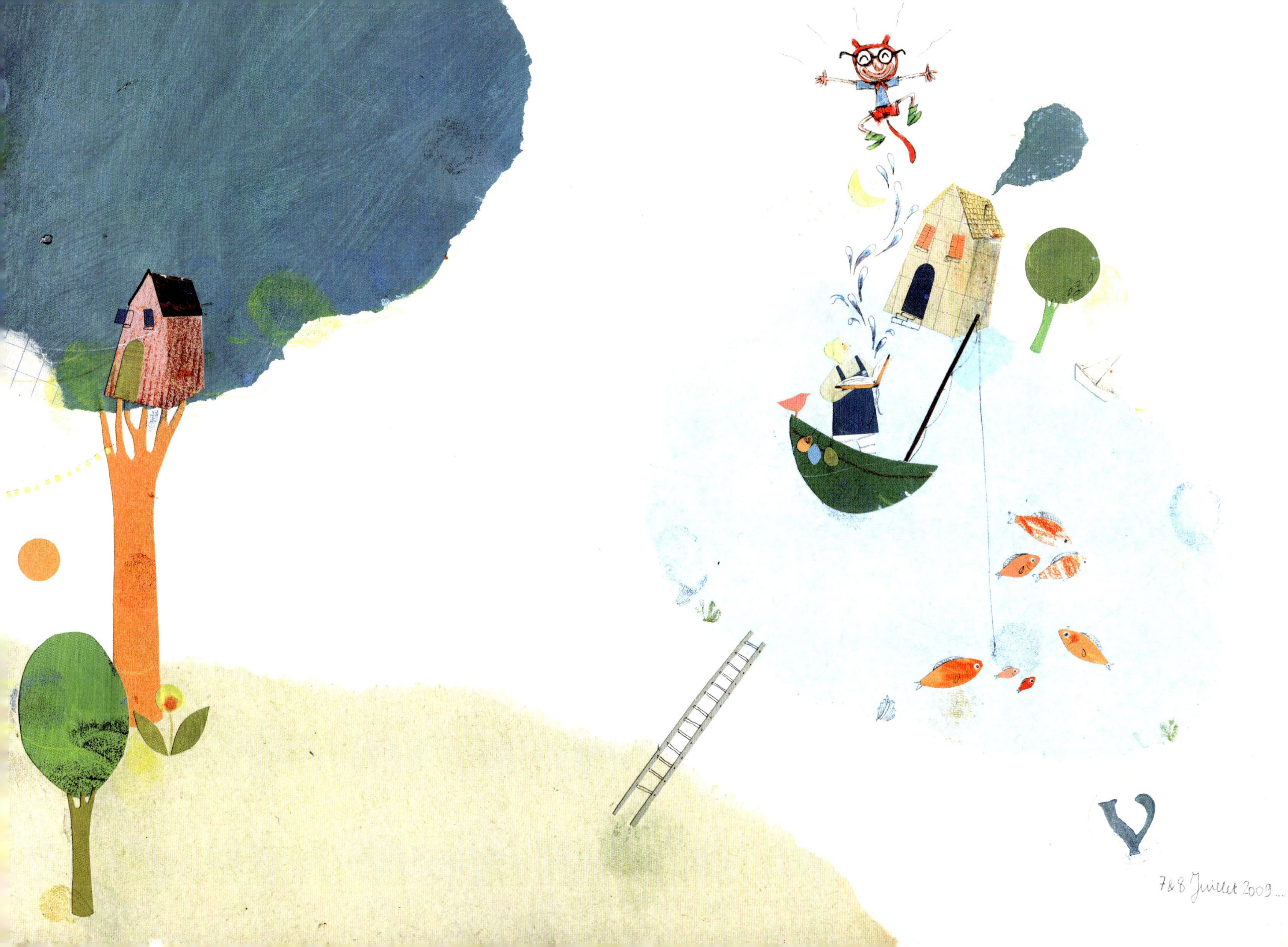
V
7&8 Juillet 2009...

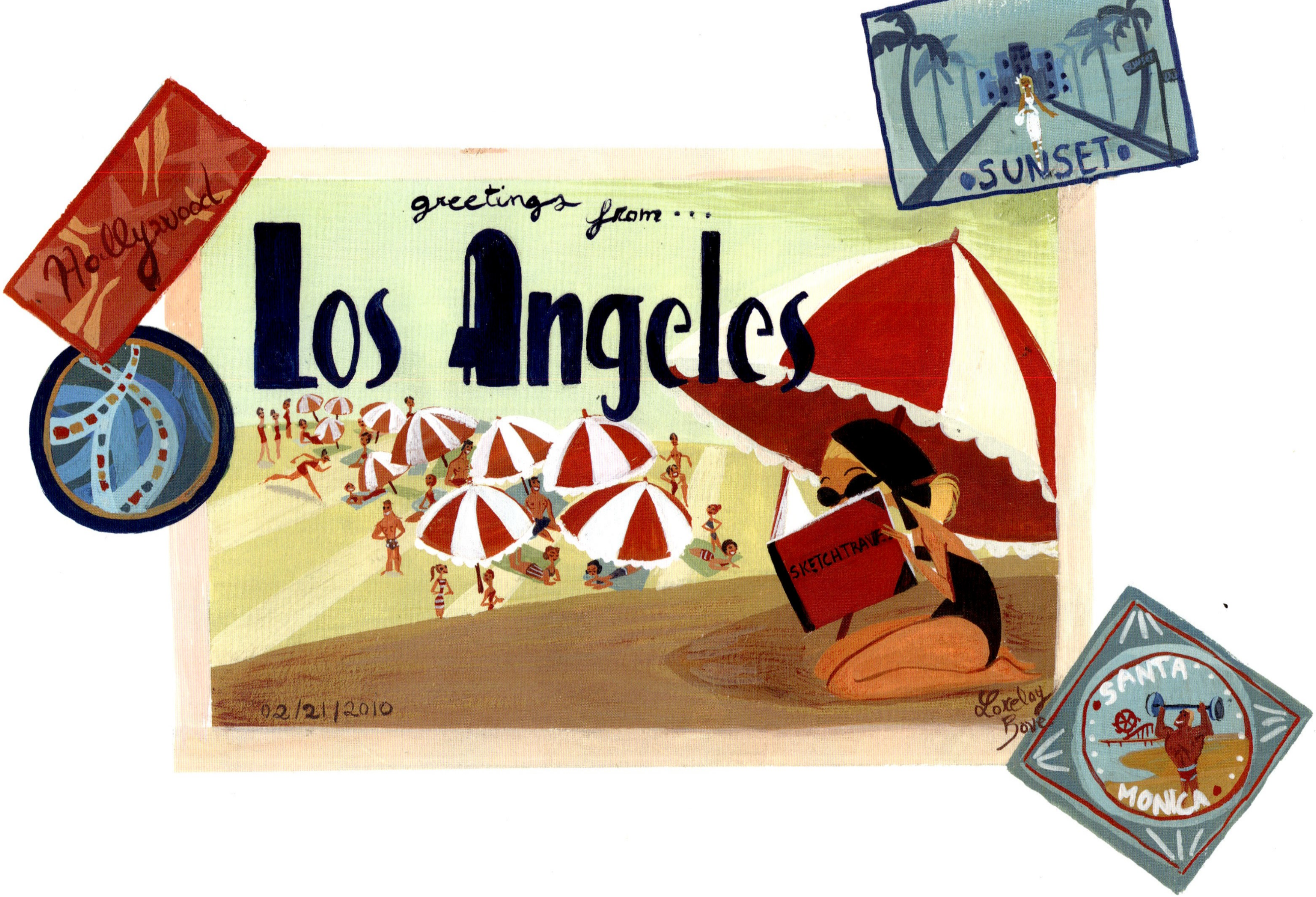
greetings from...
Los Angeles
Hollywood
SUNSET
SKETCHTRAVEL
SANTA
MONICA
02/21/2010
Loreley
Bove

Lorelay Bove

Lorelay Bove

"It is very exciting to see all these artists collaborating to realize this marvelous book, one of the most inspiring that I have had the honor of holding in my hands.

I got it just after Paul Felix and before Glen Keane; squeezed between two masters of art with my brush full of gouache, you could say that I was afraid . . ."

02/21/2010

? **Lorelay Bove** received *Sketchtravel* from the hands of **Paul Felix** on February 16, 2010, in Burbank and gave it to **Glen Keane** on February 26, 2010, in Burbank.

Stop 56 Stop 57 Stop 58

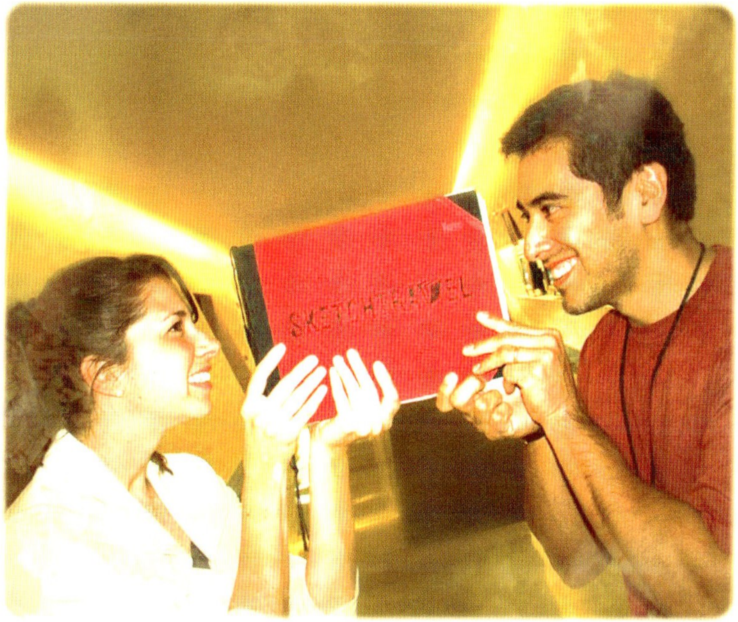

Lorelay Bove and Paul Felix

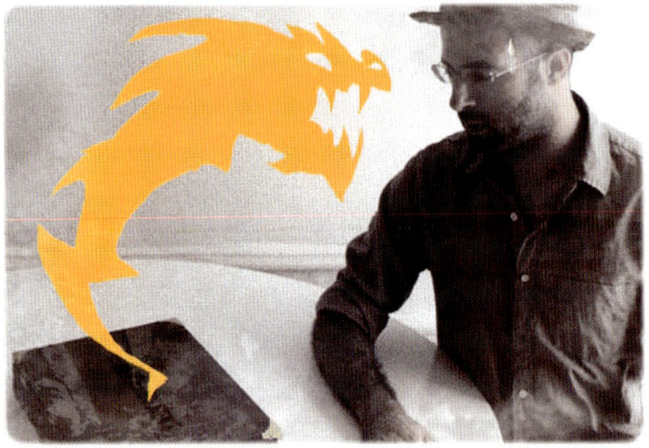

Tomer Hanuka

TH 09 N.Y.C

Tomer Hanuka

"It wasn't the fact of having to measure myself against other artists that made me afraid. They are—and remain—my heroes. It is just that I have never been very careful with my work, and I was sure that I would end up by spoiling the book and find myself with an angry horde of illustrators and animators at my heels (I am more than anything afraid of animators: they are more 'physical' . . .).

For me, it was a death sentence."

Tomer Hanuka received *Sketchtravel* from the hands of **Vincent Di Nguyen** on July 26, 2009, in New York and gave it to **Greg Couch** on July 29, 2009, in New York.

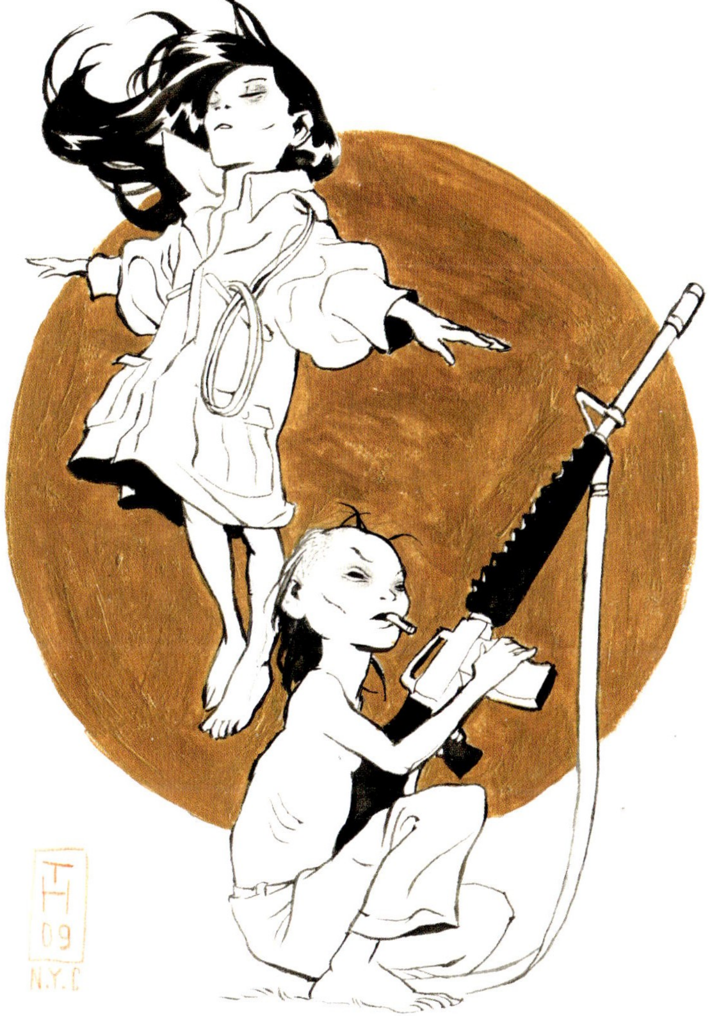
09
N.Y.C

GREG COUCH

Greg Couch

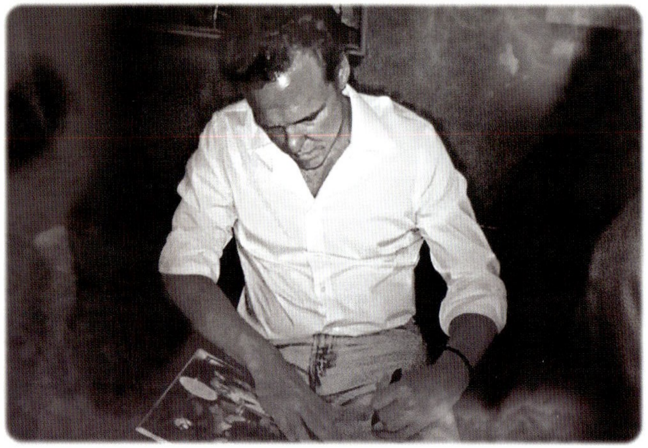

Greg Couch

"An experience both flattering and humbling: to be chosen to appear with so many artists I have admired for so long, knowing that it was for a good cause.

To get ready, I first reread my own sketchbook. I took a long time to decide, and I was terrified that I wouldn't be inspired.

Moreover, *Sketchtravel* was already quite full when I got it, and I was sure that I would end up spilling paint or coffee on it."

? **Greg Couch** received *Sketchtravel* from the hands of **Tomer Hanuka** on July 29, 2009, in New York and gave it to **Peter de Sève** on August 10, 2009, in Brooklyn.

Stop 44 Stop 45 Stop 46

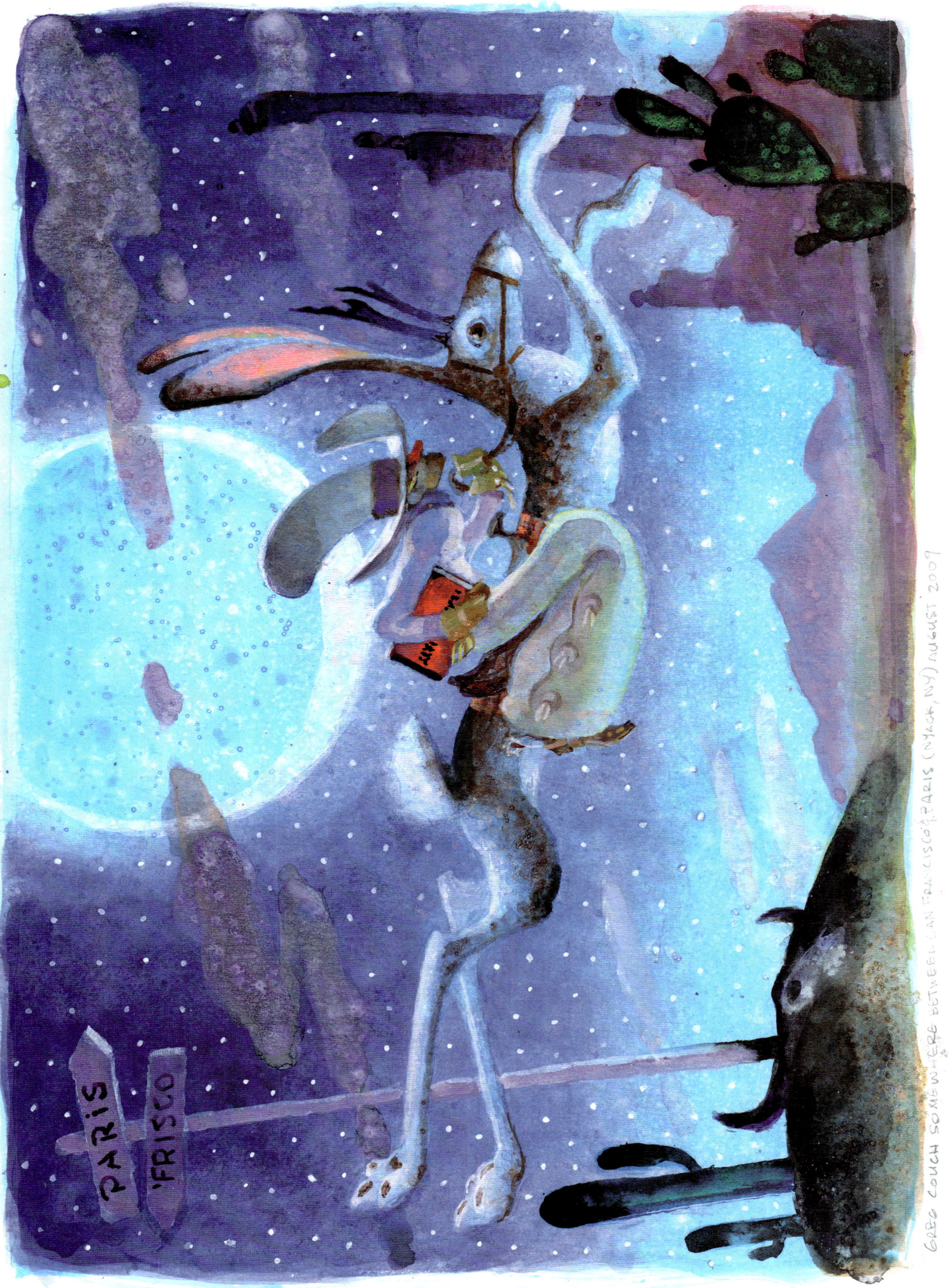
PARIS
'FRISCO
GREG COUCH SOMEWHERE BETWEEN SAN FRANCISCO & PARIS (NYACK, NY) AUGUST 2009

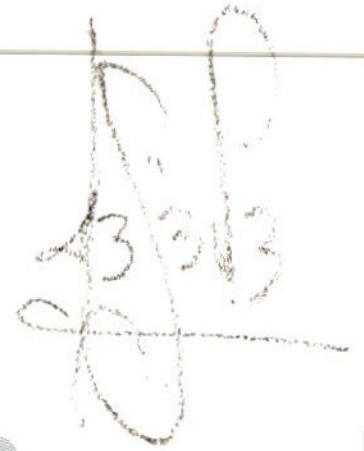

Peter de Sève

"Like all good ideas, this one began with a very simple and elegant principle: start a book, and pass it on. I am sure that the final result will be a witness to the genius of the idea.

For my part, I hesitated between making an amusing sketch that would have some relation to the project or a more general drawing that would showcase my artistic talents. I decided on the first, but I find that the final result shows my hesitation, as well as (be honest!) my terror."

Peter de Sève received *Sketchtravel* from the hands of **Greg Couch** on August 10, 2009, in Brooklyn and gave it to **Natalie Ascencios** on August 24, 2009, in Brooklyn.

Stop 45 — Stop 46 — Stop 47

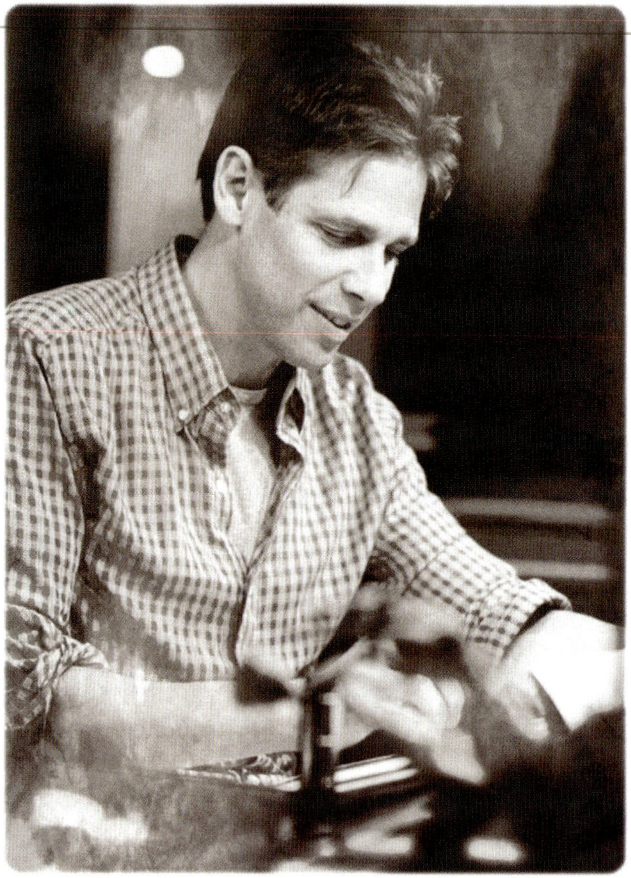

Peter de Sève

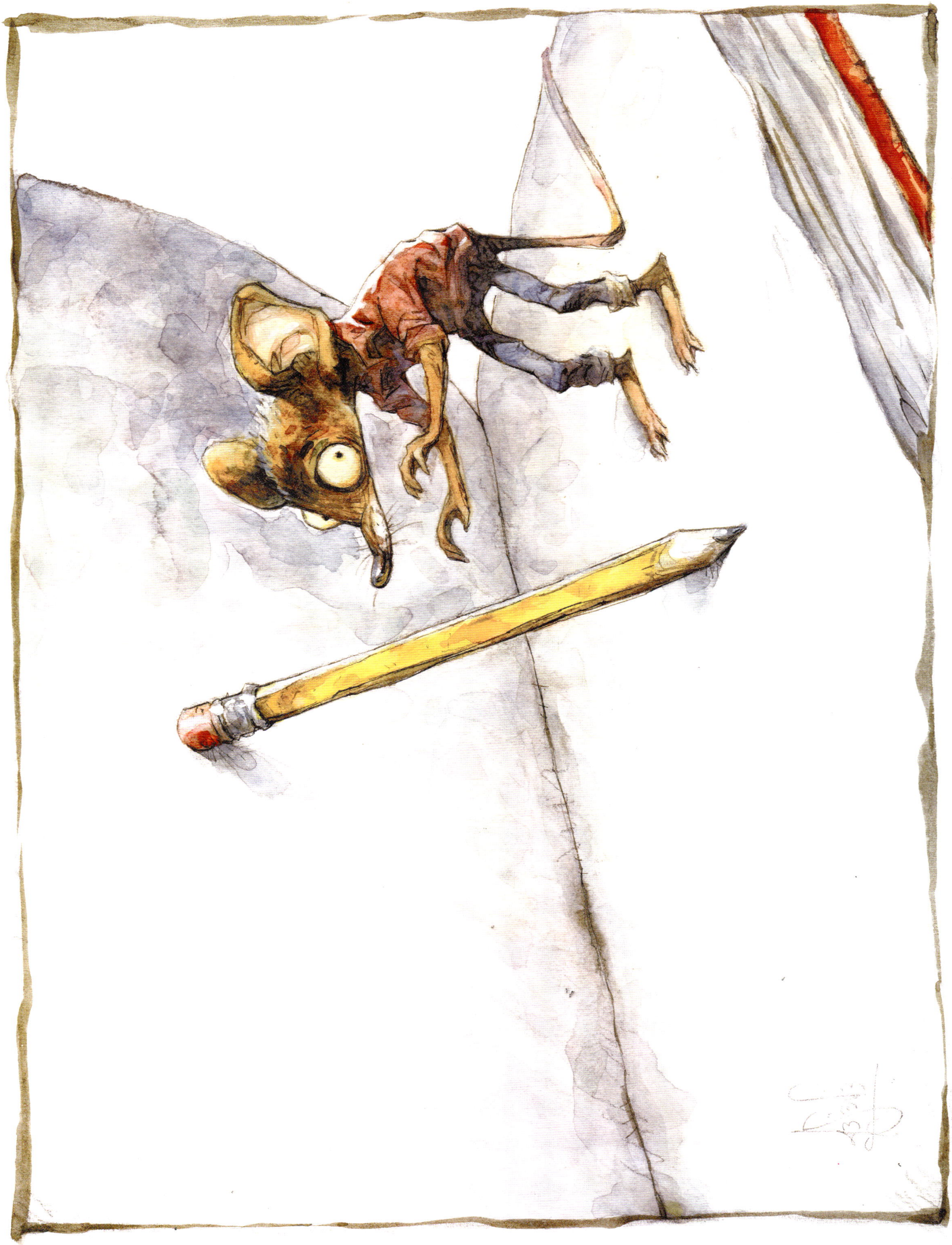

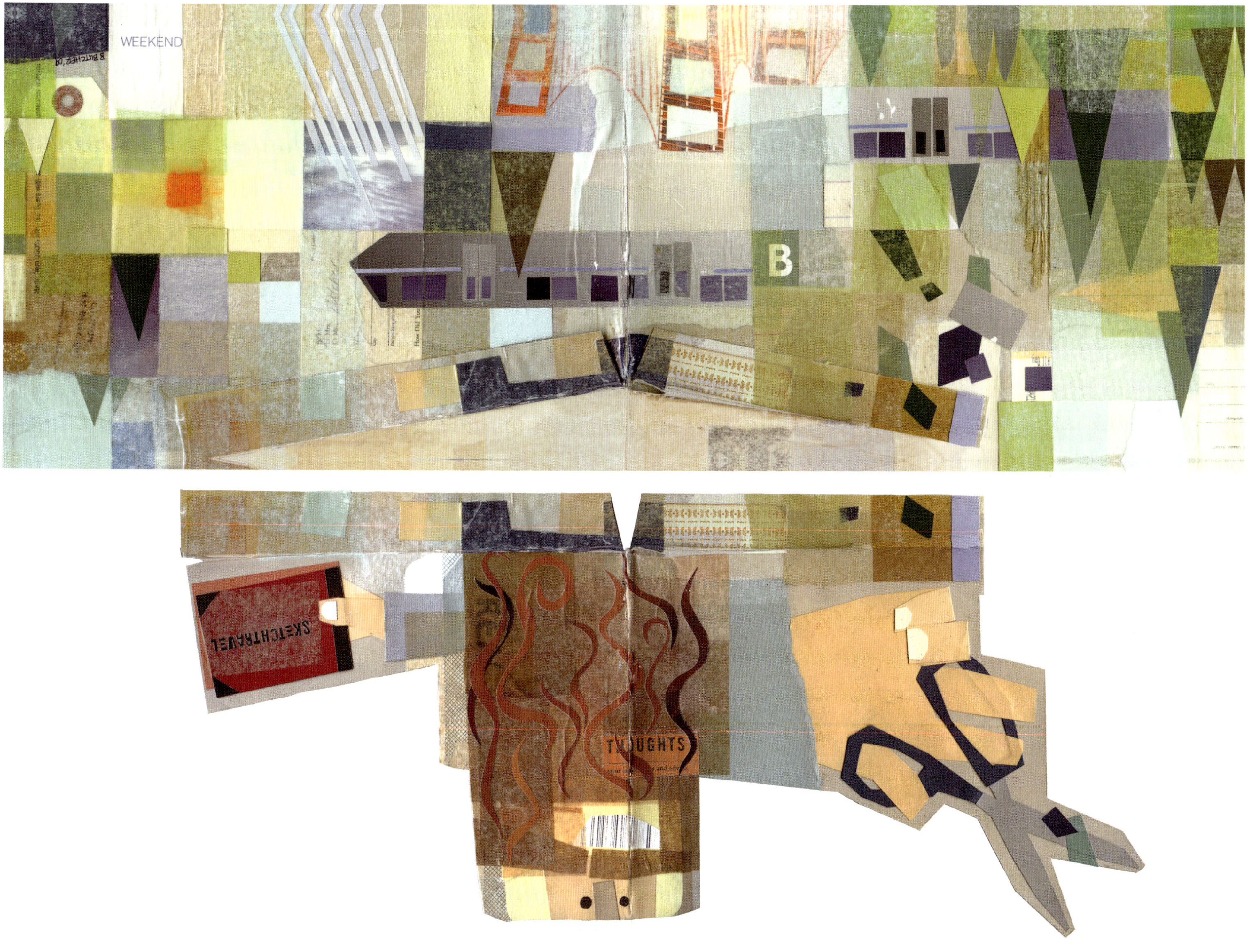
WEEKEND
B
THOUGHTS
SKETCHTRAVEL

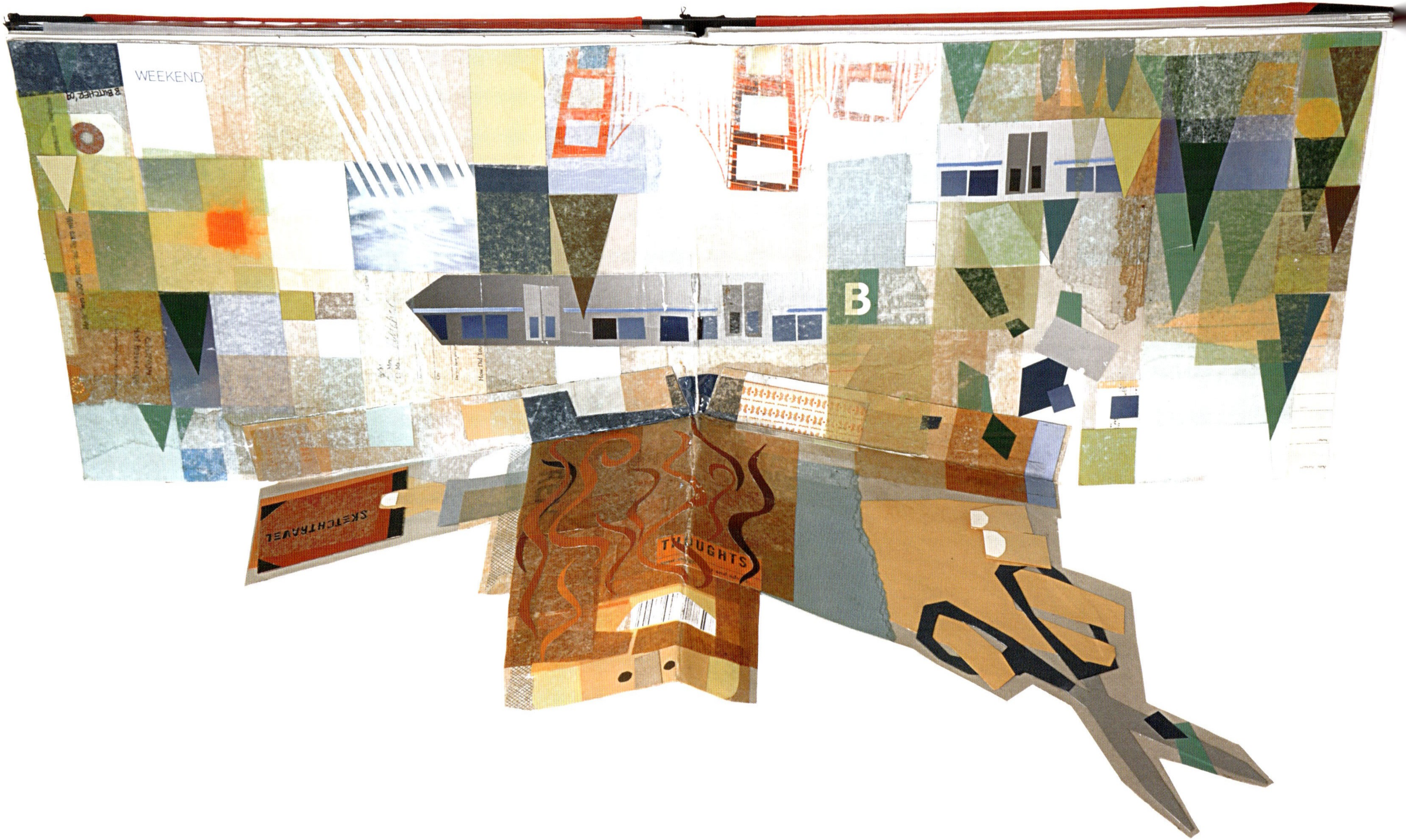
WEEKEND
B
SKETCHTRAVEL
THOUGHTS

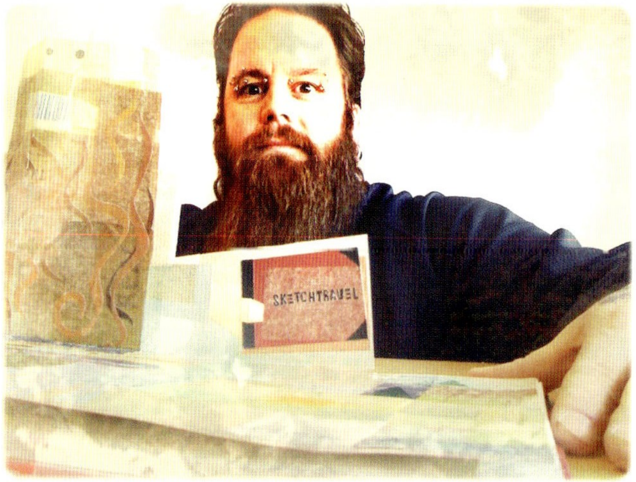

Ben Butcher

B BUTCHER '09

Ben Butcher

"When I heard about the project for the first time, I was astonished. I thought it was a great idea, but I couldn't imagine that you could really make a book travel from country to country, without something happening to it on the way.

When I got it, I was so overwhelmed that I couldn't open it for an entire day."

Ben Butcher received *Sketchtravel* from the hands of **Daisuke Tsutsumi** in November 2009 in Emeryville and gave it back to **Daisuke Tsutsumi** a few days later.

Stop 49 Stop 50 Stop 51

NATALIE ASCENCIOS

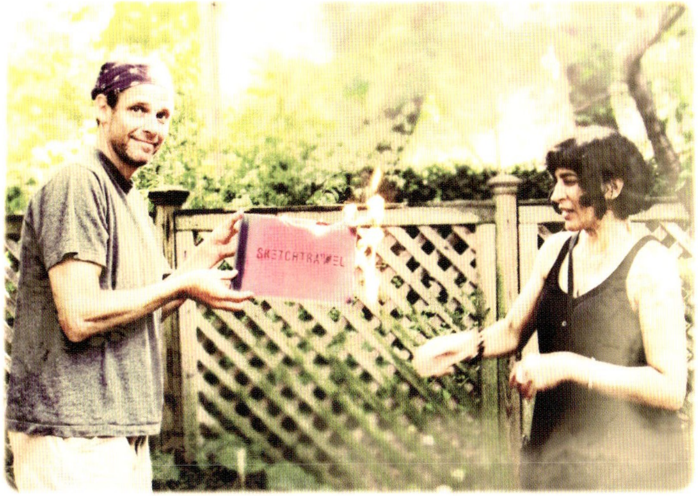

Peter de Sève and Natalie Ascencios

Natalie Ascencios

"I think this is a wonderful way to see how a group of artists, in the twenty-first century, can raise money for a charitable cause. Dice and Gérald put considerable time and effort into realizing this project, and I admire their altruism."

Natalie Ascencios received *Sketchtravel* from the hands of **Peter de Sève** on August 24, 2009, in Brooklyn and gave it to **Daisuke Tsutsumi** in September 2009, in New York.

Stop 46 Stop 47 Stop 48

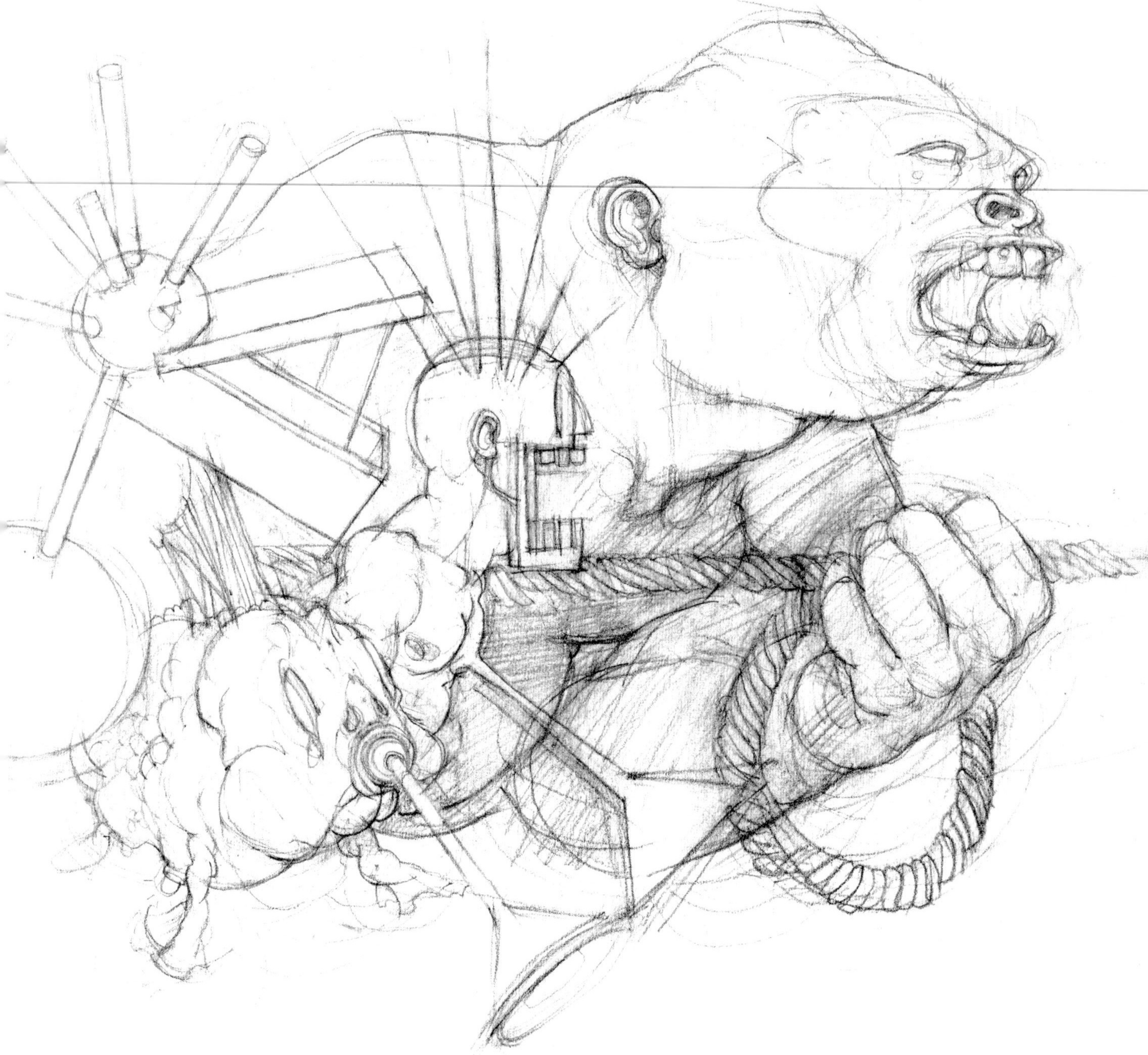

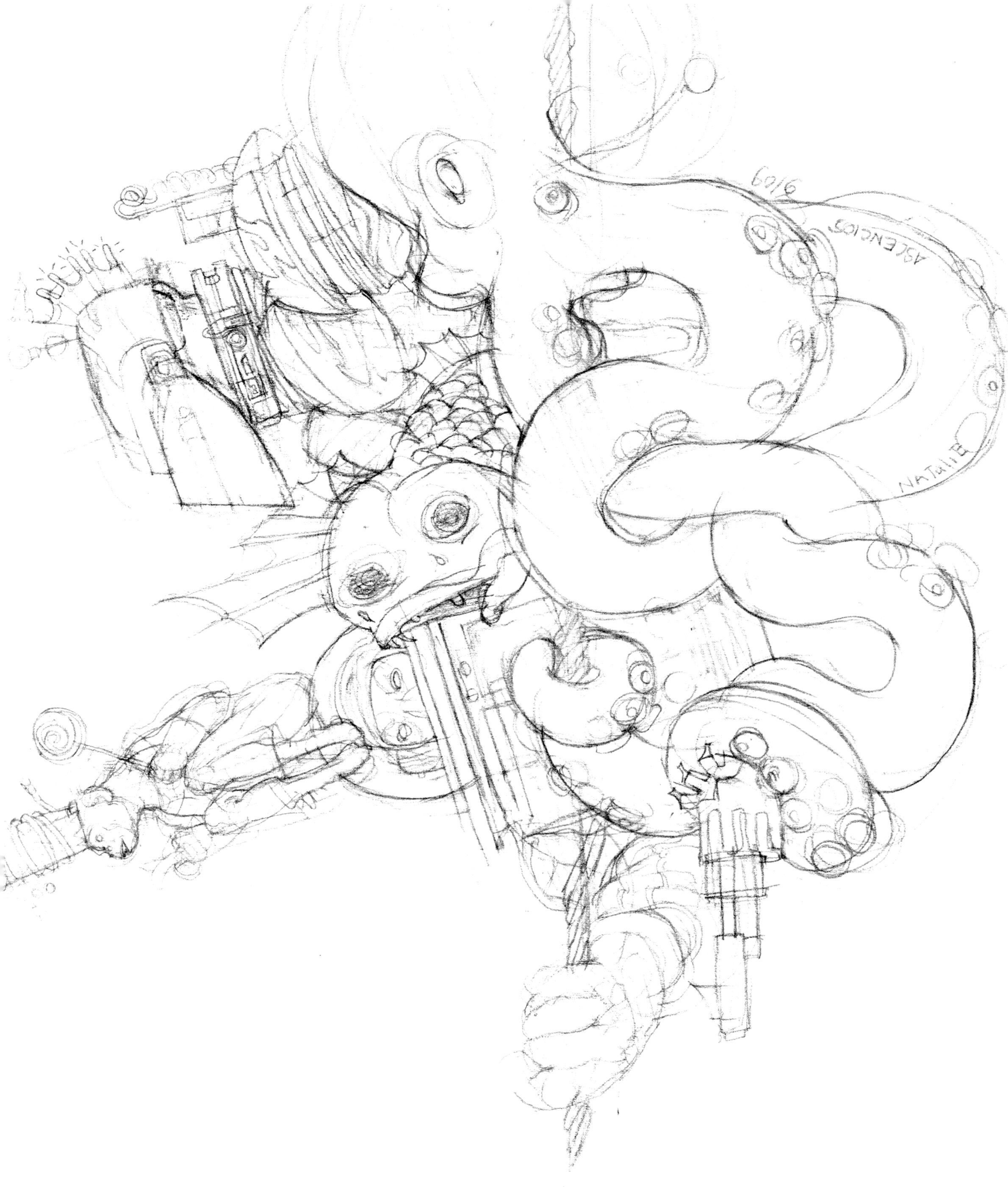

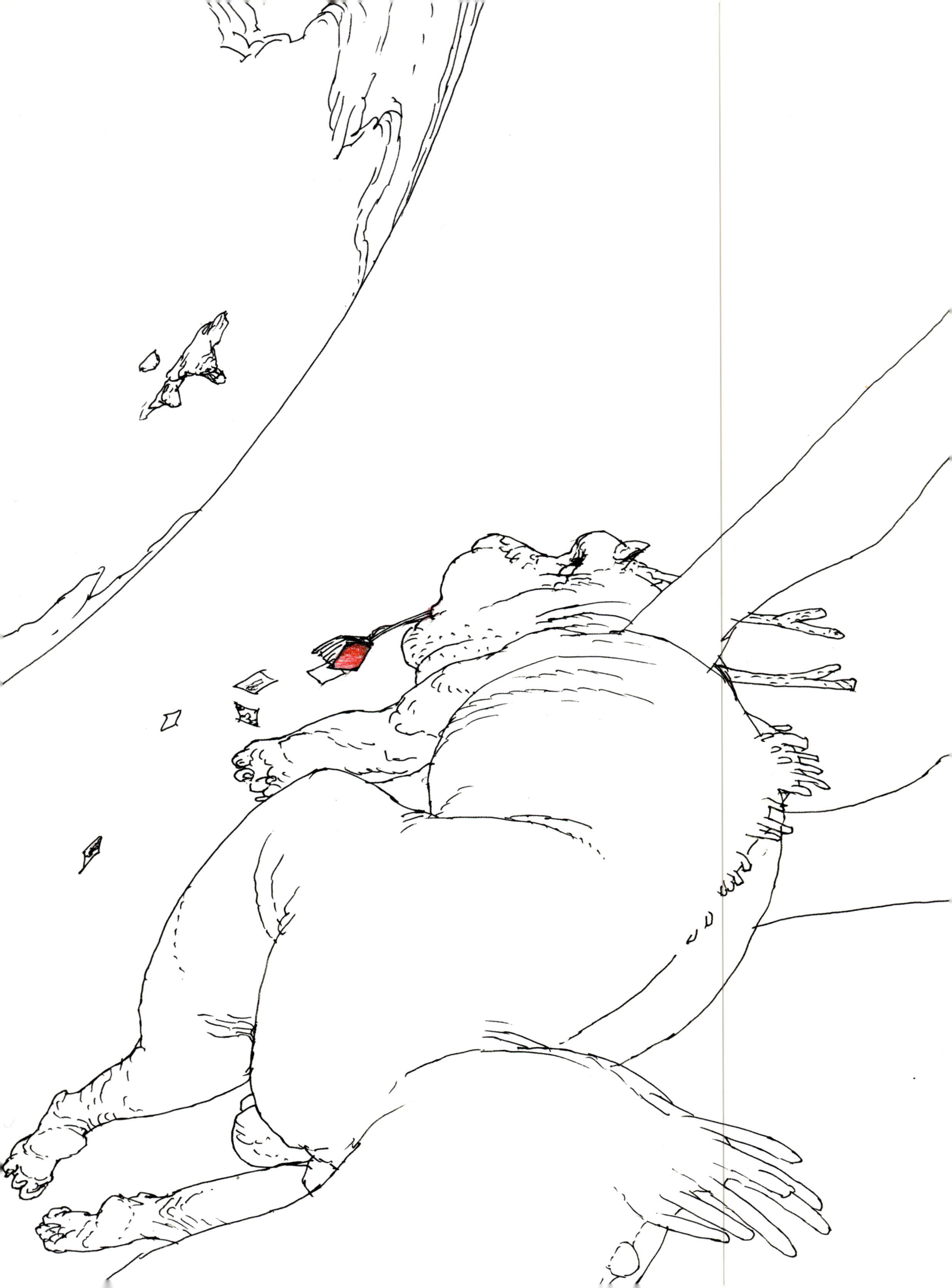

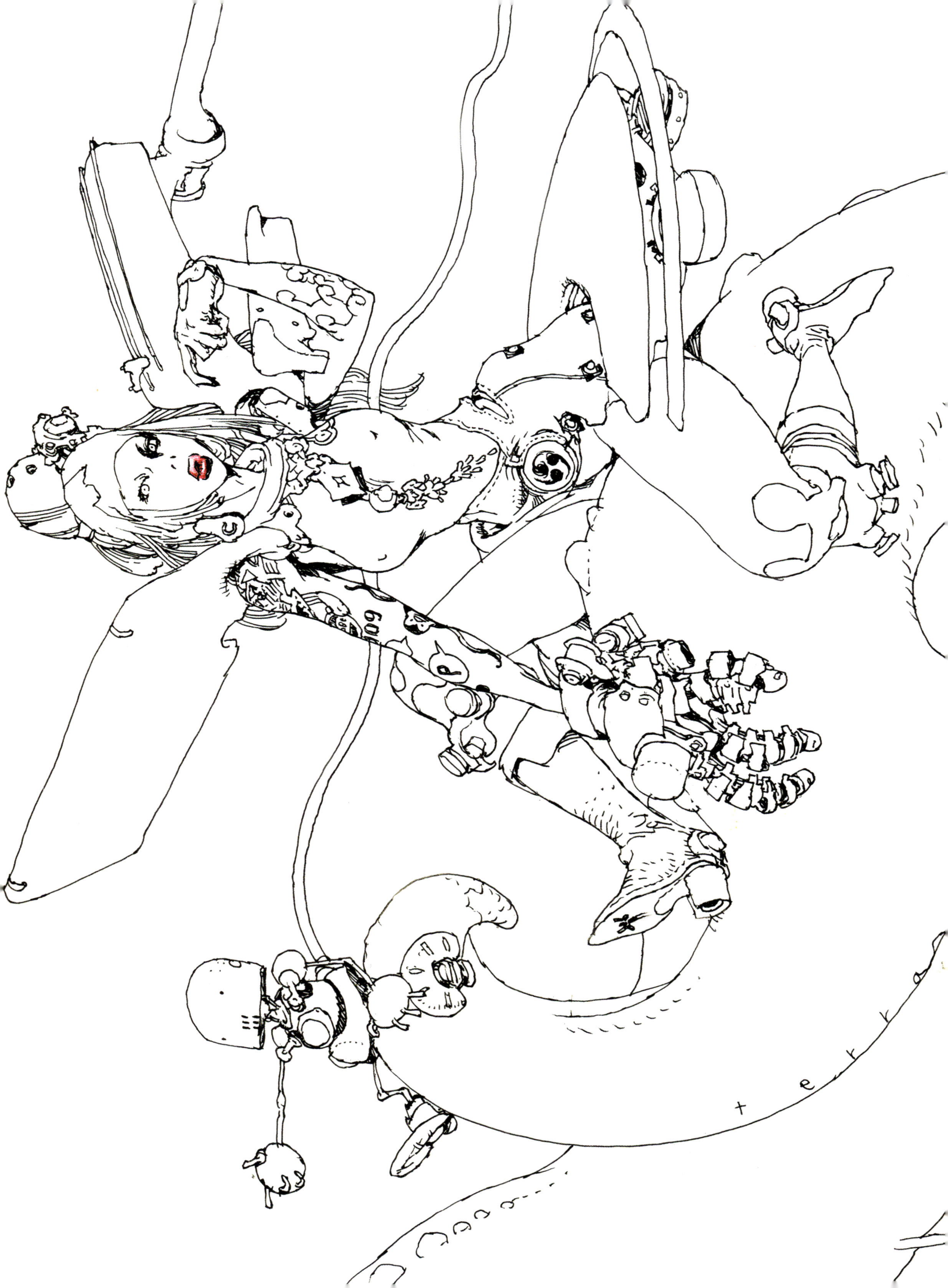
terra

"Walking, driving, riding by train, ship, and airplane; I have traveled by so many means. But now for the first time, I have traveled by sketchbook!"

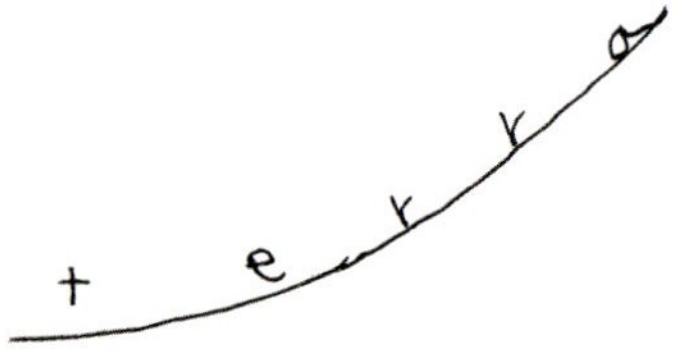

Katsuya Terada

Katsuya Terada received *Sketchtravel* from the hands of **Vincent Di Nguyen** on October 28, 2009, in Tokyo and gave it to **Daisuke Tsutsumi** November 1, 2009, in Tokyo.

Stop 50 Stop 51 Stop 52

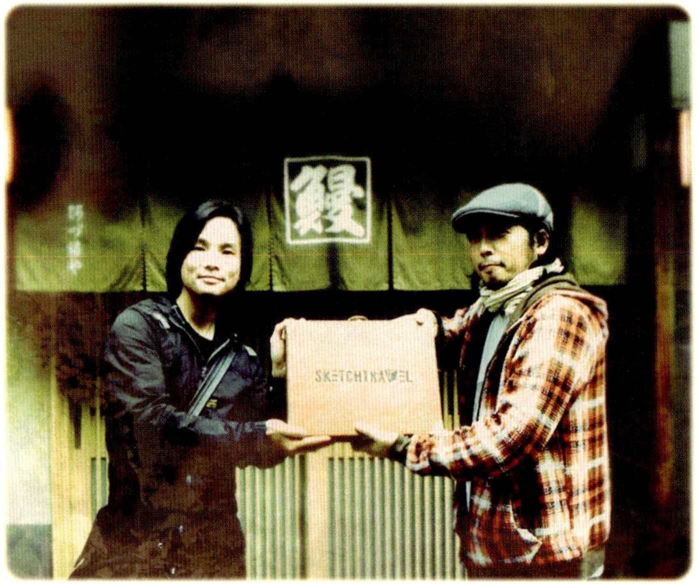

Daisuke Tsutsumi and Katsuya Terada

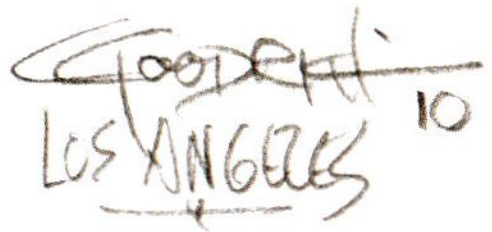

Carter Goodrich

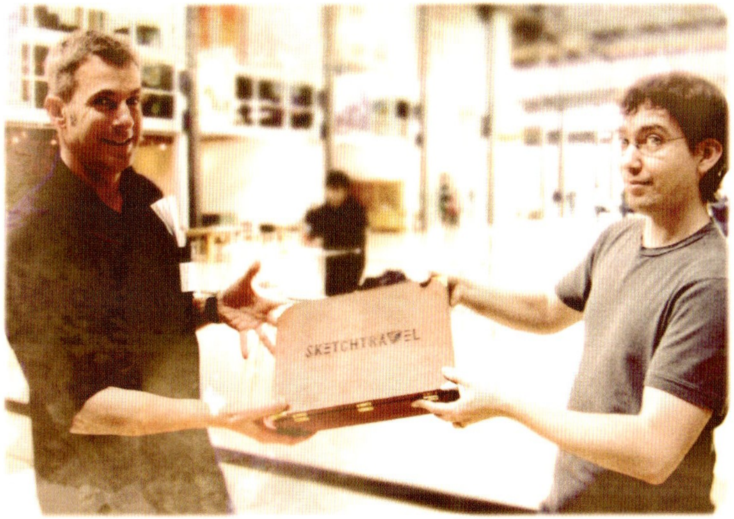

Carter Goodrich and Bill Presing

"I always thought that this was an inspired idea, but it wasn't until the moment when I found myself with the book in my hands that I recognized how difficult the task was.

After several hours spent admiring the work of other artists, punctuated with numerous trips to the fridge, I went to work. I was terrified at the idea that something would happen to the book when I was responsible for it, so I worked as fast as I could, so that I wouldn't have to live with the fear.

By the way, Bill Plympton and Carlos Nine are geniuses. I'd love to see them work."

? **Carter Goodrich** received *Sketchtravel* from the hands of **Bill Presing** on January 22, 2010, in San Francisco and gave it to **Chris Appelhans** on February 1, 2010, in Los Angeles.

Stop 53 Stop 54 Stop 55

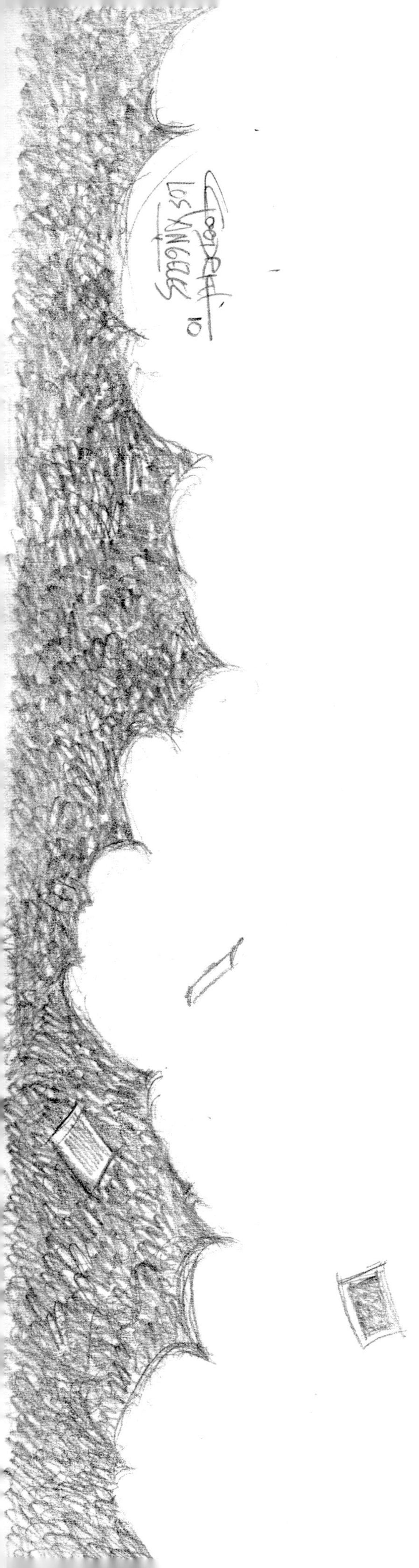

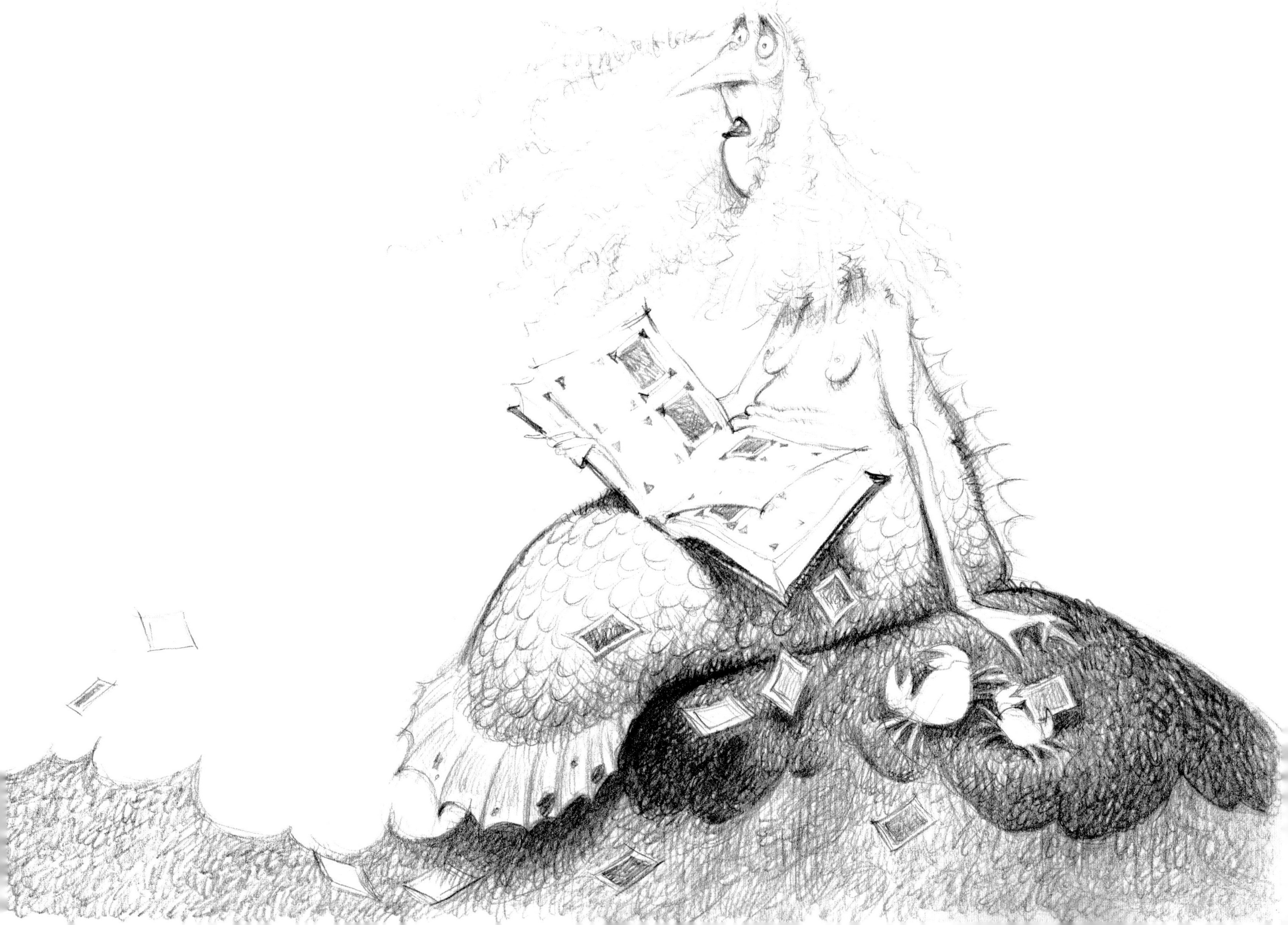

Carlos Nine

Carlos Nine

“I had never heard of such a project, and when I finally figured out what they wanted to do with the sketchbook I was skeptical about it. I liked the concept, but I was afraid that it would be impossible to carry out well because of the thousands of kilometers that separated the participants.

To try to make up for my initial lack of confidence, I wanted to make a drawing that was as perfect as possible.”

Diciembre 2009
Buenos Aires
Argentina

? **Carlos Nine** received *Sketchtravel* from the hands of **Daisuke Tsutsumi** on December 16, 2009, in Buenos Aires and gave it back to **Daisuke Tsutsumi** on December 23, 2009, in Buenos Aires.

Stop 51 Stop 52 Stop 53

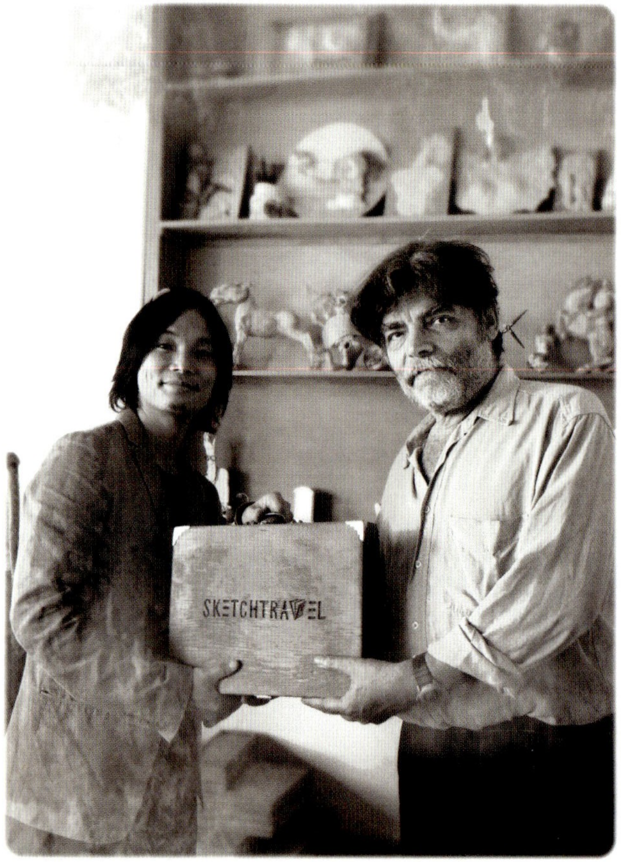

Daisuke Tsutsumi and Carlos Nine

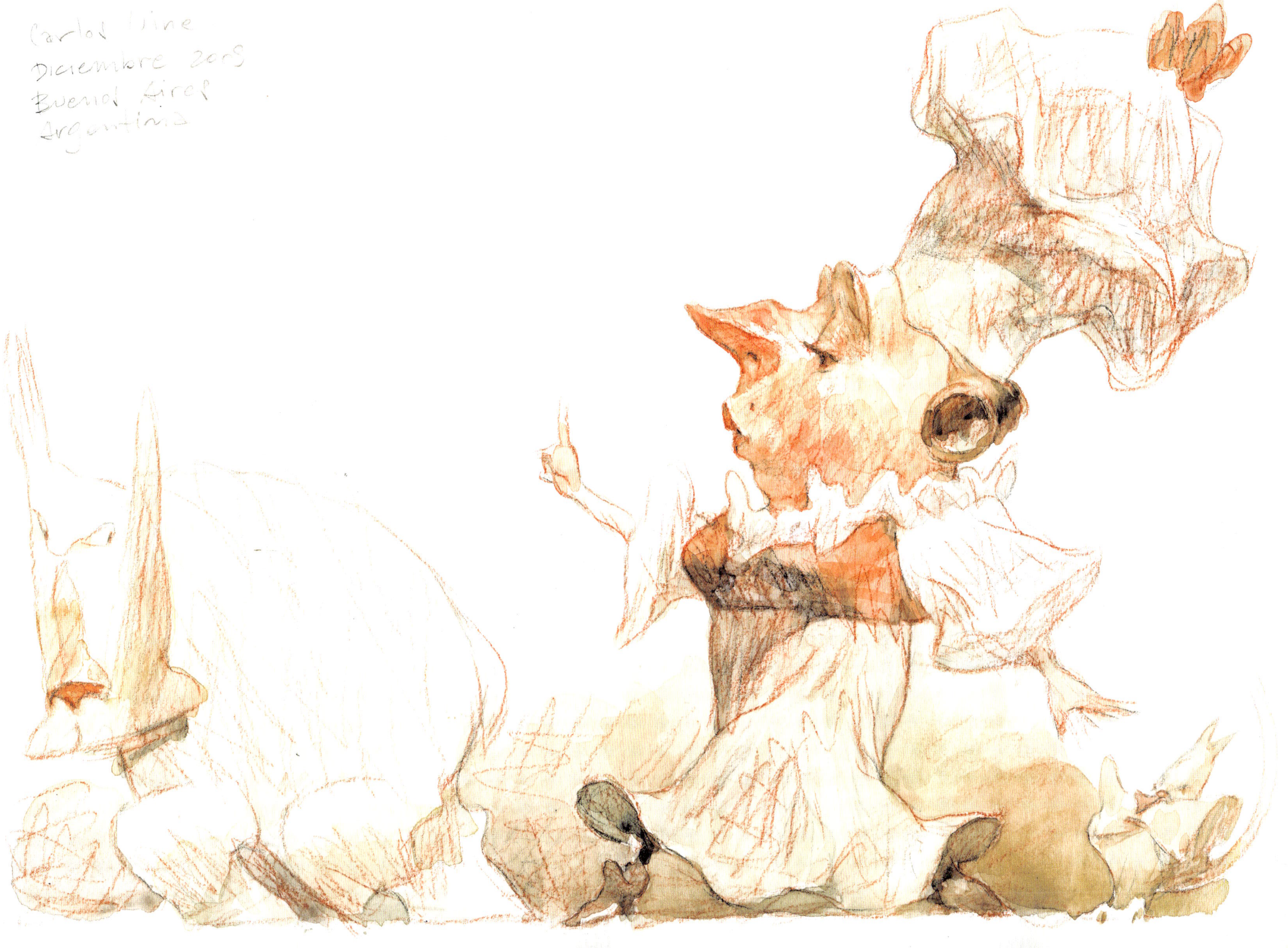
Carlos Nine
Diciembre 2008
Buenos Aires
Argentina

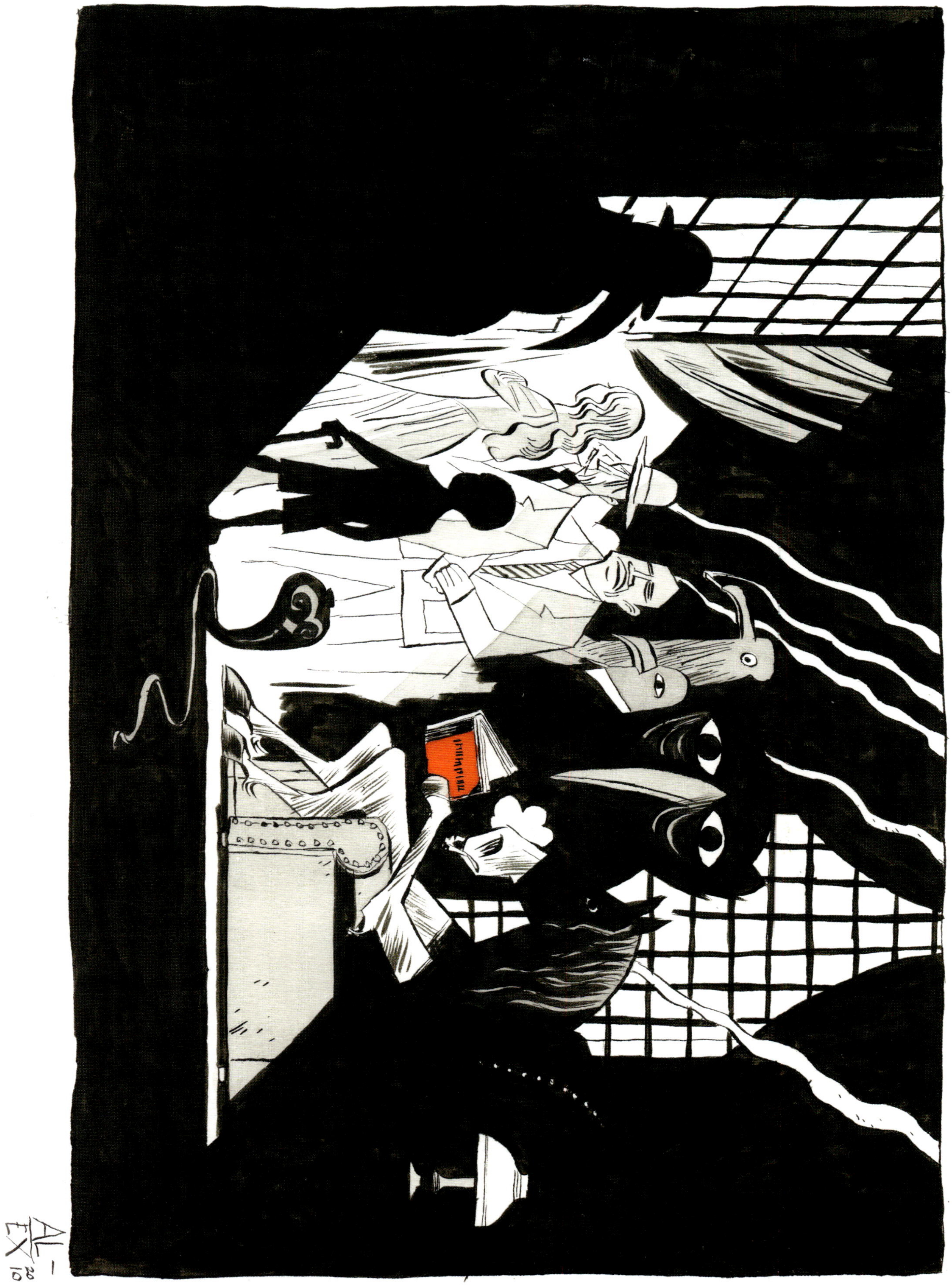

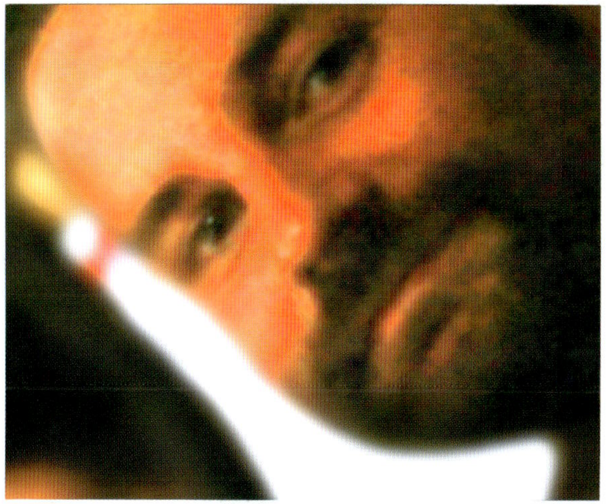

Alex Puvilland

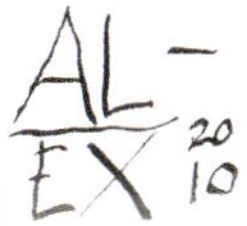

Alex Puvilland

"It's a great idea. I heard about it before Dice contacted me, but I thought it was a collection of travel sketches and I didn't think I would be part of it.

When I got it, I was delighted and very motivated; I finished my drawing in less than a day. It was exciting to see my work alongside that of so many great artists. Even though I was afraid that I would spill something on it and spoil everything!"

? **Alex Puvilland** received *Sketchtravel* from **Leuyen Pham** on October 21, 2010, in San Francisco and gave it to **Daisuke Tsutsumi** on October 23, 2010, in San Francisco.

Stop 66 — **Stop 67** — Stop 68

CHRIS

Chris Appelhans

"I love the idea of *Sketchtravel*; it is definitely something to do again. Looking at what the others had done before me, I was immediately inspired. It's true that you are always afraid to see what other great artists have done, but overall, I found it very inspiring."

Stop 54 Stop 55 Stop 56

? **Chris Appelhans** received *Sketchtravel* from the hands of **Carter Goodrich** on February 1, 2010, in Los Angeles and gave it to **Paul Felix** on February 14, 2010, in Burbank.

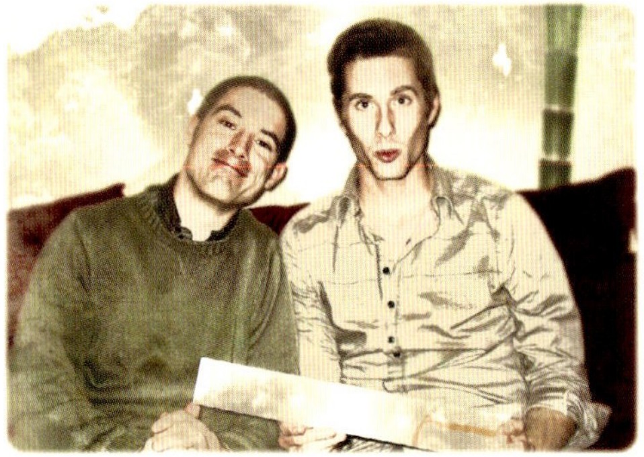

Gérald Guerlais and Chris Appelhans

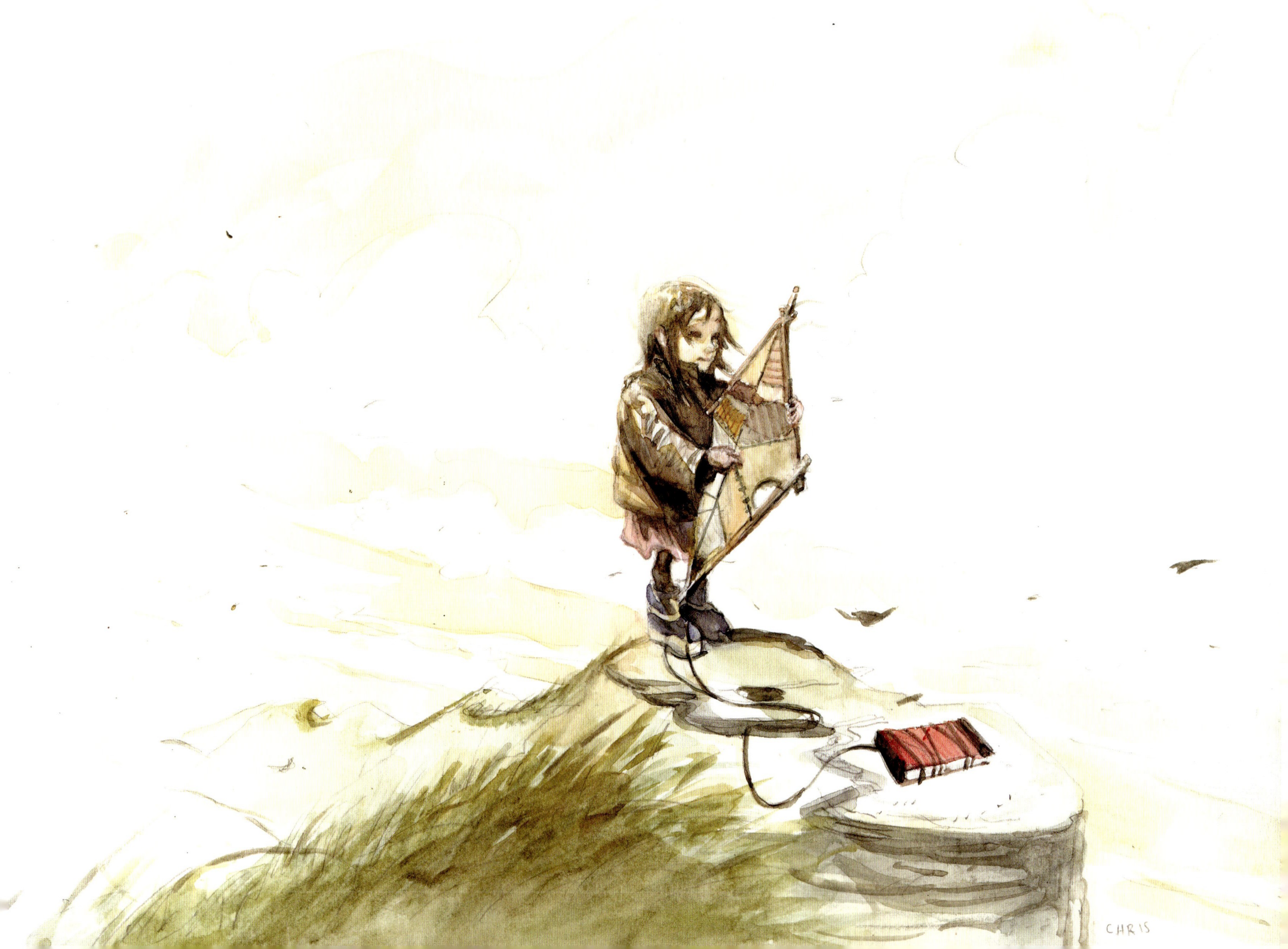
CHRIS

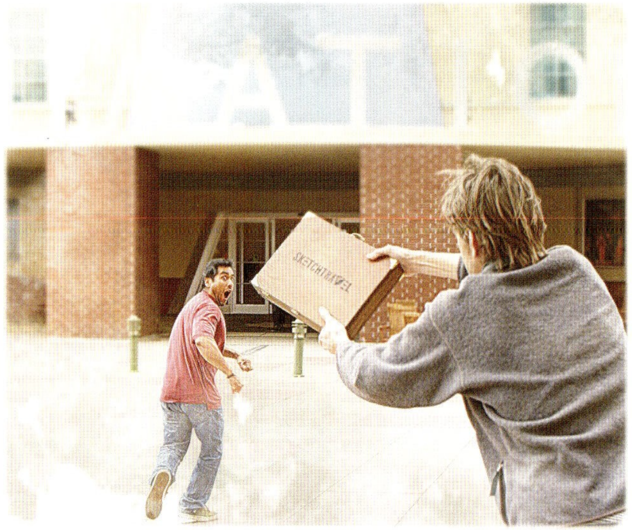

Paul Felix and Chris Appelhans

PAUL FELIX
PASADENA
FEB 15 2010

Paul Felix

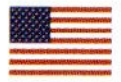

"As an artist, it's good to feel like you are part of a global community that communicates through drawing. Obviously, it was a great honor for me to have been chosen to appear with all my favorite artists.

A terrifying honor, it is true; I was really not sure I was at the same level."

? **Paul Felix** received *Sketchtravel* from the hands of **Chris Appelhans** on February 14, 2010, in Burbank and gave it to **Lorelay Bove** on February 16, 2010, in Burbank.

Stop 55 · Stop 56 · Stop 57

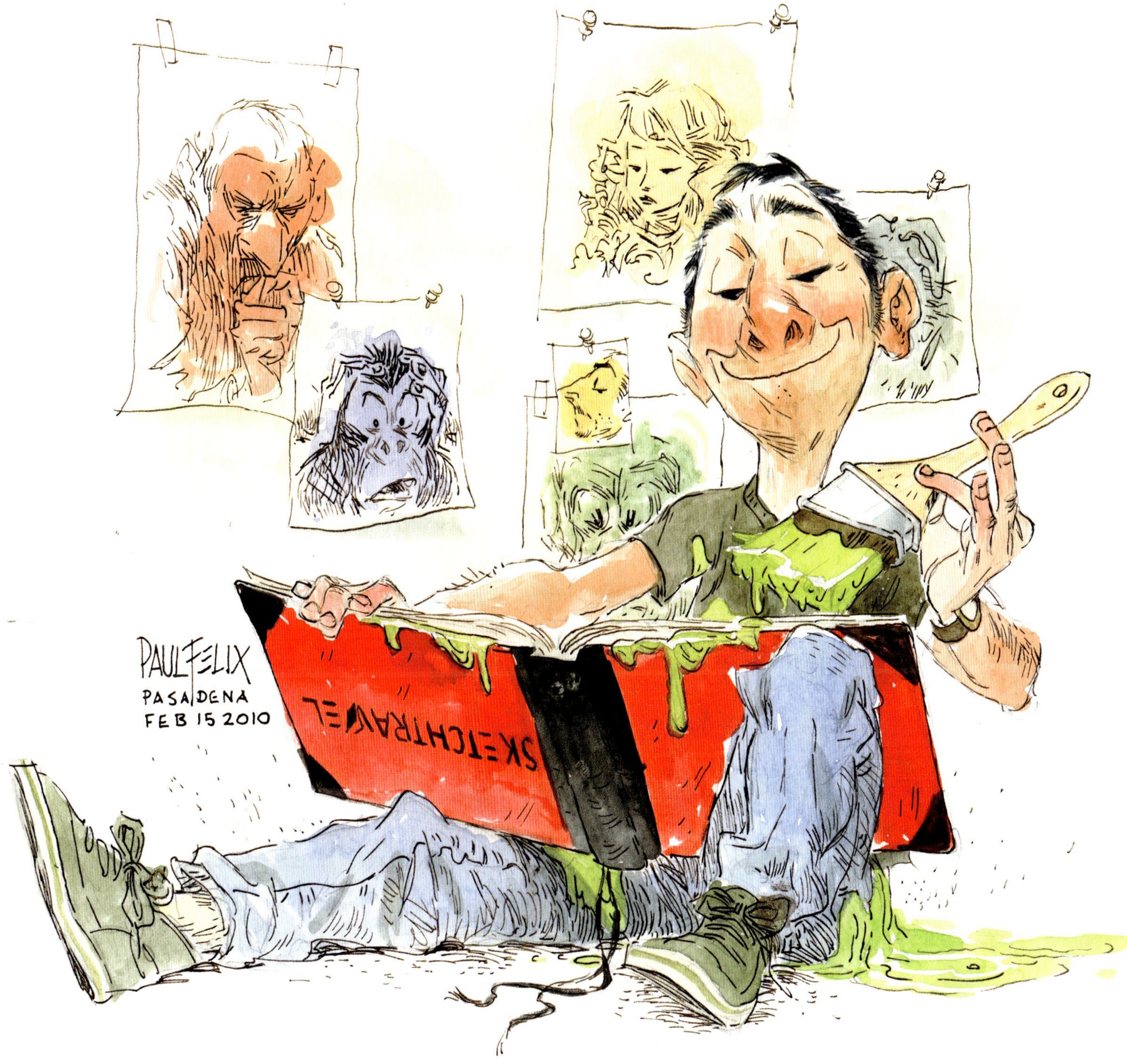
PAUL FELIX
PASADENA
FEB 15 2010
SKETCHTRAVEL

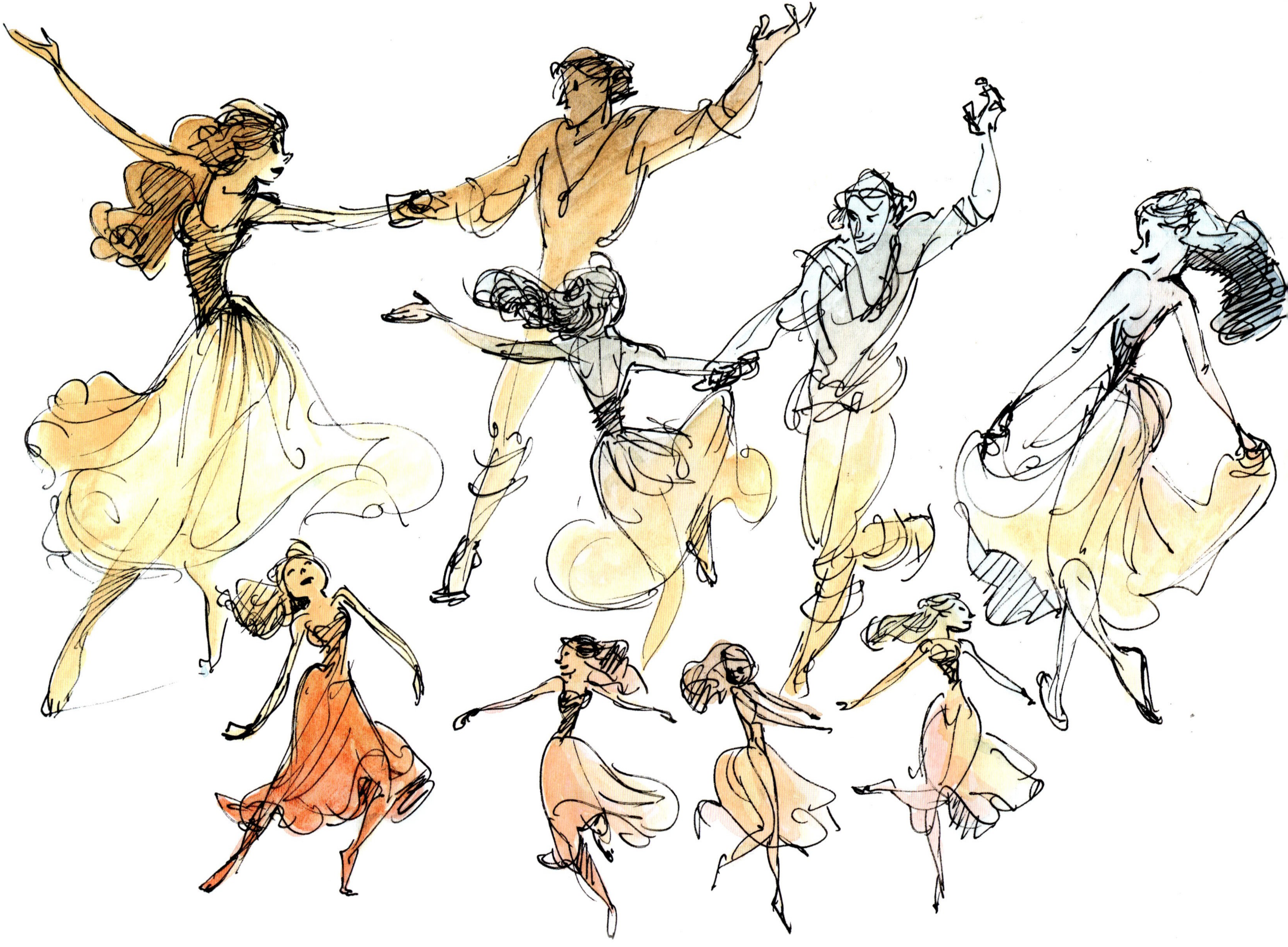

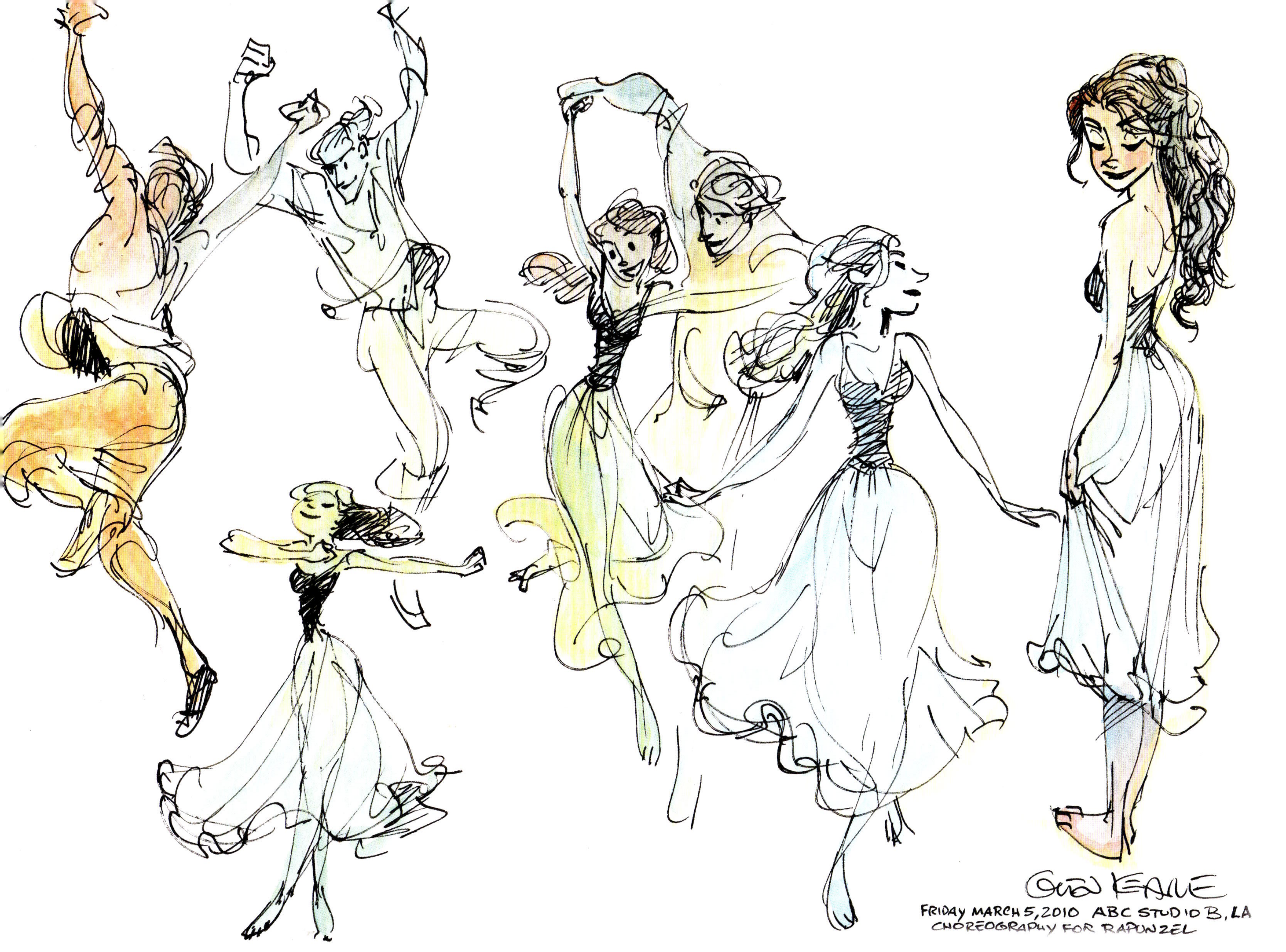
GLEN KEANE
FRIDAY MARCH 5, 2010 ABC STUDIO B, LA
CHOREOGRAPHY FOR RAPUNZEL

GLEN KEANE

Glen Keane

“It was stimulating to be part of a project with so many other people and I wanted to keep from breaking the artistic chain at any cost.

I gave the book to Robert Kondo in front of a restaurant in Hollywood; I was so afraid that a drop of water would fall on one of the pages that I held it under my jacket as if it were the Mona Lisa.”

FRIDAY MARCH 5, 2010 ABC STUDIO B, LA
CHOREOGRAPHY FOR RAPUNZEL

?

Glen Keane received *Sketchtravel* from the hands of **Lorelay Bove** on February 26, 2010, in Burbank and gave it to **Robert Kondo** on March 10, 2010, in Los Angeles.

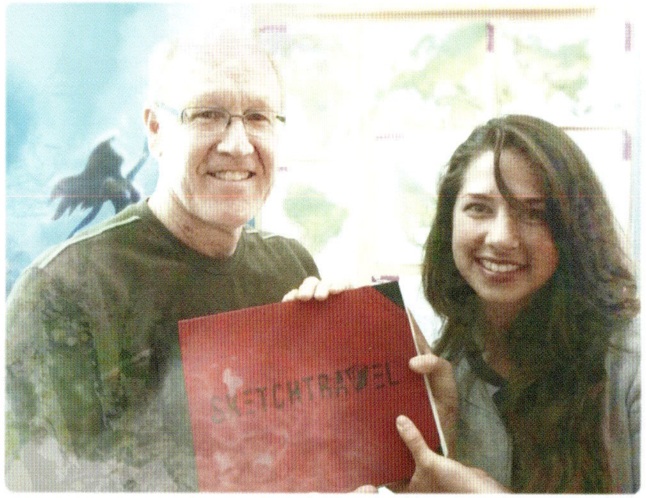

Glen Keane and Lorelay Bove

Stop 57
Stop 58
Stop 59

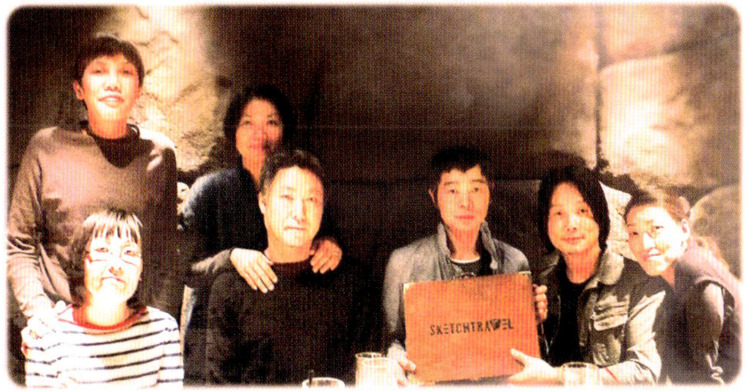

Taiyo Matsumoto (with the book) and Daisuke Tsutsumi

松本大洋

Taiyo Matsumoto

2010 4/17

?

Taiyo Matsumoto received *Sketchtravel* from the hands of **Koji Morimoto** April 19, 2010, in Tokyo and gave it to **Atsuko Fukushima** the same day.

Stop 61 — Stop 62 — Stop 63

"Is there anything I can contribute to the world? This feeling of purpose that I carry somewhere deep in my heart turned into 'doing' thanks to the red sketchbook. Thank you."

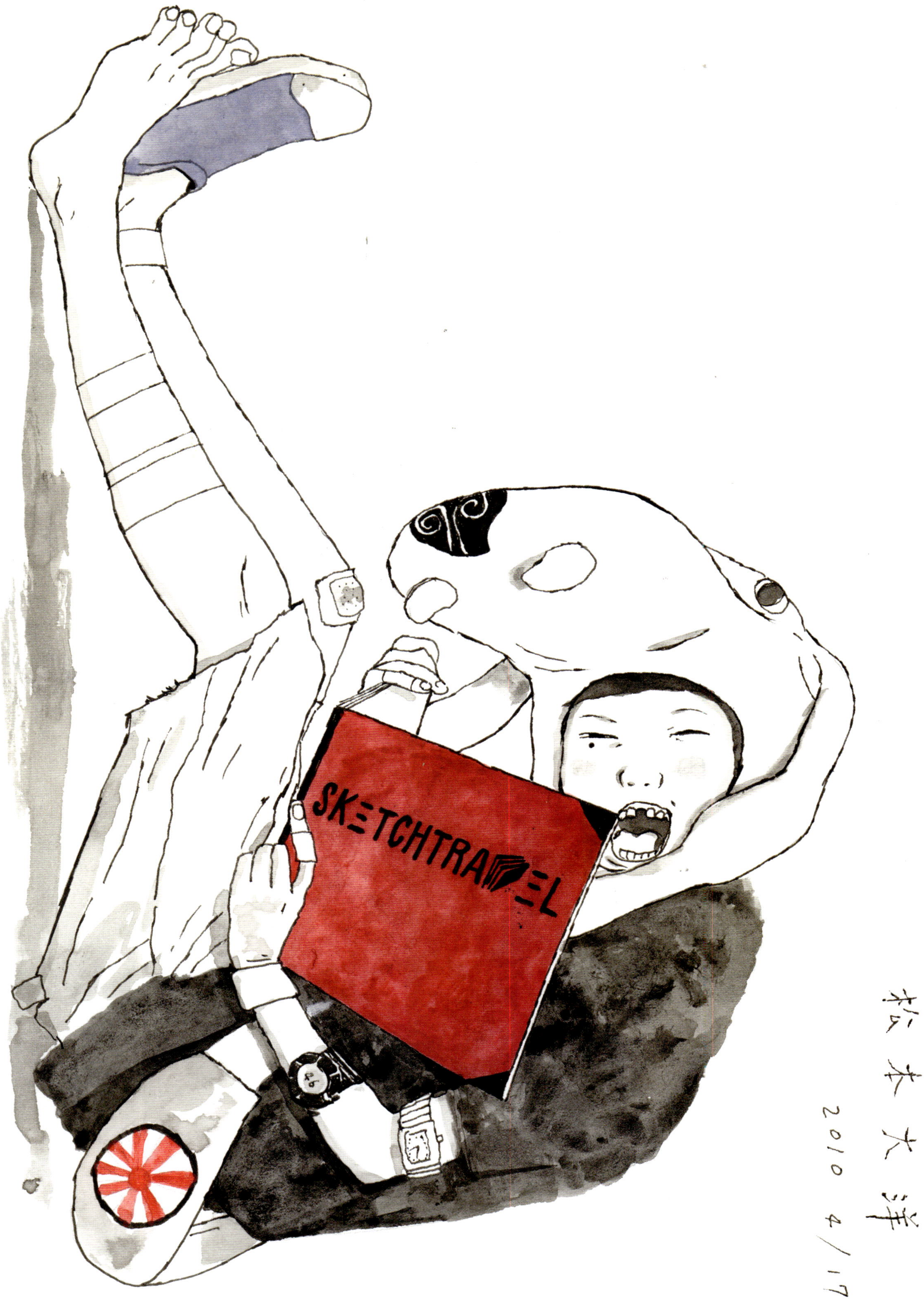
SKETCHTRAVEL
松本大洋
2010 4/17

Stop 60
Stop 61
Stop 62

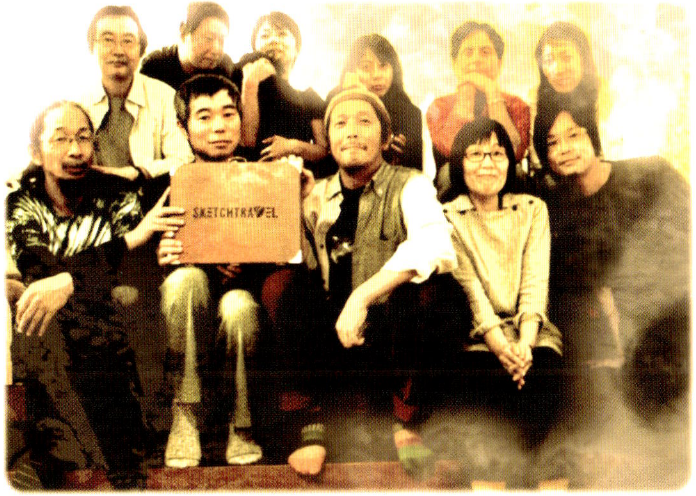

Koji Morimoto (to the right of *Sketchtravel*) and Daisuke Tsutsumi

"While this project reminded me of the pressure of a baton handed off from person to person, it gave me the precious experience of being part of something that one could not achieve on his own. I am grateful that I am an artist and could participate in this project. Thank you, Dice!"

MORIMOTO

Koji Morimoto

2010.6.7

Koji Morimoto received *Sketchtravel* from the hands of **Daisuke Tsustumi** on April 17, 2010, in Tokyo and gave it to **Taiyo Matsumoto** on April 19, 2010, in Tokyo.

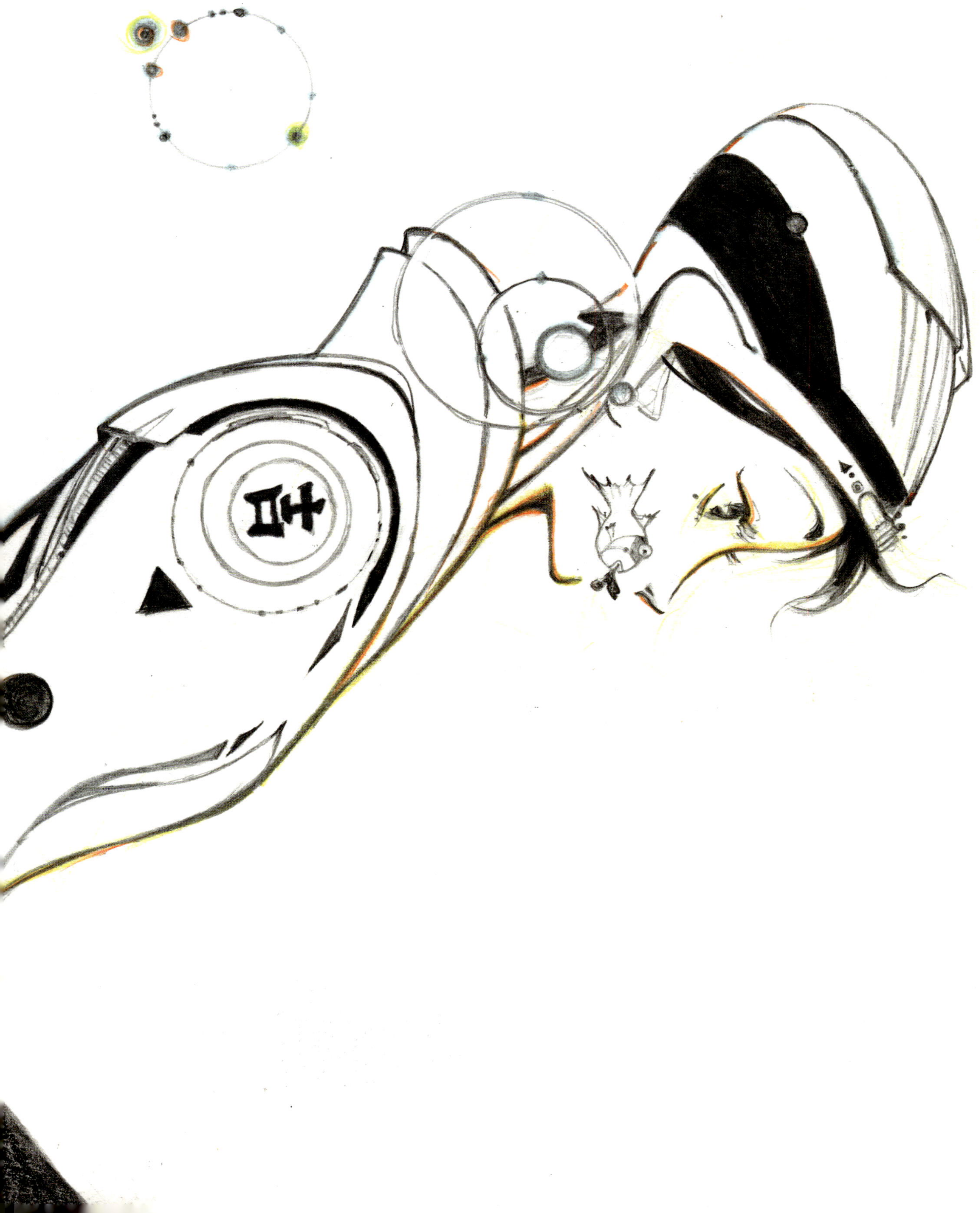

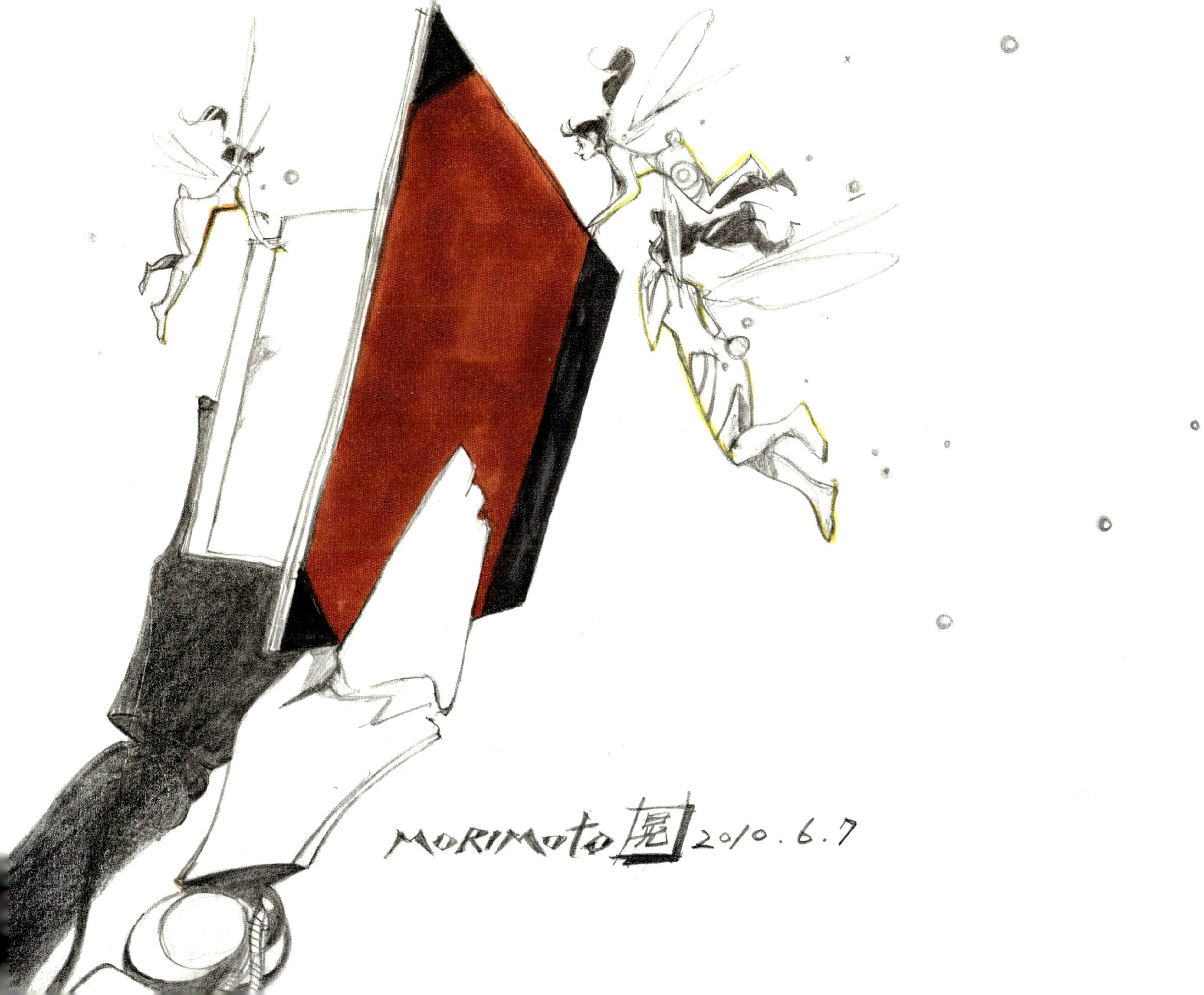
MORIMOTO 2010.6.7

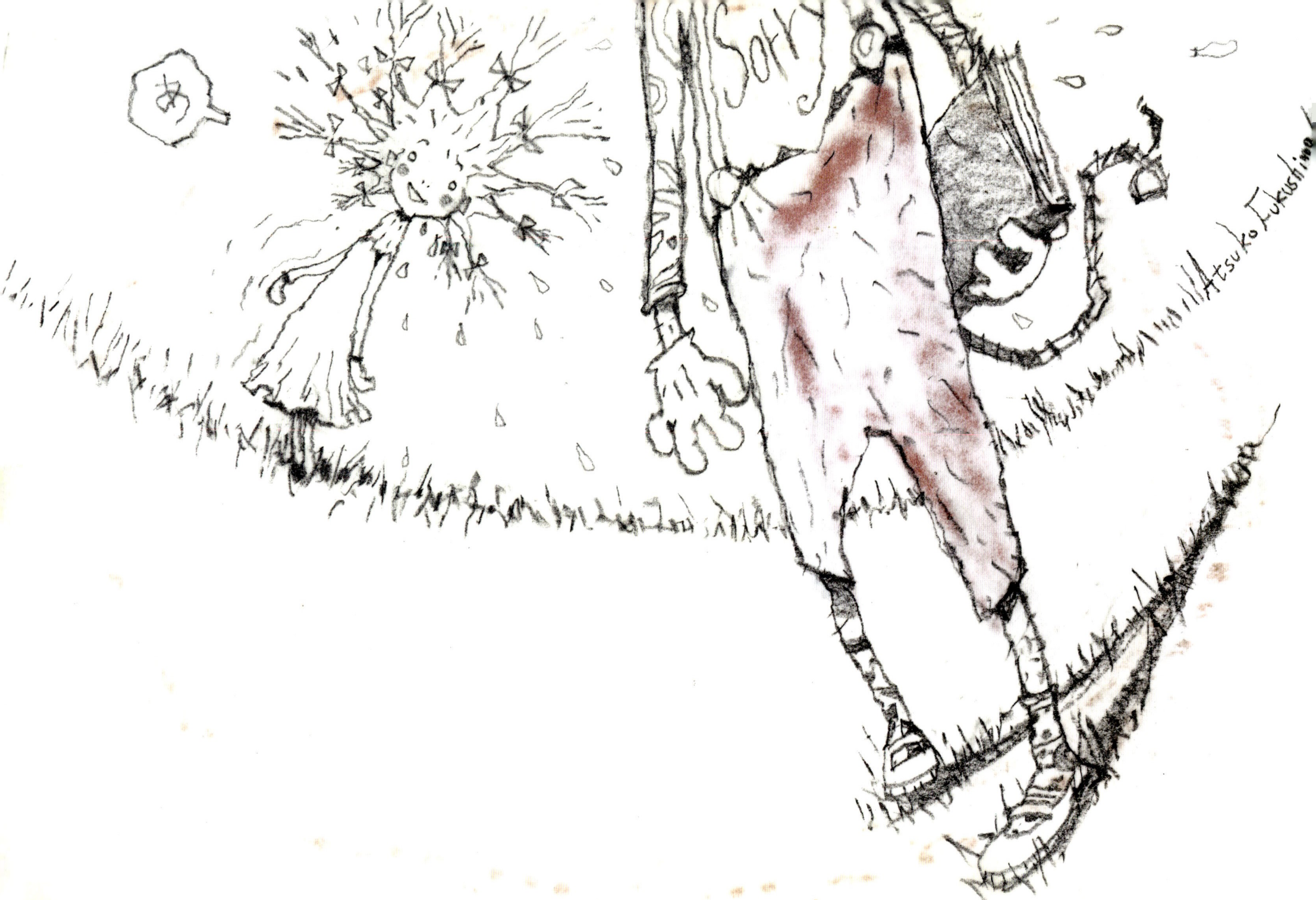
あ
Sorry
Atsuko Fukushima

“When I first held this collection of wonderful original sketches in my hand, I felt a shiver of pleasure looking at this fun and yet serious project. Only God knew that I would later feel a shiver of fear when it came to be that I, too, would contribute.”

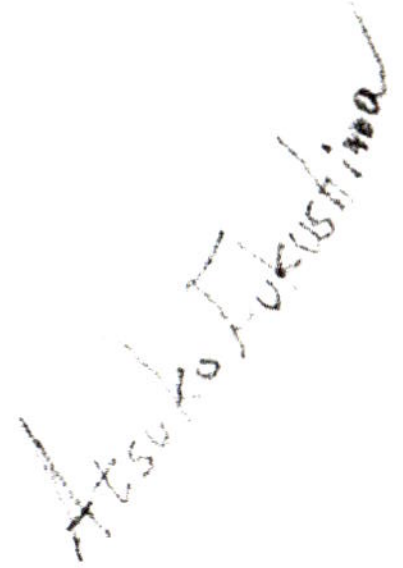

Atsuko Fukushima

Atsuko Fukushima received *Sketchtravel* from the hands of **Taiyo Matsumoto** on April 19, 2010, in Tokyo and gave it to **Daisuke Tsutsumi** on April 22, 2010, in Tokyo.

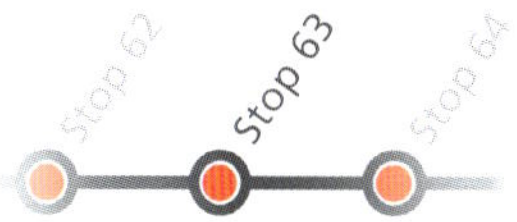

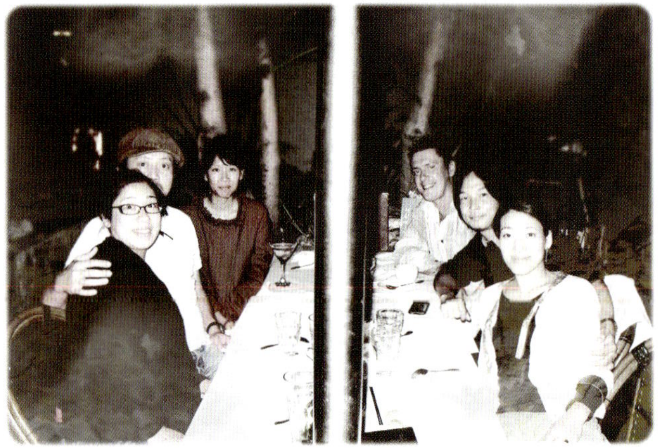

Catia Chien (left) and Daisuke Tsutsumi

Catia

Catia Chien

"An overdose of different emotions: the fear of spoiling everything by messing up my work, the excitement at the idea of participating in a meaningful humanitarian project, the honor of having been chosen by Dice, happiness to have the opportunity to make new friends around the world. An emotional roller coaster, but I was extremely motivated.

I couldn't stop saying to myself, 'It's unbelievable, this treasure that you are holding in your hands . . .'"

– Pasadena, CA
August 2010

Catia Chien received *Sketchtravel* from the hands of **Daisuke Tsutsumi** on August 15, 2010, in Los Angeles and gave it to **Nicolas Marlet** on August 28, 2010, in Los Angeles.

Stop 63 Stop 64 Stop 65

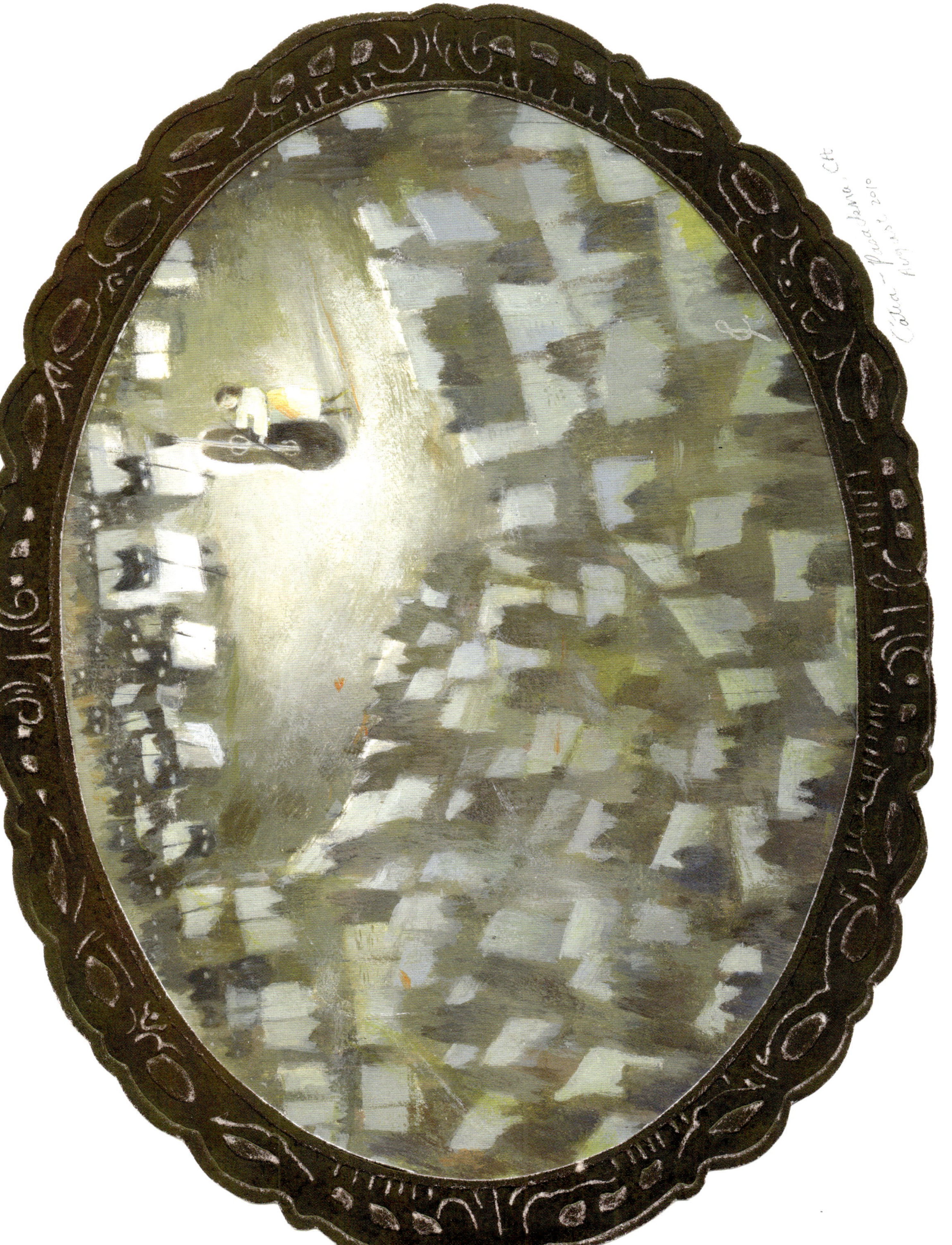

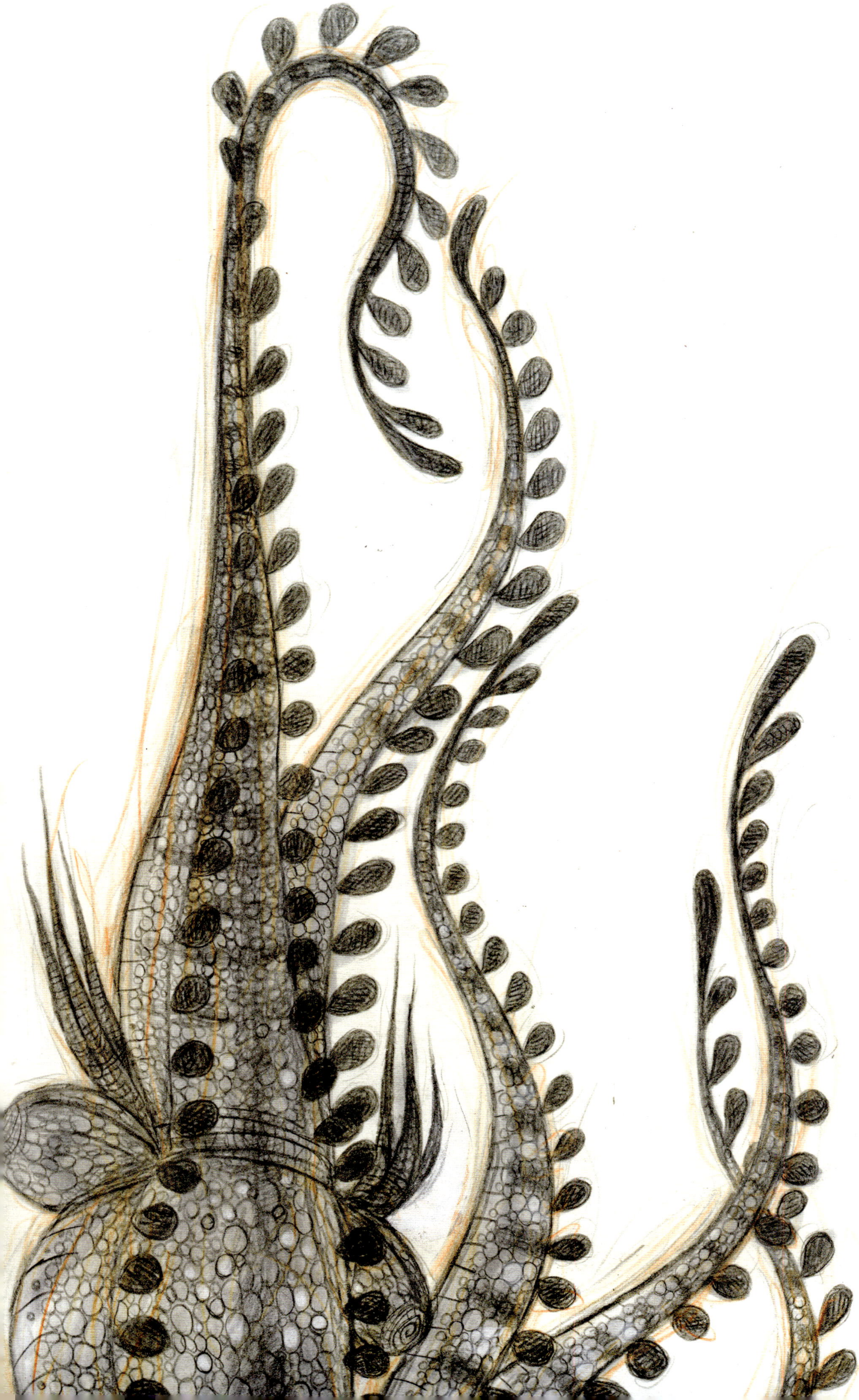

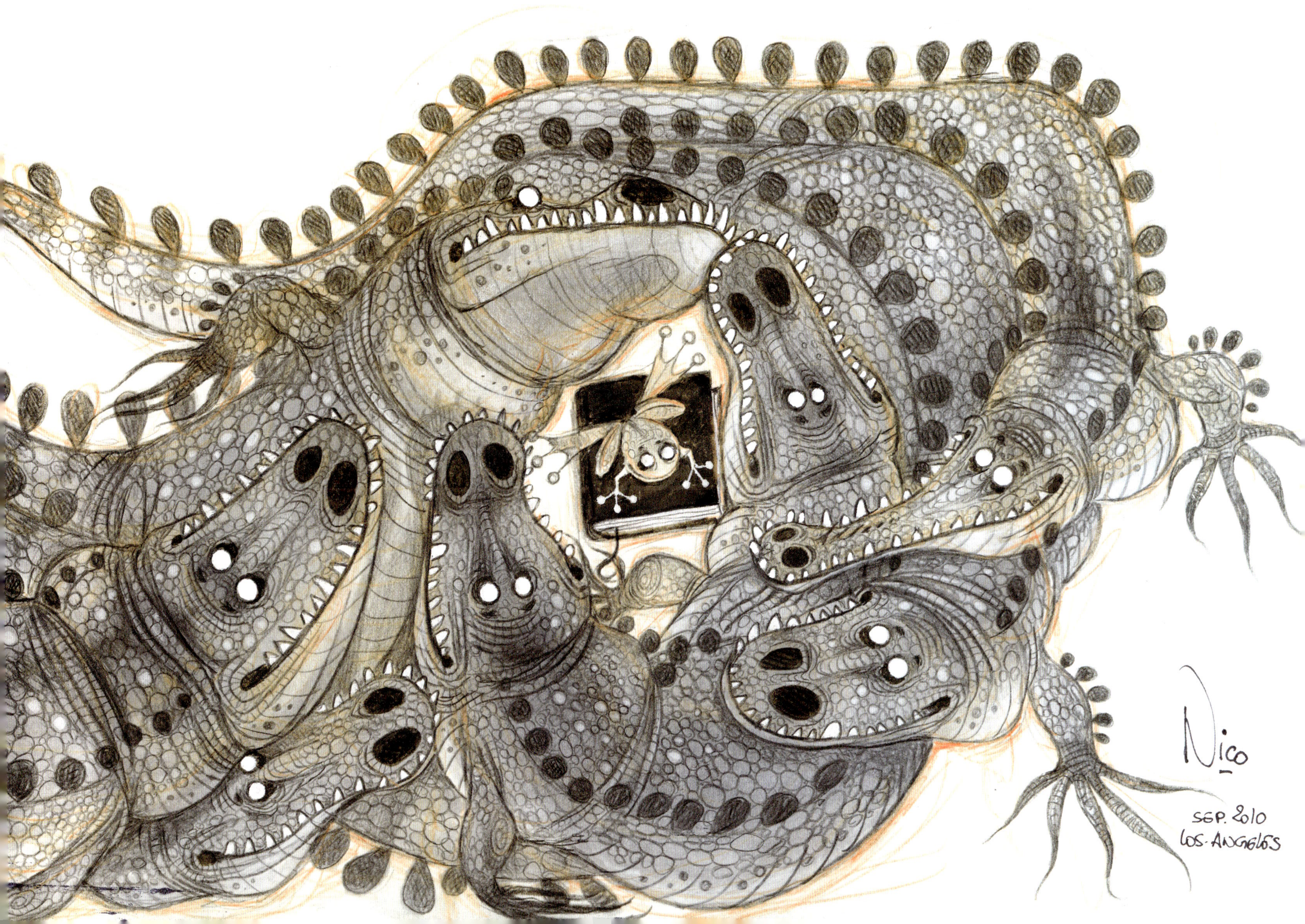
Nico
SEP. 2010
LOS ANGELES

Nicolas Marlet

Nico

"My motivation was the humanitarian cause.

My inspiration: self-portrait of Carter Goodrich as an old mermaid."

SEP. 2010
LOS ANGELES

Nicolas Marlet received *Sketchtravel* from the hands of **Catia Chien** on August 28, 2010, in Los Angeles and gave it to **Robert Kondo** on September 10, 2010, in Los Angeles.

Stop 64 — Stop 65 — Stop 66

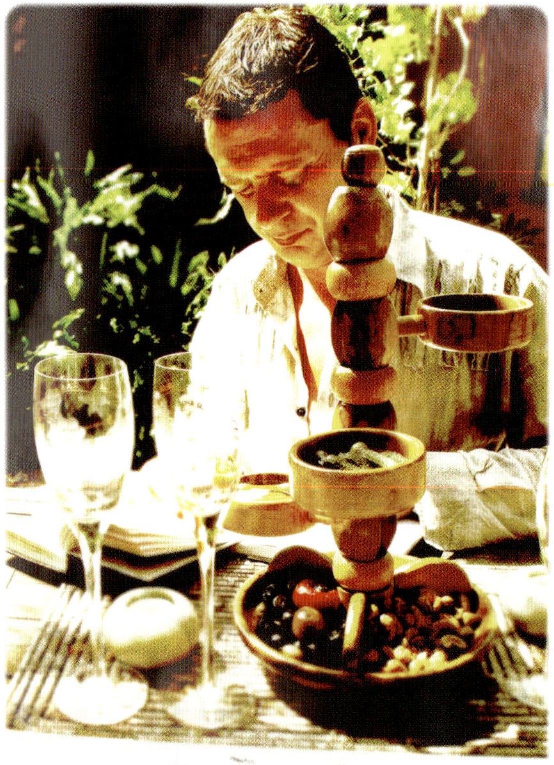

Nicolas Marlet

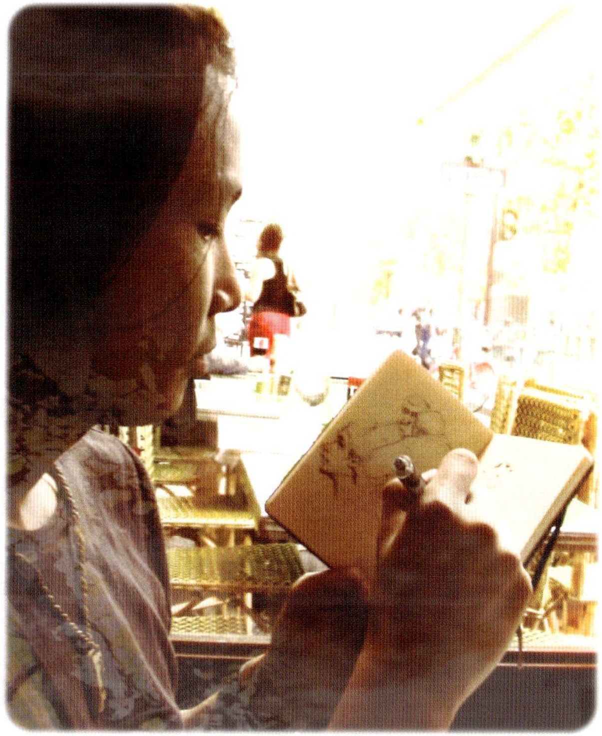
Daisuke "Dice" Tsutsumi

Daisuke "Dice" Tsutsumi

"Most of my involvement in this project consisted of making sure the sketchbook deliveries were smooth and timely. It was a big mistake for me to wait so long for my turn to actually do my page. How could I do anything that wouldn't embarrass me and show my lack of talent in the wake of all the artists that had already contributed? The terror I felt turned into the shadow monster that loomed over me."

11.6.2010

Daisuke "Dice" Tsutsumi received *Sketchtravel* from the hands of **Nicolas Marlet** on September 10, 2010, in Los Angeles and gave it to **Frédéric Back** on November 12, 2010, in Montreal.

Stop 68 Stop 69 Stop 70

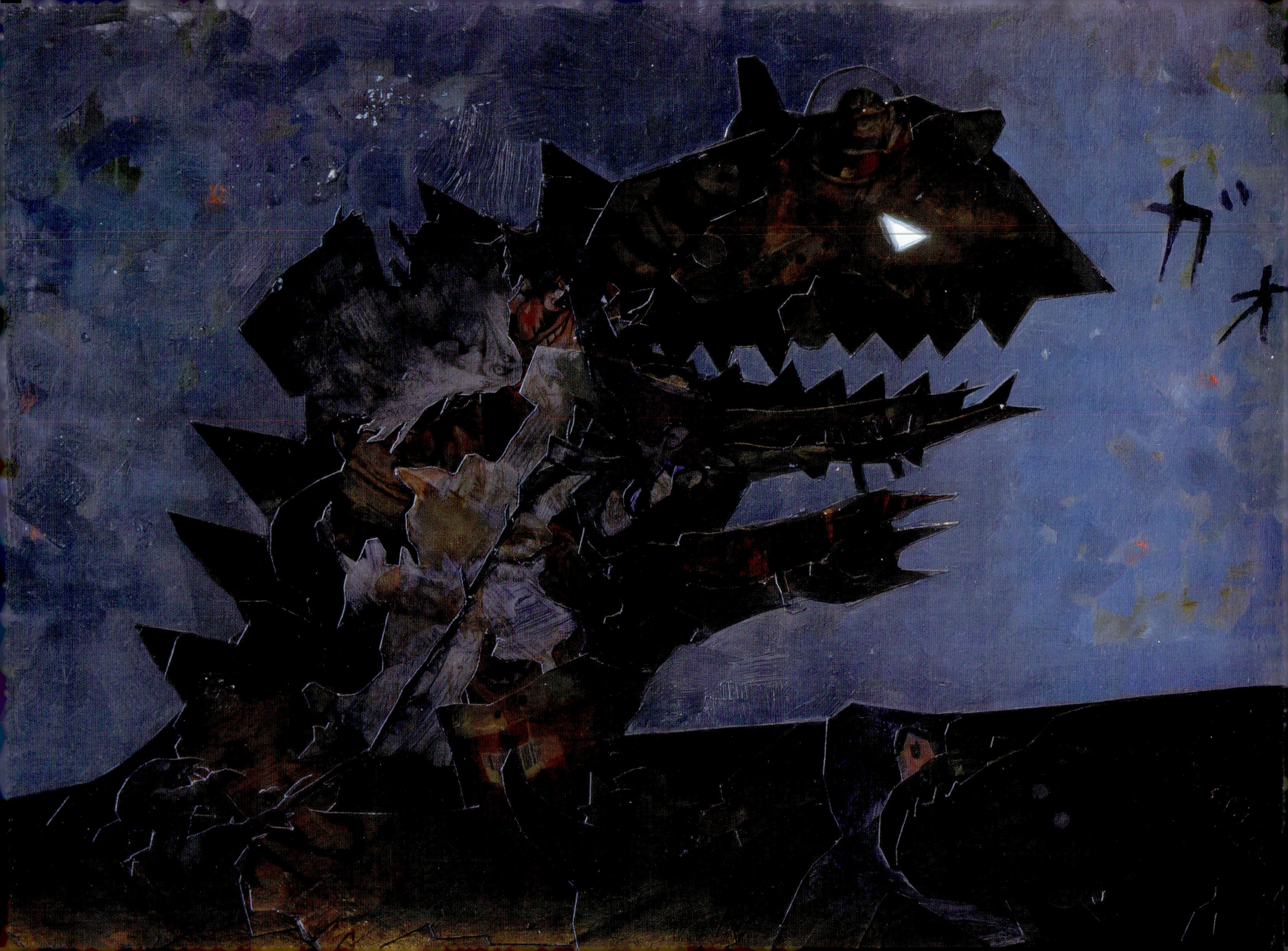
ガオ

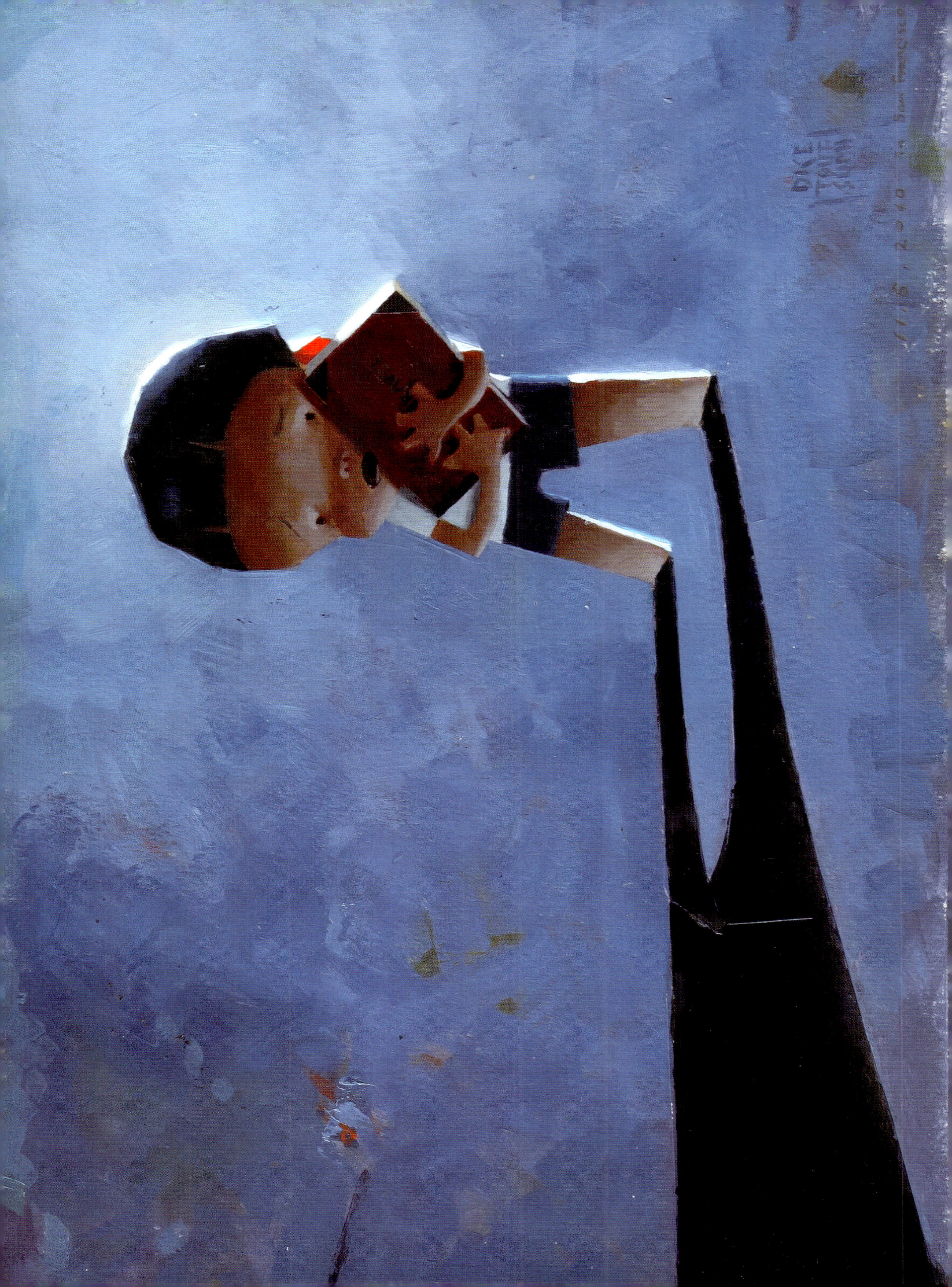

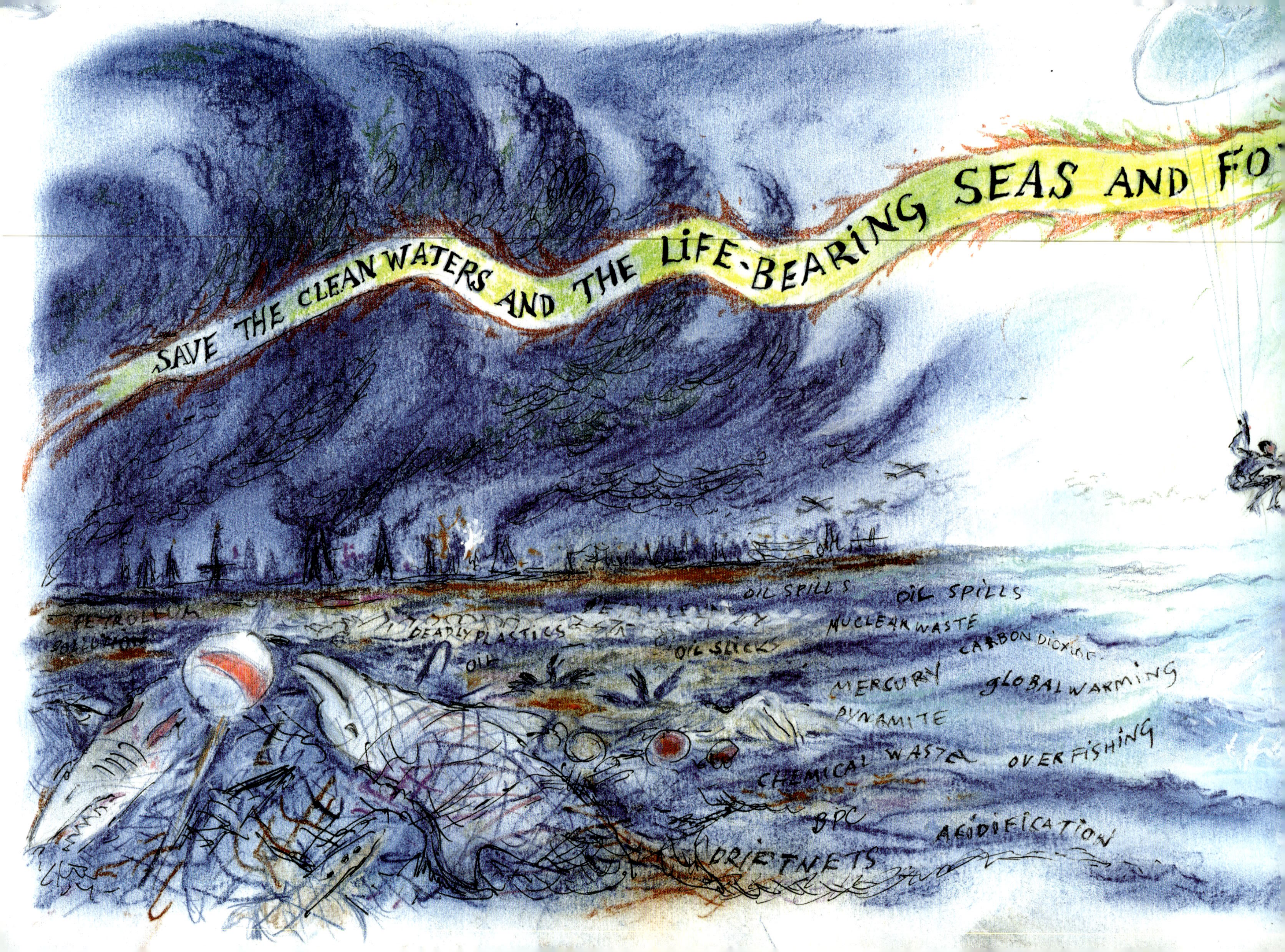
SAVE THE CLEAN WATERS AND THE LIFE-BEARING SEAS AND FO
OIL SPILLS
OIL SPILLS
DEADLY PLASTICS
OIL
OIL SLICKS
NUCLEAR WASTE
CARBON DIOXIDE
MERCURY
GLOBAL WARMING
DYNAMITE
CHEMICAL WASTE
OVERFISHING
BPC
ACIDIFICATION
DRIFTNETS

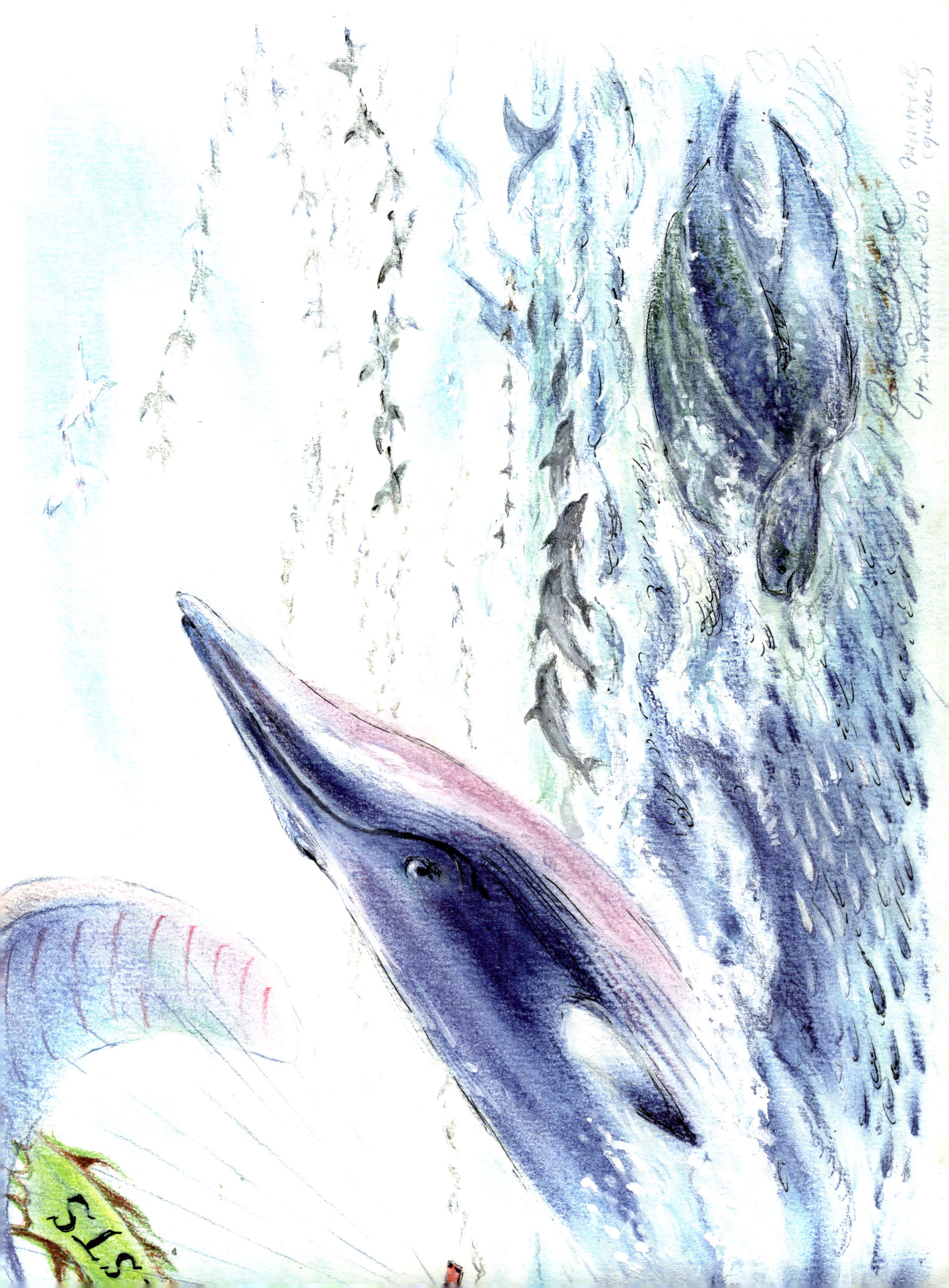

Frédéric Back

"Don't limit yourself. Let yourself be surprised. Use your talent and your art to bring hope and life to the world."

Frédéric Back received *Sketchtravel* from the hands of **Daisuke Tsutsumi** on November 12, 2010, in Montreal and gave it back to **Daisuke Tsutsumi** on November 14, 2010.

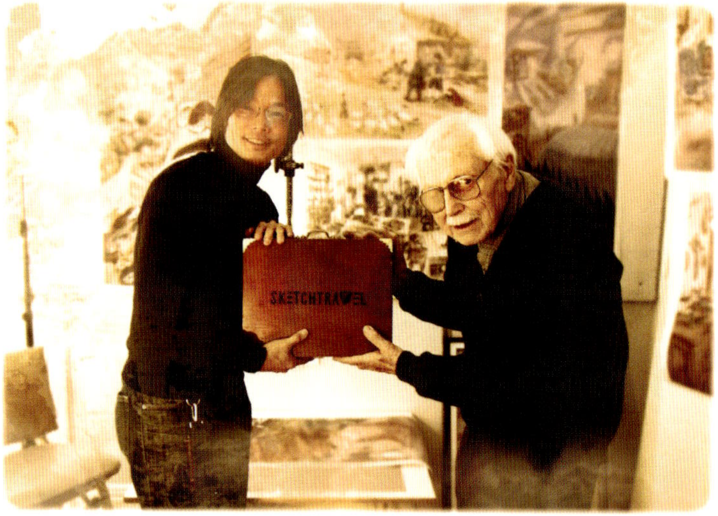

Daisuke Tsutsumi and Frédéric Back

Stop 69
Stop 70
Stop 71

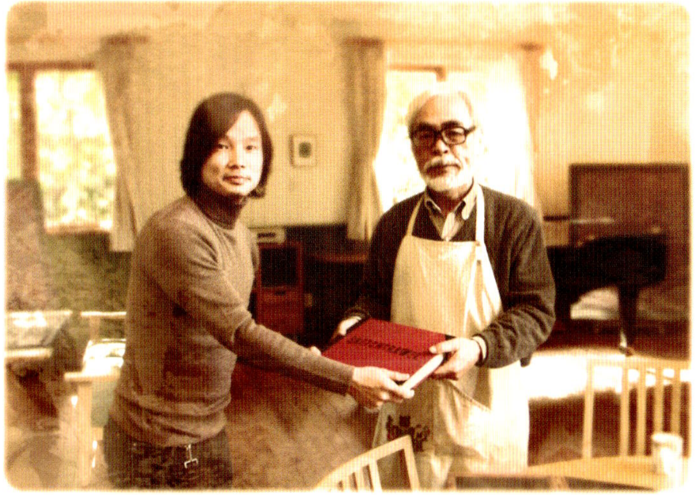

Daisuke Tsutsumi and Hayao Miyazaki

Hayao Miyazaki

Hayao Miyazaki received *Sketchtravel* from the hands of **Daisuke Tsutsumi** on January 26, 2011, in Tokyo and gave it back to **Daisuke Tsutsumi** on January 28, 2011, in Tokyo.

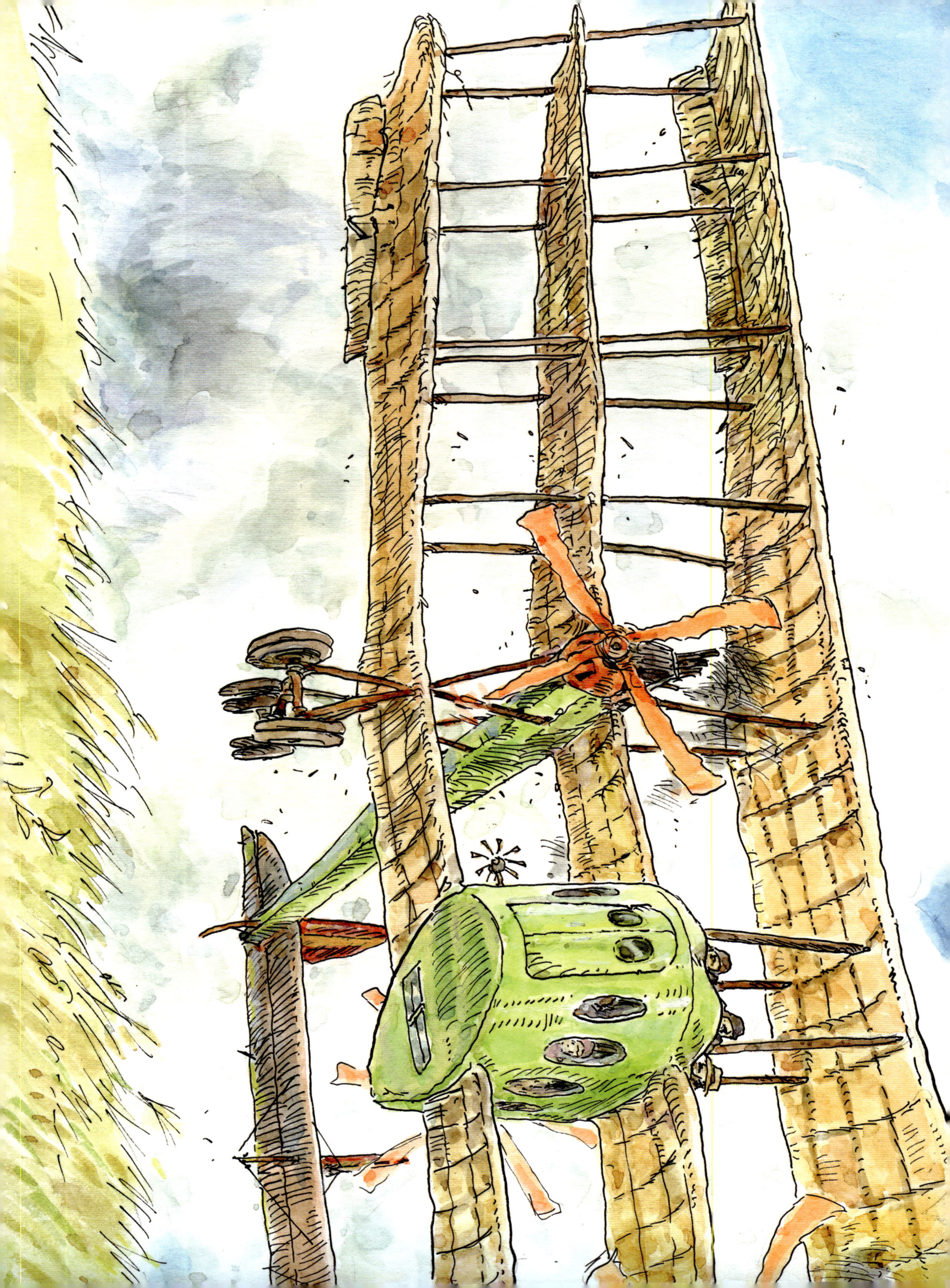

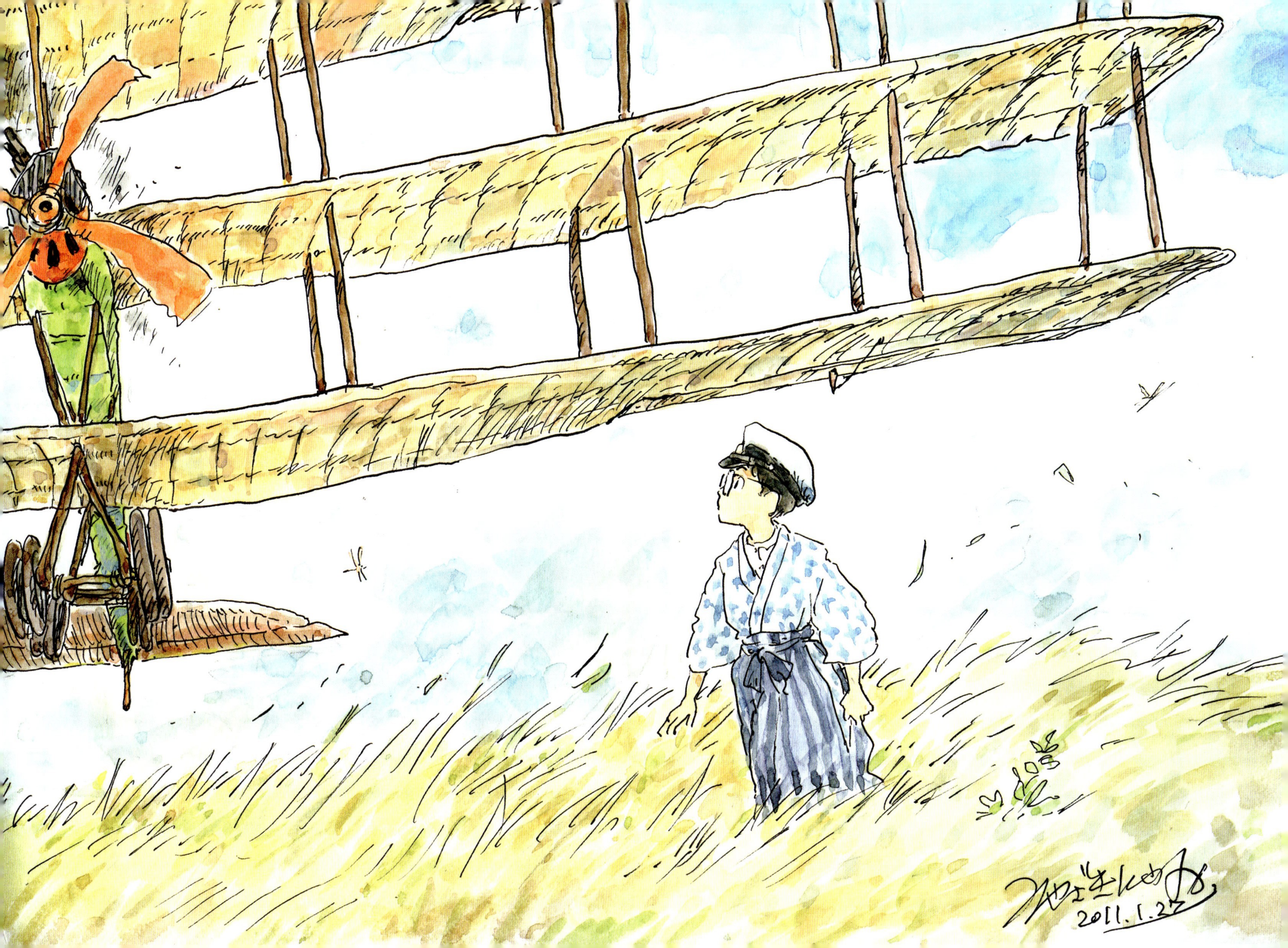

みやざきはやお
2011.1.27

The Artists

ADEL Daniel
www.danieladel.com
Daniel Adel graduated from Darmouth College. He illustrated a children's book with Jon Scieszka. His paintings have appeared in the *New Yorker*, *Vanity Fair*, the *New York Times*, *Der Spiegel*, *Forbes*, *Village Voice, Esquire*, *Newsweek*, and *Time*. Adel has painted commissioned portraits for Notre Dame University, the College of William and Mary, the New York State Court of Appeals, and Union Pacific Railroad. Adel opened the Atelier Rue Basse in Lacoste, France.

ALARY Pierre
pierrealary.blogspot.com
Pierre Alary entered the Gobelins prestigious school of graphic arts in 1991. He was then hired by Walt Disney Studios, where he spent ten years as an animator on films including *Tarzan*, *The Emperor's New Groove*, and *The Jungle Book 2* before dedicating himself to comics. His first series was *Griffin Dark*. The comics adventure has continued with *Les Echaudeurs des ténèbres*, three *Belladone* volumes, *Spider-Man Family 3* at Marvel, *Sinbad*, and *Moby Dick*.

APPELHANS Chris
froghatstudios.com
Born in Idaho, Chris Appelhans eventually fled the peaceful valleys and clean air of his birthplace and relocated to Los Angeles. His work as a concept artist for the CG movie *Monster House* confirmed his talent. Appelhans is also a comic author. His comics are available in the collective book *Flight*, Volumes 1 & 2, at Image Comics. He worked as a concept artist at LAIKA and Disney, and currently works at DreamWorks animation studios.

ASCENCIOS Natalie
www.ascencios.com
Natalie Ascencios's work has appeared in the *New Yorker*, the *New York Times Review of Books*, *Rolling Stone*, and *Time*. Ascencios created two paintings depicting the 1920s. One is on permanent display at the Algonquin Hotel in New York City and the other at the Brown Hotel in Louisville, Kentucky. The Society of Illustrators has awarded her one gold medal and two silver medals. She received first place in puppetry in the Henson design competition. Ascencios has taught drawing and painting at the School of Visual Arts.

BACK FRÉDÉRIC
www.fredericback.com
Born in Saarbrücken, The Territory of the Saar Basin, he emigrated to Canada in 1948. He began teaching at the École des Beaux-Arts de Montréal, then in 1952, he joined the graphics department of Radio-Canada and has remained there since. He created a massive stained glass mural entitled *L'histoire de la musique à Montréal* ("history of music in Montreal") at the Place-des-Arts Metro station in Montreal. Unveiled on December 20, 1967, this stained glass was the first work of art to be commissioned for the Montreal metro system. In 1980, Back was nominated for an Academy Award for Animated Short Film for his film *Tout rien* (*All Nothing* in English). In 1982, he won the Academy Award for Animated Short Film for his film *Crac*. In 1987, he won his second Academy Award for Animated Short Film for *L'homme qui plantait des arbres* (*The Man Who Planted Trees* in English). In 1994, he was nominated again for an Academy Award for Animated Short Film, for his film *Le fleuve aux grandes eaux* (*Mighty River* in English).

BERTAIL Dominique
Dominique was born in 1972 in Tours, France. He went to the Ecole des Beaux-Arts in Rennes and then Angoulême. Dominique Bertail created with writer Thierry Smolderen, a writer he met in Angoulême, the diptych *L'Enfer des Pelgram* for Delcourt in 1998 and 2000. He also maintained the site coconino-world.com for four years. He is the author of the volumes *L'Homme Tableau* (2000) and *L'Homme Nuit* (2002), both published by Alain Beaulet. He has worked recently with Smolderen on the futuristic thriller *Ghost Money* (Dargaud, 2008 onwards). Dominique Bertail is furthermore active as an illustrator (Bayard, *Fluide Glacial*, Casterman) and a story-board artist (advertising and cinema).

BLAKE Quentin
www.quentinblake.com
Quentin Blake was born in 1932. He is known for his collaboration with Roald Dahl. His books have won numerous prizes and awards, including the Whitbread Award, the Kate Greenaway Medal, the Emil/Kurt Maschler Award, and the international Bologna Ragazzi Prize. He won the 2002 Hans Christian Andersen Award for Illustration, the highest international recognition given to creators of children's books. In 2004 Quentin Blake was awarded the 'Chevalier des Arts et des Lettres' by the French Government. In 2007 he was made Officier in the same order.

BLASICH Andrea
andreablasich.blogspot.com
Born in 1967, Andrea Blasich grew up in Milan, Italy. In 1990, at the Academy of Brera, he discovered a new way of expression that would influence his entire life: animation. He worked in Germany for Munich Animation, then in London for Warner Bros. He moved to the United States and worked as a character sculptor, visual development artist, and layout artist for movies such as *The Road to El Dorado*, *Sinbad*, and *Shark Tale* at DreamWorks; and *Robots* and *Ice Age 2* at Blue Sky Studios, to name a few.

BOIGER Alexandra
www.alexandraboiger.com
Born in Munich, Germany, Alexandra Boiger studied graphic design in at the Fachlochschule Augsburg. Her work in animation brought her to Great Britain and then to the United States at DreamWorks animation studios. She now illustrates childrens books such as *Roxie and the Hooligans*, *While Mama Had a Quick Little Chat*, *The Monster Princess*, *Thanks a Lot, Emily Post*, *Doctor All-Knowing*, *The Little Bit Scary People*, and the *Mrs. Piggle-Wiggle* series.

BOVE Lorelay
lorelaybove.blogspot.com
Lorelay Bove is originally from Spain. She moved to the United States when she was fourteen years old. She studied animation in Cal Arts. She then

attended the Pixar internship for art and the Disney animation studios talent development program and apprenticeship. She is currently working at Walt Disney Studios, where she worked on *The Princess and the Frog*, *Prep & Landing*, and *Tangled*. Lorelay Bove also illustrated the *Princess and the Frog* Little Golden Book, and the *Toy Story* picture book.

BUTCHER Ben
mellowpad.blogspot.com
Ben Butcher was born into an Air Force family and spent his childhood moving all over the world, finally settling in Tacoma, Washington. After spending two years studying fine art at Cornish College of the Arts in Seattle, Ben studied animation at the California Institute of the Arts. Then he landed a job at the Walt Disney Company designing products and art. He has been creatively leading all things consumer products for the last nine years at Pixar Animation Studios.

CAMPBELL Scott
scott-c.blogspot.com
Scott Campbell's paintings have appeared in numerous shows and publications and on CDs and DVDs, such as the cover for *King of Kong: A Fistful of Quarters* and MC Frontalot's record *Final Boss*. He also creates comics including *Hickee Comics* and the stories "Igloo Head and Tree Head." His daily Web comic called "Double Fine Action Comics" lives at Doublefine.com, where he has worked as art director on games such as *Psychonauts* and *Brutal Legend*.

CASAROSA Enrico
www.enricocasarosa.com
Enrico Casarosa has been in the animation industry for nine years drawing storyboards. He is currently a story artist at Pixar Animation Studios, working on movies such as *Ratatouille* and *Cars 2*. He directed the short *La Luna*. He is the author of *The Venice Chronicles* and also did a comic for the collections *Flight*, Volume 1 and *Three Trees Make a Forest* with partners in crime Ronnie del Carmen and Tadahiro Uesugi. Enrico is also the founder of www.SketchCrawl.com, a worldwide sketching marathon event.

CHIEN Catia
www.catiachien.com
Catia Chien is a published illustrator of children's books. Her credits include *The Sea Serpent and Me* and *Princess Alyss of Wonderland*.

COUCH Greg
Greg Couch is an illustrator and artistic director at Blue Sky Studios, and has worked on films such as *Ice Age 2* and *Robots*. He is the illustrator of the books *Wild Child*, *Spring's Sprung*, *The Cello of Mr. O*, *I Know the Moon*, *Summer Vacation*, *Halloween*, and *Nothing But Trouble*. His work can be seen in *Out of Picture* Volume 1, published by Villard/Random House.

DAUTREMER Rébecca
www.rebeccadautremer.com
Rébecca Dautremer was born in 1971 in Gap, France. She attended classes at École nationale superieure des Arts Décoratifs in Paris and got a degree in graphic editing in 1995. Afterwards, she became a graphic editor and illustrator—she has since illustrated over 30 books for children, including *L'Amoureux* in 2003, which she wrote, and *Cyrano* in 2005, written by her husband. Her book *L'Amoureux* was adapted for the stage and performed by children. It was awarded the Prix Sorcière (Witch Prize), a French award for children's literature. Her book *Princesses* is a best-seller in the French children's book industry.

DE CRÉCY Nicolas
Born in 1966, in Lyon, France, Nicolas de Crécy graduated from studies in applied art in 1984 in Marseille. He then completed a three-year course of comic classes at Angoulême Fine Arts. He imposed his unique style in comic form with the acclaimed *Foligatto*. He can't stop drawing and is a prolific comic author with many books including *Leon la Came*, *Prosopopus*, *Glacial Period*, *Monsieur Fruit*, *New York on Loire*, and *Lisbonne, Imaginary Trip*. Nicolas also worked at the Japanese animation Studio 4°C.

DE SÈVE Peter
www.peterdeseve.com
Peter de Sève's work has been published by *Time*, *Newsweek*, *Atlantic Monthly*, *Smithsonian*, *Premiere*, and *Entertainment Weekly*. He also frequently contributes covers to the *New Yorker*. He has designed characters for animated feature films produced by Disney, DreamWorks, Pixar, and 20th Century Fox. His credits include *The Hunchback of Notre Dame*, *The Prince of Egypt*, *Mulan*, *A Bug's Life*, *Tarzan*, *Monsters*, and *Ice Age 1*, *2*, and *3*. He received the Hamilton King Award from the Society of Illustrators.

DEL CARMEN Ronnie
www.ronniedelcarmen.com
Ronnie del Carmen is currently working for Pixar Animation Studios in Emeryville, California. Prior to that he worked at DreamWorks and Warner Bros. as a story artist, story supervisor, character designer, and illustrator. There's documentation that shows he's been dabbling in comics over the years for DC and Dark Horse among others. He self-publishes his comic book *Paper Biscuit* and worked on the collective book *Three Trees Make a Forest* with partners in crime Enrico Casarosa and Tadahiro Uesugi.

DUNNIGAN Nash
nash-dunnigan-art.blogspot.com
Nash Dunnigan made his way to art school in 1987, to the moderately sized city of Richmond, Virginia, only to be prematurely ejected after four years and a BFA diploma in 1991. In 2003, life began again: a studio named Blue Sky took him in as a layout artist. There, he grew up among art giants, practiced the art of cinematography on wondrous moving pictures like *Ice Age 2* and *Robots*, and he is now art directing *Ice Age 4*. They even let him be in their super-cool art book, *Out of Picture* Volumes 1 and 2.

FELIX Paul
Paul Felix has been with Walt Disney Animation Studios since 1995. He has worked as a visual development designer on *Mulan*, *Tarzan*, *The Emperor's New Groove*, and *Brother Bear*. Paul was

production designer for *Lilo and Stitch* and art director of *Bolt*. He is a 1987 graduate of Harvard College and hails from Arizona.

FERNÁNDEZ Enrique
enriquefernandez0.blogspot.com
Born in Barcelona in 1975, Enrique Fernández left fine arts for the Spanish animation industry in 1997. His work as a storyboard artist, animator, and layout man can be seen in movies like *El Cid* and the upcoming *Nocturna* (both from Filmax Animation). He is now a full-time comic book artist whose works include *Libertadores*, *OZ Magician*, *Mother of Victories*, and *L'Ile sans sourire*, to name a few.

FUKUSHIMA Atsuko
Atsuko Fukushima, born in Japan, is well-known for her incredible opening five-minute animation for the film anthology *Genius Party*. She also directed *Robotto Kânibaru* (segments "Coming Soon" and "See You Again"). She worked as animator on movies such as *Akira*, *Kiki's Delivery Service*, and *Robot Carnival*, to name a few.

GOODRICH Carter
cartergoodrich.com
Carter Goodrich's editorial illustration work has been featured in *Time, Newsweek, Playboy*, and on sixteen published covers of the *New Yorker*. He is a two-time recipient of the gold medal from the Society of Illustators, NY. He's won several Annie awards for Character Design in an Animated Feature. He's done character design for the DreamWorks films *Prince of Egypt*, *Shrek*, *Spirit*, and *Sinbad*; Pixar films *Finding Nemo, Monsters, Inc.*, and *Ratatouille*; Sony Pictures Animation film *Open Season*; and Illumination Animation film *Despicable Me*. His illustrations appear in the books *Nutcracker*, *A Christmas Carol*, *A Creature Was Stirring*, *Hermit Crab*, and *Say Hello to Zorro*.

GORDON David
www.illustrationranch.com
Dave Gordon is a children's book author and illustrator. He attended Parsons School of Design in New York. Then he moved to California, where he created concept art for many of Pixar's films including *Toy Story 1* and *2*, *A Bug's Life*, and *Monsters, Inc.* He also worked on the acclaimed animated television series *SpongeBob SquarePants* and Blue Sky Studio's *Robots*. Dave has authored and illustrated three vehicle fairy tales for HarperCollins: *The Ugly Truckling*, *The Three Little Rigs*, and *Hansel and Diesel*.

GOSSELET Éric
mister-egg.blogspot.com
Éric Gosselet was born in 1971 in Châlons en Champagne, in France. Éric began his career at Disney studios in Paris working on *Tarzan*. He then worked in various studios as a character designer. He created the character Lulu Capisco for *Milan Edition*, and is a member of the collective Rendez-Vous. He co-created the series *Rekker the Rabbit* at Marathon Media. His work has been exhibited in the Arludik gallery in Paris and Nucleus gallery in Los Angeles.

GRANÉ Luis
luisgrane.blogspot.com
Animator Luis Grané worked on animated features such as *Ratatouille* at Pixar Studios, and *Road to Eldorado* and *The Prince of Egypt* at DreamWorks. His contribution "They Are Waiting" was selected as the cover of the worldwide acclaimed collective *The Art of Totoro Forest Project* book.

GUARNIDO Juanjo
Juanjo Guarnido's illustrations have been published in *Comics Forum* (Planeta DeAgostini). He worked in Madrid for the TV animation industry. In 1993, he moved to Paris, joining Disney Studios at Montreuil, and worked on film such as *Tarzan*, *Hercules*, and *Atlantis: The Lost Empire*, as a layout artist and animator. When the studio finally halted productions in France, he naturally came back to his first love: comics. *Blacksad*, his first volume at Dargaud, quickly became a phenomenon.

GUERLAIS Gérald
www.geraldguerlais.com
Gérald was born in 1974 in Nantes, in France. He graduated from the National School of Applied Art in Paris in 1998. Gérald is a versatile artist and worked in multimedia, publishing, advertising, and animation. He initiated the *Sketchtravel* project with Dice Tsutsumi, as well as the collective comics *Rendez-Vous*. He also illustrated *Les Trois Microbes*, a children's book written by Tai-Marc Le Thanh, who designed the published version of the *Sketchtravel* book.

HANUKA Tomer
www.thanuka.com
Award-winning illustrator and cartoonist Tomer Hanuka was born in Israel. At age twenty-two he moved to New York. He quickly became a regular contributor to many national magazines. His clients include *Time* magazine, the *New Yorker*, *Spin*, the *New York Times*, *Rolling Stone*, MTV, and Saatchi & Saatchi. He is the winner of multiple medals from the Society of Illustrators and the Society of Publication Designers as well as from *American Illustration* and *Print* magazine.

HARRIS Eli
www.eliwharris.com
Eli Harris is an award-winning editorial, commercial, and gallery artist based out of Oakland, California. He's designed several seasons' worth of merchandise for apparel giant Gama-Go, and has worked with *California* magazine, *SF Weekly*, *Bay Area Alternative Press*, and Rex Goliath wines. His work has been recognized by the Society of Illustrators and American Illustration. Eli just finished preparation for his third solo show, "Dance the Collapse," in San Francisco.

HOWE John
www.john-howe.com
John Howe (born August 21, 1957 in Vancouver) lives in Neuchâtel, Switzerland. He studied in a college in Strasbourg, France, then at the École des Arts Décoratifs. He is best known for his work based on J. R. R. Tolkien's worlds. Howe and Alan Lee were the lead artists of Peter Jackson's *The Lord of the Rings* movie trilogy. Howe also re-illustrated the maps of *The Lord of the Rings*, *The Hobbit*, and *The Silmarillion*. His work includes images of myths such as the Anglo-Saxon legend of Beowulf.

JEAN James
www.jamesjean.com
James Jean is an award-winning illustrator living in Los Angeles. He was born in Taiwan in 1979. He quickly became an acclaimed cover artist for DC Comics, garnering three consecutive Eisner awards, two Harvey awards, two gold medals and a silver from the Society of Illustrators of LA, and a gold medal from the Society of Illustrators of NY. His clients include *Time* magazine, the *New York Times*, *Rolling Stone*, *Spin*, ESPN, Atlantic Records, Target, *Playboy*, and Knopf, among others.

JOFFRE Véronique
verossignol.blogspot.com
With a sophisticated simplicity, Véronique Joffre tackles emotions and concepts at the core of life and the world around us. The young French artist graduated from École Estienne in Paris and École des Arts Décoratifs in Strasbourg and has a budding career in popular French children's books such as *La chèvre de monsieur Seguin* (Lito) and *Contes du Monde* (Collectif, Amaterra), to name a couple.

KEANE Glen
theartofglenkeane.blogspot.com
Animation supervisor Glen Keane is widely regarded as one of the top talents working in animation today. His bold expressive style and innovative character designs have been compared favorably by critics and colleagues alike to the legendary masters of the art. During his illustrious thirty-five years with the Disney studio, he has been responsible for creating the characters of Ariel, the Beast, Aladdin, Pocahontas, Tarzan, John Silver, and Rapunzel.

KERASCOËT
www.kerascoet.fr
Kerascoët is the French name of a comics and animation artist couple, composed of Marie Pommepuy, born in 1978 in Brest, and Sébastien Cosset, born in 1975 in Paris. The name of this pair of authors comes from the village of Kerascoët in Brittany where Marie Pommepuy grew up. They met at the Olivier de Serres Art School.

KNAPP Michael
www.michaelknapp.com
Michael Knapp worked as a designer on the animated films *Robots*, *Ice Age*, and *Horton Hears a Who*, and art-directed the Academy Award-nominated short *No Time for Nuts*. His work can be found in the *Art of the Totoro Forest Project*, *Spectrum* 12 and 13, and the *Society of Illustrators Annuals* 48 and 49. He is the book designer, coproducer, and story contributor for the anthologies *Out of Picture* Volumes 1 and 2. He art-directed *Ice Age 3* and is currently helping develop one of Blue Sky's upcoming films.

KONDO Robert
www.dopw.us/blog/gallery
Robert Kondo is an art director for Pixar Animation Studios. Born and raised in Southern California, he graduated from the Art Center College of Design in 2002. His first job was with Oblique Strategies as a sketch artist working on film posters. He went on to work at Angel Studios for three months before joining Pixar. He worked on *Ratatouille* and *Toy Story 3* as a sets art director. Occasionally he updates his blog with gallery work and illustration work.

LEE Mike
mikeleeart.blogspot.com
Originally from Southern California, Mike Lee received his BFA from Otis College of Art and Design. Upon graduating, he moved to San Francisco to work for Lucas Arts as a conceptual designer as well as freelance for various commercial and television studios. A few clients include Disney, Psyop, and Hornet Inc. He now lives in New York City working as a color key artist for animated feature films such as *Ice Age* and *Rio*.

LEE Sang Jun
www.sangjunart.com
Sang Jun Lee was born in Korea. He did creature design for *Men in Black II*, *Hulk*, *Peter Pan*, and *Pirates of the Caribbean*. Specializing in character, costume, and creature design for *Star Wars Episode III*, Lee has been exploring depths and details of cultures and worlds that have long fascinated *Star Wars* fans as well as ones never imagined. Sang Jun Lee is currently working at Blue Sky Studios, where he designed characters for *Hortons Hears a Who* and *Rio*.

LE PENNEC Benoît
www.outofpicture.com
Born in France in 1962, Benoît worked on the animated movie *Balto* for Amblimation, London. When that company dissolved into DreamWorks, he moved to the United States, where he worked on all of DreamWorks' 2-D movies (from *The Prince of Egypt* to *Sinbad*) as a layout artist. He also worked at Blue Sky Studios on *Robots*. His work can be seen in the comic anthology *Out of Picture*, Volume 1.

LÓPEZ MUÑOZ Daniel
daniellopezmunoz.blogspot.com
Daniel López Muñoz grew up in Córdova, Spain. At age five a wandering pencil fell into his hands. Enchanted by its magic, Daniel never let it go. The happy pair, after several years at Blue Sky Studios, where he worked on the movie *Robots*, are now found at Pixar Animation Studios, where Daniel worked on *Wall-E* and *Up*. He is a member of the Out of Picture collective. His work can be seen in *Out of Picture* Volume 1. Daniel designed and built the official *Sketchtravel* case with red oak circa 1920.

LOUIS Dominique
Dominique Louis was born in 1967 in Burgundy, France. After graduating from Gobelins School of the Image he started his career in animation in London. He then joined Disney-France on *A Goofy Movie*. He worked on Brad Bird's *The Iron Giant*, art directed at Pixar Studios on *Monsters, Inc.* and *Ratatouille*, and contributed to *Finding Nemo*, *Wall-E*, *Up*, and *Toy Story 3*. He joined DreamWorks on *How to Train Your Dragon*. He is a passionate hiker, traveler, and an accomplished photographer.

MACKENZIE Robert
robert-mackenzie.blogspot.com
Robert MacKenzie grew up in San Mateo, California. In 1998, Robert graduated from San Jose State University with a degree in illustration and has worked as a concept, visual development, and color

key artist at Lucasfilm, PDI/DreamWorks, and Blue Sky Studios on movies including *Hulk*, *Shrek 2*, and *Ice Age 2*. His first comic can be seen in *Out of Picture* Volume 1. He has also illustrated children's books.

MARC Sylvain

polyminthe.blogspot.com

Born in 1982 in Vincennes near Paris, France, Sylvain won the Alph-Art award of the school comic contest at the International Comics Festival at Angoulême in 2000. He got his degree at Estienne with high honors and his degree at Gobelins school. His clients include Framestore, Cartoon Network, and Laika. He won the best TV pilot award at the 2010 Cartoon on the Bay festival. Sylvain is also a freelance illustrator and character designer.

MARLET Nicolas

Annie Award-winning animator Nicolas Marlet graduated from Gobelins School of the Image and moved from his native France to California in the 1990s. Joining DreamWorks Studios, he became quickly one of the best character designers in the industry. Nicolas Marlet has lent his unique talents as a character designer to several DreamWorks productions over the past fifteen years including *Over the Hedge*, *Kung Fu Panda*, and *How to Train Your Dragon*.

MATSUMOTO Taiyo

Born in 1967, Taiyo Matsumoto is best known for his works with Kodansha's rival publisher Shogakukan, including *Tekkonkinkreet*, *Ping Pong*, and *Number Five*. He has received critical praise for his unconventional art style. *Ping Pong* and *Aoi Haru* have been adapted into live-action feature films, and acclaimed animation studio Studio 4°C adapted *Tekkonkinkreet* into an animated feature film. In 2007 he received an Excellence Award for manga at the Japan Media Arts Festival for the art of *Takemitsu Zamurai*.

MIGNOLA Mike

www.hellboy.com

Mike Mignola (born in Berkeley, California,1960) is an American comic book artist and writer. He worked on animated movies such as *Atlantis: The Lost Empire*, and on covers and backup features for various DC and Marvel comics. Mignola has influenced a new generation of comics artists since he began working on *Hellboy*. Where others would draw muscular men and slim, well-endowed women, Mignola's characters were usually bulky and rough-looking, and more often than not defined by large shadowed areas rather than fine details.

MIYAZAKI Hayao

www.ghibli.jp

Hayao Miyazaki is regarded as one of the greatest creators of animated films, and his work certainly stands as some of the best the genre has to offer. Miyazaki and Takahata cofounded Ghibli Films, a name that would become synonymous with quality. Miyazaki's works contained more of his own personal vision. *Nausicaä of the Valley of the Wind*, and others including *Kiki's Delivery Service*, *The Crimson Pig*, *Princess Mononoke*, and *My Neighbor Totoro*, contain elements of fantasy and often reveal humanist, ecological themes. *Spirited Away* won the Academy Award for Best Animated Feature.

MORIMOTO Koji

www.kojimorimoto.net

Born December 26, 1959, Koji Morimoto is an animator and one of Japan's premier anime directors. Morimoto collaborated with Takashi Nakamura, most notably in Katsuhiro Otomo's "The Order to Stop Construction" segment of the anthology film *Neo-Tokyo*. He worked on *Akira* and directed a short for the *Robot Carnival* anthology. Around this time he founded Studio 4°C with producer Eiko Tanaka and Yoshiharu Sato. He directed "Beyond," a segment of *The Animatrix* shorts.

NGUYEN Peter

saigonradio.blogspot.com

Born in Philadelphia and raised in Texas amongst a family of artists, Peter spent his childhood drawing and painting on whatever he could get his hands on. Currently working as a color key artist at Blue Sky Studios, his work has influenced feature films such as *Horton Hears a Who* and *Ice Age*. His artwork can also be found in *Out of Picture* Volume 2 and in numerous DC Comics publications, achieving a boyhood dream to be a comic artist. In addition to his printed projects, Peter's art has been exhibited in galleries domestically as well as internationally, in cities such as Paris, France. Peter currently resides in New York City and continues to work on animation and comic books.

NGUYEN Vincent Di

vincentdi.blogspot.com

Vincent Di Nguyen grew up in Houston, Texas. He attended the School of Visual Arts in New York, where he earned his BFA in illustration. He illustrated the children's books *Louis and the Dodo*, *Not Another Tea Party*, *Jungle Bullies*, *Whoosh Went the Wind!*, *Stella the Star*, and *The Crabfish* before joining the art department at Blue Sky Studios, where he worked on movies such as *Robots*, *Ice Age 2*, and *Horton Hears a Who*. His work can also be seen in *The Art of Robots* and the comic anthology *Out of Picture*, Volumes 1 and 2.

NINE Carlos

www.carlosnine.com

Carlos Nine was born in 1944 in Buenos Aires, Argentina. He graduated from the Fine Arts School in Buenos Aires. Nine works as an illustrator, comics author, painter, sculptor, and writer. His work has been published in Argentina, Spain, Italy, France, Belgium, The United Kingdom, Germany, The United States of America, Brazil, Taiwan, and Hong Kong. He is a national icon in Argentina and an inspiration for many *Sketchtravel* contributors.

OPEÑA Jerome

artofcrom.blogspot.com

Jerome Opeña first came to be noticed for his work on Rick Remender's *Fear Agent*. But prior to this series he also penciled issues of Image's *Strange Girl* and Dark Horse's *Star Wars Tales*. Jerome was then noticed by Marvel and signed an exclusive deal with them. He penciled the first arc of the *Punisher* and Moon Knight's latest series. In 2010, Jerome was announced as the penciler on Marvel's new ongoing *Uncanny X-Force*, being re-united with Rick

Remender. The series has received much publicity and coverage.

PHAM Leuyen
www.leuyenpham.com
Leuyen Pham used to work as a layout artist at DreamWorks animation studio. She is the illustrator of such best-selling children's books as *Can You Do This, Old Badger?*, *Big Sister, Little Sister*, and *Freckleface Strawberry* (written by Julianne Moore). By her best guesstimate, she has illustrated about thirty books. She does three or four each year and has authored one herself, *Big Sister, Little Sister*. Written as a gift to Pham's older sister, LeChi, the book was an instant success when it was published in 2005. She lives with her husband Alex Puvilland and their kids in California.

PLYMPTON Bill
www.plymptoons.com
Plympton's illustrations and cartoons have been published in the *New York Times*, the *Village Voice*, *Vogue*, *Rolling Stone*, *Vanity Fair*, *Penthouse*, and *National Lampoon*. Plympton has created twenty-six animated short films and five animated features. His short *Guard Dog* was nominated for an Academy Award for Best Animated Short Film. Plympton animated the music video for Kanye West's "Heard 'Em Say" and created the music video for Weird Al Yankovic's "Don't Download This Song."

PREDAL Aurélien
aurelien-predal.blogspot.com
Aurélien Predal was born in 1984 in Suresnes, France. He attended the prestigious Gobelins school in Paris. He codirected *Burning Safari*, a promising 3-D masterpiece, shown during the Annecy 2006 Animation Festival. After working as a character designer at Method Films for a few months he got involved as an animator on the full-length feature *Nine*. He is currently art directing at Onyx Films.

PRESING Bill
billpresing.blogspot.com
Bill Presing's work has been recognized by a number of award committees and institutions. The Lugz commercial spot he illustrated was nominated for an Annie Award, and his work on the animated opening for *The Rosie O'Donnell Show* won him a prestigious Daytime Emmy Award. Bill is the cocreator of *Rex Steele: Nazi Smasher*, a comic book for which he received a nomination for the 2000 Ignatz award for outstanding artist. Bill Presing is currently a storyboard artist at Pixar Animation Studios.

PUVILLAND Alex
alexpuvilland.com
Having grown up in France in the eighties, Alexandre Puvilland may have mad cow disease and holes in his brain. He might also be perfectly normal. While waiting to be seventy-five to find out, he works for DreamWorks Animation and does comics whenever he has a moment. Alexandre lives in San Francisco with his ridiculously talented wife Leuyen Pham and their no less spectacular sons Leo and Adrien.

ROCA François
François Roca was born in Lyon in 1971. He attended the National School of Applied Arts Olivier de Serres in Paris, in the Image and Communication department, and then École Emile Cohl to study illustration. In 1996, he started doing illustrations for children including *The Queen of Ants Has Disappeared*, based on a text by his friend Fred Bernard. François Roca has illustrated more than twenty books. He regularly collaborates with the news magazine *Télérama*.

ROMANO Lou
louromano.blogspot.com
Lou Romano was born in San Diego in 1972. After graduating high school in 1990 he studied animation at the California Institute of the Arts. Since then he has worked as an illustrator and designer on *The Powerpuff Girls* and *The Iron Giant*. He was also the production designer of Brad Bird's *The Incredibles* for Pixar Animation Studios. He did his first cover for the *New Yorker* magazine on June 25, 2007. He also published *The Ancient Book of Myth and War* with AdHouse Books.

SHIMIZU Yuko
yukoart.com
Yuko Shimizu is a freelance illustrator based in New York City and an illustration instructor at School of Visual Arts. *Newsweek Japan* chose her as one of the 100 most respected Japanese people in the world in 2009. Yuko graduated with an MFA from New York School of Visual Arts' Illustration as Visual Essay Program in 2003 and has been illustrating since. She also teaches a BFA illustration course and occasionally advises MFA students at SVA.

TANJI Yoko
www.tanji.jp
Yoko Tanji graduated from Tokyo National University of Fine Arts and Music with a degree in design, and started to work as an illustrator in 1997. Since then she has been contributing her works to magazines and books, most of which are available through Amazon. Her recent interests extend to character designs and movie productions.

TERADA Katsuya
Katsuya Terada (born December 7, 1963), is a Japanese illustrator and cartoonist from Tamano (Okayama). He is the character designer for the animated film *Blood: The Last Vampire*. He has also done work related to American comics, such as *Iron Man* and *Hellboy*. He has done very little group-drawn work, an exception being the manga *Saiyukiden Daienou* (Monkey King), his principal activities being illustration and character design.

TIEMENS Erik
www.watersketch.com
Erik Tiemens worked as a senior art director at Industrial Light and Magic and as a concept design supervisor on *Star Wars Episode II* and *III*. He is now working at Lucasfilm Animation Ltd. in the new features division. His awards include an honorary Emmy for matte painting on the *Young Indiana Jones* series, and an Emmy nomination for designing the opening of the *Star Trek: Voyager* TV series.
He was part of the Oscar-winning effects team on both *Jurassic Park* and *Forrest Gump*, working as a concept artist.

TRÉBUTIEN Claude-William

singeclub.blogspot.com

Claude-William Trébutien was born in 1981 in Caen, France. After passing his A-levels with a major in literature and a minor in English, he attended Caen's Beaux Arts classes for a year. Unsatisfied with the average level of the teaching he then got at a Brussels school, he produced a homemade traditional animated movie which he hopes to be his key to the prestigious school Les Gobelins in Paris. He codirected *Burning Safari*, and worked as animator on CGI movies such as *Nine* and *Rio*.

TSUTSUMI Daisuke (Dice)

www.simplestroke.com

Born and raised in Tokyo, Japan, Daisuke moved to New York in 1993, where he enrolled at the School of Visual Arts. He graduated in 1998. Daisuke started his career as a staff illustrator for Lucas Learning Ltd. in San Francisco. Two years later, he moved back to New York to work for Blue Sky Studios as a visual development/color key artist on their film projects such as *Ice Age, Robots*, and *Horton Hears a Who*. In 2007, he accepted the new challenge to join as an art director at Pixar Animation Studios. Dice was the color and lighting art director of Pixar's latest feature, *Toy Story 3*. His first children's book, *I Can Hear*, was published in Japan in 2009.

USUEGI Tadahiro

www10.big.or.jp/~tuesugi

Tadahiro Uesugi was born in 1966 in Miyazaki on Kyuushuu Island, Japan. He studied fashion illustration at the Tokyo Art School's Setsu Mode seminar. He worked as an assistant for manga artist JiroTaniguchi and made his debut as an illustrator for *Magazine House*. His work can be seen in Japan, Europe, and the United States on magazine covers, in books, and in a variety of other commercial products, including advertising campaigns and even the movie *Coraline*.

VALLADE Maïlys

mailysvallade.blogspot.com

Maïlys Vallade was born in1985 at Châtenay Malabry, France. She graduated from the Gobelins school in Paris, and won a prize at Annecy Festival for her contribution as codirector on the short movie *The Lighthouse Keeper* in 2010.

VALLEY Robert

www.robertvalley.com

Robert Valley is from Vancouver. He is one of the founders of the collective Maverix Studios. His work as director and animator includes clients such Passion Pictures London, Curious Pictures, ILM, and Warner Bros. Animation. He collaborated with Jamie Hewlett on Gorillaz video clips and with Peter Chung on *Aeon Flux*. Valley is a Wild Brain studio director. He is also an acclaimed comic author for DC Comics and *Heavy Metal*.

VILLERMAUX Grégoire

gregoirevillermaux.blogspot.com

Grégoire Villermaux was born in Lyon, France in 1976. He attended the National Applied School of Art (Olivier de Serres, Paris) and then École Emile Cohl in Lyon. Known for his strong ability to adapt his style to many French TV animation productions, he bounces from one place to another. His clients include Vivendi Universal Publishing, Futurikon, Method Films, and Ankama. He travels a lot, doing many sketchbooks.

Acknowledgments

Dice Tsutsumi would like to thank:
All seventy-one participating artists, Gérald Guerlais for his initiative and leadership, Yukino Pang and Maureen Fan for their master project management, as well as Jeremy McCracken, Zach Johnston, and Dan Govier. For their incredible talent, Toshio Suzuki, Koji Hoshino and everyone at Studio Ghibli. Suzel Buck, Charles Solomon, Karen Paik, Sophie Guerlais, Kuro Uesugi, Seth Van Booven, and Catherine Bonvalot and her French documentary team. Nicky Rigg and Room To Read for their generous help and collaboration. Emily Haynes, Neil Egan, Becca Cohen and the team at Chronicle Books. And finally, Dice offers his biggest thanks to his wife Mei and his son Senju for their unbelievable patience and support.

Gérald Guerlais would like to thank:
Sophie Guerlais, Daisuke Tsutsumi, Mei Tsutsumi, Rébecca Cautremer, Taï-Marc Le Thanh, Catherine Bonvalot, Charles Solomon, Fabienne Kriegel, Amélie Poggi, Nathalie Lefebvre, Sabine Houplain, Anne Schuliar, Sherri Aldis, Isabelle des Courtils, Hélène Maurice, Benjamin Desmet, Bruno Tomalak, Jean-Rémi Perrin, Yukino Pang, Thibaut Castan, Fanny Chalot, Vincent Benoit, Benjamin Barker, Louise Terseur, Diane and Jean-Jacques Launier, Marc Aguesse, Anne-Laure Falkman, Valérie Jarry, François Dupuy, Charlotte Moundlic, Arnaud Bouron, Fanny Bensussan, Maud Remy, David Panzo, Redha Zaïm, Prakash Topsy, Céline Gobinet, Damien Gallas, Randall de Sève, Ellie Walsh, Jessica Roulston, Jonathan Buisson, David Gilson, Anne Calandre, Geneviève Godbout, Olivier Pouchelon, François Maumont, Caroline Charles, Nathalie Saint-Oyant, Jean-Louis Vandestoc, Christophe Lautrette, Stéphane Kardos, Claire Keane, Pierre-Olivier Vincent, Kim Mackey, Shelley Page, Serge Bromberg, Tina Price.

Library of Congress Cataloging-in-Publication Data

Sketchtravel.
pages cm
Introductions by Dice Tsutsumi and Gérald Guerlais.
ISBN 978-1-4521-1245-9
1. Artists' books. 2. Notebooks. 3. Group work in art. I. Tsutsumi, Daisuke, 1974- writer of added text. II. Guerlais, Gerald, writer of added text.

N7433.3.S57 2012
709.04'082—dc23

2012009316

Manufactured in China

10 9 8 7 6 5 4 3 2 1

Chronicle Books
680 Second Street
San Francisco, California 94107
www.chroniclebooks.com

Partenaires

ACTUAL   august & debouzy avocats   CATSUKA   Room to Read

www.editionsduchene.fr

Directrice : Fabienne Kriegel
Responsables éditoriales : Nathalie Lefebvre /Amélie Poggi
Assistante d'édition : Fanny Martin
Directrice artistique : Sabine Houplain, assistée de Claire Mieyeville
Conception graphique : Taï-Marc Le Thanh
Fabrication : Nicole Thieriot-Pichon
Lecture-correction : Isabelle Macé et Clémentine Sanchez
Traduction : Louis Brutton

Photogravure : Taï-Marc Le Thanh et APS Chromostyle
Achevé d'imprimer en Chine
Dépôt légal : octobre 2011
ISBN : 978-2-81230-504-7
34/8286/6